Agency and Embodiment

AGENCY AND EMBODIMENT

Performing Gestures/Producing Culture

CARRIE NOLAND

Harvard University Press
Cambridge, Massachusetts
London, England
2009

Copyright © 2009 by the President and Fellows of Harvard College
All rights reserved
Printed in the United States of America

Library of Congress Cataloging-in-Publication Data

Noland, Carrie, 1958–
   Agency and embodiment : performing gestures/producing culture / Carrie Noland.
     p.   cm.
   Includes bibliographical references and index.
   ISBN 978-0-674-03451-8 (alk. paper)
   1. Body, Human—Social aspects. 2. Gesture—Social aspects. 3. Mind and body—
Social aspect. 4. Culture. I. Title.
   HM636.N65 2009
   306.4—dc22   2009005476

Dedicated to my loving mother,
Dorothy Wiener Noland

Contents

Introduction

MAGINE THE GRAFFITI writer. He swings his arm up over his head following the vertical extension of his body, then sweeps it in a half moon back down to his feet. His gesture, extended by the length of a spray-can, leaves behind a haloed line of paint, a *D* on the wall. In the magnified scope of the graffiti gesture, writing affords the writer an opportunity to impress the individual shape and vitality of the body's motor power onto the contours of the cultural sign. Yet if the writer performs the motion repeatedly, his own body will eventually be inscribed, the muscles and ligaments physiologically altered, by the gestural routine that expresses and confines his body at the very same time.

It was while watching a graffiti writer that I first began to perceive how agency might work. As I observed the writer, his gestures revealed themselves to be simultaneously a repetitive routine and an improvisational dance; a script was obviously at the root of the performance and a script was its ultimate, durable product, but in between, as I could plainly see, a body was afforded a chance to feel itself moving through space. I knew at that moment that this singular performance had something to teach me, that it was offering a response to a set of questions I, and many others in my field, had been formulating with an urgency that had not diminished over the years. How does individual human agency exert itself despite the enormous pressure of social conditioning? What *is* human agency? Does it in fact exist? If so, then where does it come from? The libido? The soul? If not, and we are no more than products of social conditioning, then why do we not simply repeat what we are conditioned to do? If our agency is governed by *systèmes de signification* (in one account) or anonymous power structures (in another), then why do variation, innovation, and resistance occur? Why do scripts differ and meanings evolve? In short, why aren't humans more like machines?

The moving body of the graffiti writer suggested to me that innovation is more than mere chance, but also that agency cannot spring from an autonomous, undisciplined source. What I saw as I watched was that *gestures,* learned techniques of the body, are the means by which cultural conditioning is simultaneously embodied and put to the test. Further, the source of that testing is not the "subject" in a classic Cartesian sense, but rather the sensate motor body, the medium, if you will, on which the gestural regime—and the "subject"—necessarily builds. It occurred to me that motor challenges to acculturated behaviors are themselves a form of agency, one that arises from the experiences of movement afforded, paradoxically, by acculturation itself. This book is therefore a study of the ways culture is both embodied and challenged through corporeal performance, that is, through kinetic acts as they contingently reiterate learned behaviors. Gestures are a type of inscription, a parsing of the body into signifying or operational units; they can thereby be seen to reveal the submission of a shared human anatomy to a set of bodily practices specific to one culture. At the same time, gestures clearly belong to the domain of movement; they provide kinesthetic sensations that remain in excess of what the gestures themselves might signify or accomplish within that culture. Just what is this excess, and what kind of work does it do? How does embodying socialized gestures produce an experience of movement—its texture and velocity—that ends up altering the routine, the body that performs the routine, and eventually, perhaps, culture itself?

The body we observe in the act of writing may indeed be communicating a message or completing a task, but it is simultaneously measuring space, monitoring pressure and friction, accommodating shifts of weight. These kinesthetic experiences that exceed communicative or instrumental projects affect the gestures that are made and the meanings they convey. As a motor phenomenon, gesturing not only sculpts the moving body, transforming it into a technical prosthesis (an extension of the stylus) or a type of sign (the sign of belonging to a certain gender, class, subculture, or gang). Gesturing also affords an opportunity for *interoceptive* or kinesthetic awareness, the intensity of which may cause subjects to alter the very ways they move. If bodily motility is, as Henri Bergson once claimed, the single most important filtering device in the subject's negotiations with the external world, then a theory of agency that places movement center stage is essential to understanding how human beings are embodied within—and impress themselves on—their worlds.

The hypothesis I advance in this book is that kinesthetic experience, produced by acts of embodied gesturing, places pressure on the conditioning a body receives, encouraging variations in performance that account for

larger innovations in cultural practice that cannot otherwise be explained.
In these pages I will speak of "variations in performance" and not only instances of "resistance," in order to avoid the agonistic overtones of Michel
Foucault's highly influential but largely binary account of power, which
reduces the field of cultural practices to techniques of "strict subjection."[1]
Rethinking the cultural field as differential rather than oppositional alone
allows me to study a whole range of deviations from normative behavior—
from slight variation to outright rejection—while simultaneously con-
struing the *normative* as equally wide-ranging in its modes of acquisition.
Normative behavior may be coercively imposed (as in Foucault's account)
or actively sought, imitated during infancy or gained incrementally throughout one's entire life. Further, "normative" should be understood as normative within a particular context: a hip-swaying gait might be normative for
a classed or gendered subject at a certain place and time, but balletic turn-
out is normative for a self-selected group of skilled bodies that have acquired flexibility in the hip joints under voluntary duress. My point here
is that the embodiment of the *habitus* generates a far greater number of
variations than the hazards of simple iteration can explain. These variations
can accumulate and cascade into forms of innovation and, yes, resistance
that produce profound effects on behavior, effects that spread out and ra-
diate into realms of conscious decision-making and other, supposedly
more mindful areas of cultural and political practice. "The possibility of
a body that is written upon *but that also writes,*" Susan Leigh Foster ventures, "asks scholars to approach the body's involvement in any activity
with an assumption of potential agency to participate in or resist whatever
forms of cultural production are underway."[2]

    To be sure, not all innovative or resistant acts can be attributed to the
body's ability to feel itself move, and I might be accused of making too
much of a zone of sensation of which we are seldom, if ever (according to
some), aware.[3] Nevertheless, I intend to privilege corporeal performance
and the sensory experience it affords in the hope of yielding a theory of
agency fully implicated in embodiment, which I take to be that ambiguous
phenomenon in which culture both asserts and loses its grip on individual
subjects. Drawing on resources found in art, philosophy, and anthropology as well as psychology, cognitive science, and neuroanatomy, each chapter argues from a different angle that kinesthetic experience—the sensory
awareness of one's own movement—can indeed encourage experiment,
modification, and, at times, rejection of the routine. Clearly, subjects make
conscious decisions to resist or conform, and the principles according to
which they do so have been theorized at length. But subjects also make
motor decisions that challenge cultural meanings in profound ways, and

the principles governing such gestural deviance have hardly been studied at all. Even the relatively new and promising field of "affect studies" has confined itself to exploring the ways emotions rather than kinesthetic sensations function in the process of individuation. Emotive affects (such as anguish, disgust, or envy) have received significant critical attention, but the more directly somatic affects (such as discomfort, strain, or the calm acquired through skeletal alignment) fly largely under the theoretical radar screen.[4] For the most part, kinesthetic experiences and the motor possibilities they sketch out have remained beyond the purview of theorists invested in subjective individuation as primarily a psychic phenomenon. However, insofar as theorists of affect have approached feelings as *experiences* (unsettling rather than reassuring to the unified subject), they offer support for the arguments I will be advancing here.

Kinesthetic sensations are a particular kind of affect belonging both to the body that precedes our subjectivity (narrowly construed) and the contingent, cumulative subjectivity our body allows us to build over time. Because these sensations are also preserved as memories, they help constitute the "embodied history of the subject," a history stored in gestural "I can's," that determines in large part how that embodiment will continue to unfold.[5] Kinesthesia allows us to correct recursively, refine, and experiment with the practices we have learned. The knowledge obtained through kinesthesia is thus *constitutive of*—not tangential to—the process of individuation. And yet despite the central role kinesthetic sensation plays, it is rarely treated as vital to the development of forms assumed by either culture or the self. Constructivist theories of subjectivity tend to view the entire domain of the kinetic as constructed by cultural or industrial regimes, while affect theories consign kinesthesia to the primitive order of sense impressions ("affections") and focus on emotions ("affects") instead.[6] Thus, neither constructivist nor affect-centered theories of agency have much to say about kinesthetic experience and motor intentionality, the dynamic engagement of the body in a specific context that invites subjects to effect change. In this book, I address this critical neglect, creating a new paradigm for analyzing the role of the moving body in the transmission and transformation of subjectivities, expressive practices, and bodily techniques.

To develop this paradigm, the first shift I operate is to replace the term "movement," favored by theorists of many stripes, with "gesture," my term for the organized forms of kinesis through which subjects navigate and alter their worlds. There are several advantages to be gained by this shift, some of which will only become clear as the book proceeds. At the outset, however, I will claim that "gesture" is preferable because it evokes a line of thought on the body that until now has remained marginal but that firmly lays the groundwork for the kind of holistic approach required. This line of thought draws its founding insights from Marcel Mauss and continues through the works of his two most important students, the philosopher Maurice Merleau-Ponty and the paleoethnographer André Leroi-Gourhan, who viewed the body as a sensorium extending itself prosthetically through gesture into the world. While Leroi-Gourhan has begun to receive some attention, it is clearly Merleau-Ponty's more familiar works that have provided a rich resource for renewing theories of agency, offering contemporary scholars a nuanced account of gestural construction that urges them to recall the *specific* moving body inevitably inflecting acquired gestural routines and instantiating them in a revised form. As significant as this interest in Merleau-Ponty has proved to be, however, the genealogy of the phenomenological tradition and the treasures it holds have by no means been exhausted. The following chapters therefore draw attention to a history of theorizing embodiment as it has evolved in the (largely) French phenomenological context—from Bergson, Mauss, Merleau-Ponty, Leroi-Gourhan, Jean-Paul Sartre, and Frantz Fanon to Pierre Bourdieu, Judith Butler, and Jacques Derrida. Ultimately, my ambitions are both historical and theoretical in nature; by exploring this genealogy, I seek new support for insights that scholars in dance, especially, have been developing for decades— arguments that are highly relevant but, due to disciplinary boundaries, less familiar than they ought to be. One of the most remarkable discoveries I have made while writing this book is the extent to which both dance scholars and contemporary neuroscientists (or at least a substantial subset of them) rely on the tradition I follow in these pages. Alain Berthoz, for instance, quotes Husserl and Bourdieu; Francisco Varela and Marc Jeannerod (the father of "motor cognition") explicitly echo Merleau-Ponty; and the famous neuroscientist of emotion, Antonio Damasio, clearly owes a debt to Bergson. At times, however, it appears that the sensitivity to history and social context demonstrated by philosophers of the phenomenological tradition has not been sufficiently developed in their late twentieth-century scientific heirs. In other words, scientists occasionally (but certainly not always) neglect the social component of movement acquisition as well as the cultural framing of qualitative kinesthetic feedback. In contrast, dance scholars, while attentive to the anatomical substrate of what they study, manage to remain far more observant of interactions between biological and cultural variables. The tradition initiated by Mauss and nourished in many dance ethnographies teaches that *socially acquired* techniques of the body bring biological bodies into being. Accordingly, embodiment through qualitative kinesthetic feedback is a matter of cultural performance as well as genetic destiny. In this light, performativity, as a theory of how bodies achieve social recognition (and sensual materiality), should be understood as relevant to more than verbal phenomena. Reiterated *corporeal* performatives produce a wide range of qualitative interoceptive experiences (as well as gendered, classed, and raced bodies); and it is these experiences that are responsible for inspiring new gestural routines. Building on insights derived from Mauss, Merleau-Ponty, and Bourdieu, phenomological dance scholarship proposes that culturally framed interoceptive experiences constitute a type of knowledge—and engender a variety of agency—to which far more critical attention should be paid.[7]

Along with evoking a specific phenomenological tradition associated with Mauss and Merleau-Ponty, the term "gesture" also encourages us to view all movements executed by the human body as situated along a continuum—from the ordinary iteration of a habit to the most spectacular and self-conscious performance of a choreography. "Gesture" reminds us that movements of all kinds can be abstracted from the projects to which they contingently belong; accordingly, they can be studied as both discrete units of meaning *and* distinct instances of kinesis. As Rudolf von Laban established in the 1920s, the performance of any gesture—involving the torso, limbs, facial features, or digits—possesses its own peculiar momentum, velocity, rhythm, and scope. Gestures can be intentional or involuntary, crafted or spontaneous. They can be in the service of aesthetic, expressive, instrumental, or survivalist goals. But in all cases, gestures manifest a wide range of "effort qualities" (Laban's terms)—tentative or firm, bound or flowing, lethargic or rushed—that affect their meaning, both for others and for ourselves.[8] Of course, the ability to sense these qualitative differences, to abstract movement from its social "frame,"[9] is itself not natural, but rather a learned skill, one of the culturally elaborated "somatic modes of attention" that are designed to alert us to the *qualities,* not the results, of our acts.[10] Laban, after all, was interested in developing a cadre of professionals able to analyze and record movement; most of us do not attend to our gestures in this way, but instead go about our daily routines without being aware of what our bodies are sensing as we perform them, or how our movements—abrupt or gentle, effortless or forceful—make others feel. As specialized as Laban's perspective might seem, however, his way of attending to movement is potentially available to us all, albeit to differing degrees. When we perform gestures, it is possible to sense qualitative distinctions in tonicity, even as we become aware of the constructed and iterative nature of our acts. And it is precisely because our acts are learned and iterable, because cultural conditioning has been inscribed on our muscles and bones, that we are able to experience such distinctions in tonicity at all. Ultimately, it is because we experience differentiated movement qualities in the course of performing gestures that we are inspired to alter the rhythm, sequence, and meaning of our acts.

From this perspective, an additional reason why the term "gesture" is more analytically productive comes to light. Even while evoking the flesh of performance, "gesture" also recalls the carapace of routine, the inscription on the body of skills that allow individuals to traverse space in the first place. Implying *organized* kinesis, "gesture" serves as a reminder that movement is not purely expressive but is culturally shaped at every turn. That such a reminder is necessary is made evident by the increasingly abstract use of the term "movement" in works that study new media and embodied perception in technological environments.[11] Along with dance and performance studies, the discipline of new media studies has offered an important resource for the development of an alternative to constructivist approaches to the body. In the past few decades, a neovitalist tradition stemming from Nietzsche's *Will to Power* and gaining momentum in Gilles Deleuze's aesthetics has focused critical attention on a "virtual body" that is putatively related to and parallels the cultural-biological one. As provocative as these speculations are, they require qualification (and empirical exempla), for it is clear that no "virtual" potential can emerge without the restraining and enabling intervention of social conditioning. As Mauss observed nearly a century ago, the body's motility is the first vehicle societies employ to express their values and perpetuate themselves. The acquisition of a *habitus,* a set of bodily techniques, inevitably shapes the unfolding of virtual kinesis and constrains the types of kinesthetic sensation that will be available for inspiring innovation or resistance. Unfortunately, the critical recourse to an order of virtuality, while liberating in certain respects, has threatened to eclipse the dialogic and recursive relation of kinetic potentials to social forms that is the very subject of this book. If moving bodies perform in innovative ways, it is not because they manage to move without acquired gestural routines but because they gain knowledge *as a result of performing them.* The "practical enskilment" of the human subject involves, as Tim Ingold has claimed, both the disciplining of the body and the *discovery* of the individual body's singular "capacities of awareness and response."[12]

My interest in the moving body grows out of a desire to find a way beyond the impasse of constructivist theory, which I take to be the inability, after Foucault, to produce a convincing account of agency. I begin with the observation that despite the very real force of social conditioning, human subjects continue to invent surprising new ways of altering the inscribed behaviors they are called on to perform. Individual bodies generate "tactics"[13] that successfully belie the "durable" body *hexis* to which they have been subjected, the disciplining that, if we were to follow a long Marxist tradition, should make humans into gesturing machines.[14] To enable a better understanding of how this happens, why such myriad variations arise, I provide in each chapter a close reading of a cultural or artistic practice in which a gestural regime is at once enacted and put to the test. In Chapter 1, Marcel Mauss confronts everyday resistances to the *habitus;* in Chapter 2, Maurice Merleau-Ponty illuminates the protentive quality of kinesthesia captured in Bill Viola's video installation *The Passions;* in Chapter 3, André Leroi-Gourhan is called on to account for the persistence of gesture in contemporary digital writing; in Chapter 4, Henri Michaux experiments with the gestures of sign making in order to find a performing body beyond them; in Chapter 5, Judith Butler and Frantz Fanon propose challenges to the phenomenological assurance that interoceptive experience can be achieved and exert agency; and in the conclusion, Jacques Derrida discovers the unique present through the reiterated act of inscription. Building on the works of these philosophers, ethnographers, and artists of the gestural, I offer a model that is capable of navigating between the two most influential theories of subjective agency in circulation today: on the one hand a determinist, constructivist theory that depicts subjects as pliant material on which culture inscribes and on the other a neovitalist approach that tends to exaggerate the subject's capacity to express and fashion itself.

In this book, then, I treat gesture as the nodal point where culture (the imposition of bodily techniques), neurobiology (the given mechanics of a human sensorimotor apparatus), and embodied experience (the kinesthetic experience specific to an individual body) overlap and inform one another. Joining a growing number of humanists concerned with the foreclosure of empirical inquiry, I integrate contemporary developments in cognitive psychology and neuroscience into a theoretical approach that relies heavily on both phenomenological and constructivist accounts of embodiment as a *historical* (not simply biological) condition. My objective is to balance an entrenched historical determinism with recent scientific findings not for the purpose of affirming the existence of a transcendent agency predicated on a timeless biological body but rather to make available for theory *what scientists themselves are discovering:* a biological body that unfolds its unpredictable (as opposed to predetermined) possibilities as they are pruned or expanded through variables that are primarily historical and social in nature.

Clearly, scientists in many domains are far from eschewing the dialectic of culture and nature at the heart of much twentieth-century philosophizing. There is cause, then, to celebrate the dismantling of the wall between empirical research and poststructuralist theory; but in truth, this wall has never been a formidable obstruction. We need merely consider the huge impact of Henri Wallon's clinical studies of infant behavior on Jacques Lacan (and the generations of feminist theorists who followed his lead) to realize how co-dependent empirical and speculative modes of inquiry frequently are. Clinical studies dating from the 1930s have held a surprisingly firm grip on poststructuralist thought, despite the fact that their findings have been revised or discredited by later research. Where would much of contemporary theory be without Wallon's experiments with babies and mirrors, his postulation of a "gestural disorder" confronted at the "mirror stage"?[15] In truth, certain varieties of positivism have always been admissible, as long as they appeared to abet the linguistic turn. I too will welcome empirical research, but this time to theorize kinesthetic sensation as a point of intersection between cultural, biological, and personal imperatives. I believe it is possible to theorize human agency through the philosophical and scientific means presently available while remaining aware that ideas and experimental findings gleaned from contemporary empirical research are falsifiable, and that such research might evolve in unpredictable and perhaps unaccommodating ways.

A few words are in order concerning the principal terms of my analysis—*kinesthesia, gesture,* and *performative*—all of which enjoy rich histories in the disciplines consulted. I have already sketched out a brief definition of *embodiment,* the process whereby collective behaviors and beliefs, acquired through acculturation, are rendered individual and "lived" at the level of the body.[16] *Agency,* it follows, is the power to alter those acquired behaviors and beliefs for purposes that may be reactive (resistant) or collaborative (innovative) in kind. Throughout the book, I will expand on these lapidary definitions, but it should be recognized from the start that the existence of both depends on the role of *kinesthesia,* without which the subject would not be able to distinguish her own body from other bodies; would have no capacity for independent movement; and thus would be incapable of assuming any agency at all. Accordingly, the most urgent task is to clarify the meaning of *kinesthesia,* which I take to be fully a sixth sense, a source of sensations of which the subject is more or less aware.

Kinesthesia—and my claim that we have access to it—will probably provoke the most objections, so defining it requires some fine-grained analysis. Derived from the Greek *cineo,* "to put in motion," and *aisthesis,* "sensation" or "impression," the term "kinesthesia" refers to the sensations of movement transmitted to the mind from the nerves of the muscular, tendinous, and articular systems. First introduced by H. C. Bastian in *The Brain as an Organ of the Mind* (1880), "kinesthesia" was coined to replace the looser phrase "muscular sense,"[17] in circulation at the time. In 1906, Charles Scott Sherrington (also the originator of the distinction between *interoception* and *exteroception*) decided to add a new term to the emerging field of neurophysiology: *proprioception,* by which he referenced receptors charged with conveying stimuli provided by the body *proper* to the brain, insofar as these stimuli guide the body in its various automatic processes or habitual behaviors. Much has been written on the distinction between the two (in some accounts kinesthesia is folded into proprioception, in others the reverse), but most authors reserve *kinesthesia* to refer to sensations of movement (rather than balance) available to the conscious mind. Sherrington in fact wrote that kinesthesia, as opposed to proprioception, is bodily sensation "considered in its own right *and functioning for introspection.*"[18] Kinesthetic sensation is thus in league with the mind's attempt to experience its embodiment as an animate form. That kinesthesia might be seen as providing sensory experience for the purposes of "introspection" is of course highly relevant, for it implies that the way movement feels ("sensation in its own right") can indeed become the object of intentional consciousness (to evoke Husserl's terms). Such an implication has begun to be explored by scientists in Sherrington's wake; the contemporary neuroscientist Alain Berthoz has even expounded a thesis on "enactive perception" the cornerstone of which is the agentic, decision-influencing role of kinesthetic sensation.[19] Empirical findings from a number of sources suggest that we should treat kinesthesia as a sixth sense, one that, like sight, informs conscious as well as unconscious behaviors. If *proprioception* designates sensory stimulation produced *by* the self, *kinesthesia* designates sensory stimulation produced *for* the self; as such, it opens up a field of reflexivity in which the subject becomes an object (as body) of her own awareness. The kinesthetic body sense, then, is vulnerable to the intervention of culture at the very moment when the situated subject must make propositional sense (meaning) of what she feels. That is, it is precisely when sensations produced by holding a posture or executing a gesture become available to "introspection," or conscious awareness, that they must be mediated by language or by equally culture-specific systems of visual imagery. The intervention of culture is necessary to transform the inarticulate workings of the nervous system into the *experience* of a particular subject.

A strong formulation of this point would replace the word "intervention" with the word "construction," thereby reducing kinesthetic sensation to a mere image supplied from without. In his account of twentieth-century dance, Andrew Hewitt implicitly effects such a reduction when he writes that "nothing could be more ideological" than "to celebrate the somatic—

the seamless experience of embodiment—as the truth."[20] To his mind, crediting kinesthetic sensations with the capacity to speak "truth" about the body is tantamount to reestablishing an essentialist paradigm that veils the historical construction of bodies *and* their "truths." My question, though, is how, without according value to kinesthesia, we can explain why so many movement practitioners, yogis, dancers, and mimes seek recourse to kinesthetic sensation to improve coordination, balance, contact, and skeletal alignment? And how are we to respond when the efficacy of kinesthetic feedback proves to be an experimentally registered fact?[21] To be sure, it would be an exaggeration to state, as Martha Graham famously did, that "Movement never lies." As scholars and movement practitioners have long known, images and discourses provided by culture can indeed influence what a subject thinks she feels. But we must guard ourselves from assuming constructivism's most undialectical posture. Clearly, bodily sensations do not *always* lie. At times they offer valuable information about our culture and its disciplines, information that we can draw on to develop new ways of moving through and inhabiting space.[22]

There are good reasons to remain skeptical with regard to the purported immediacy of somatic experience; and yet it is now time to explore how the body might speak to us—not beyond but *through* cultural frames. I am by no means alone in advancing this argument; indeed, a new wave of theorists—in visual studies, performance studies, and anthropology (not to mention cognitive science)—now seek our provisional acceptance that a kinesthetic sense not only exists but also provides valuable intelligence concerning the state of one's body and world. That such an acceptance must still be solicited is suggested by a brief glance at the number of recent works striving to identify an area of sensation not thoroughly saturated by culture (or, in another version, discourse). We find Elizabeth Grosz, for instance, protesting in *Volatile Bodies: Toward a Corporeal Feminism* that radical constructivism may have thrown the baby out with the bathwater by making it impossible to credit as authentic a subject's experience of her own body. "It is clear," she writes, "that experience cannot be taken as an unproblematic given. . . . Nevertheless, I would contend that without some acknowledgement of the formative role of experience in the establishment of knowledges, feminism has no grounds from which to dispute patriarchal norms."[23] To her credit, Grosz identifies the "experience of the lived body" as a potential area of resistance to "patriarchal norms," but her ultimate decision to treat the body as a "surface of inscriptions" dilutes the strength of her initial retort. Like many scholars in the humanities, she entraps herself in a linguistic metaphor and thereby forecloses the possibility of exploring alternative, non-text-based vocabularies and concepts for approaching the body's own experience of itself.[24]

Richer resources can be found in the emerging field of "sensuous scholarship," practiced by anthropologists Sally Ann Ness, Paul Stoller, and Deidre Sklar, among others.[25] For these scholars, the "experience of the lived body" is by no means an abstraction but instead takes precise, if multiple, forms, such as tasting, hearing, and feeling the body move. As opposed to Grosz (and most of the feminist theorists who have sought in the wake of Butler's work to advance the category of the somatic), anthropologists, archeologists, and dance ethnographers have been exacting in their search to understand just how the body's experience of itself might play a role not only in the emergence of subjectivity but, further, in the process of meaning construction in which cultures are involved. In this vein, no study has been more successful in bringing to the fore the types of awareness that constitute an "experience of the lived body" than Kathryn Linn Guerts's *Culture and the Senses: Bodily Ways of Knowing in an African Community.*[26] If continental philosophy has had to wait for neuroscience to confirm the existence of a sixth sense, the people Guerts studies, the Anlo-Ewe-speaking people of Ghana, have long possessed a word in their everyday vocabulary, *"seselelame,"* to designate "feeling in or through the body"; further, they have made *seselelame* central to their cultural self-understanding, repeatedly referring to it in their proverbs, their judgments, and their reasoning. For them, kinesthesia is as significant for the construction of knowledge as sight or hearing. Guerts maintains that if Anlo-Ewe speakers refer to *seselelame* with great regularity it is not because the sensations it names are products of some discursive formation peculiar to that culture. Rather, cultures merely differ from one another with respect to the sense experiences they privilege. Experiencing *seselelame* is not something the Anlo-Ewe-speaking people alone can do; it is something Guerts claims is available to her—and to us. Although our culture might not encode kinesthetic sensations in the same way, that does not mean that they do not enter our self-understanding and play a large role in constructing—and challenging—our *habitus.* "Humans," Guerts writes, "are capable of experiencing and manifesting a multitude of kinesthetic motions and postures but the predilection for essentializing and labeling these patterns is limited to those cultural traditions that have placed a high premium on kinesthesia and proprioception" (81).

One of the larger implications of Guerts's research, pertinent to my project here, is that the category of kinesthesia is worth our attention not because kinesthetic sensation is more truthful than any other modality of experience (it "cannot lie") but because it has as much epistemological weight as any other (it might not lie). It can be used to judge the accuracy of other knowledges and beliefs and thus merits respect as one among many voices of reason. For Guerts, as well as for the community she studies, kinesthetic sensations are neither inventions of discourse nor prereflexive "affections" forever unavailable to consciousness. They are, in short, tools for understanding the properties of self, other, and world. From the perspective Guerts opens up, it would seem perverse to deny the contribution of organic sensitivities, however they are framed. Only an academic prejudice could incline us to disregard bodily sensations because they have, supposedly, been constructed by discourse; only an academic prejudice could incite us to consider the material body to be abject and foreclosed.[27] The existence of words like *seselelame* indicate that, of course, sensory experience is inevitably mediated by signifiers; however, "mediated" should be taken to mean that signifiers provide *a medium of access to*—and not a fabrication of—experience. We can rely on John Lucy's notion that the linguistic terms available to a cultural group inflect the apprehension of, *but do not construct,* a material given. In Lucy's felicitous expression, specific languages "volunteer" categories of experience (such as *seselelame*).[28] The existence of a great number of languages each of which offers a slightly different way of classifying the senses attests to the fact that "immediate bodily experience is not understood or defined in any universal way."[29] Yet this by no means implies that the material body as a region of sensation and knowledge is forever unavailable to discourse or conscious apprehension. Bodily experiences may be culturally shaped ("not understood or defined in any universal way"); however, whether privileged or bracketed, they wield a force that shapes linguistic—and other choices—in a recursive process we call history and change.

There exist, to be sure, subcultures within Western culture (and many other cultures throughout the globe) that do not question kinesthetic experience as a significant resource for knowledge about the self. Dancers and movement practitioners explicitly credit kinesthetic experience with the capacity to produce skilled bodies while inspiring audiences to resonate to dance and other movement performances in acts of empathy that may have an ethical, socializing function in human communities. An excursus on kinesthesia would not be complete without mention of its role in intersubjective relations, its crucial function in establishing both the individual's body schema (a sense of the body as bounded and discrete) and the imagination we are able to exercise with respect to the feelings another embodied subject might have. As dance analyst John Martin argued in the 1930s, kinesthesia is a unique sense in that it provides the subject with a greater awareness of both her own body *and* that of the other.[30] In "Reading Dancing: Gestures toward a Semiotics of Dance," Susan Leigh Foster examines this paradox, asserting that deeper awareness of one's own movements—logically, an intensely interoceptive and therefore private "lived experience" of one's own body—actually allows access to understanding how *another* moving body might feel, a body that is external yet at the same time continuous with the subject in imaginative and sensual terms. In light of this paradox, Foster considers the word "kinesthesia" to mean not only "the feeling of moving which the person experiences in the body in the act of moving" but also the sensations experienced while "imagining moving," or while "watching another move."[31] She states that kinesthesia "includes the feelings which allow us to guide our movement in the dark, which prompt us to shift from an uncomfortable position, or which [permit us to] respond with overall bodily tension as we watch a runner cross the finish line or an angry child throwing a tantrum." Kinesthesia, in short, implies an intimacy with the other that is sustained by an intimacy with the self.

Foster's examples, however, suggest a further reason why a definition of kinesthesia is in order. When, in Foster's example, one is prompted "to shift from an uncomfortable position" one's bodily awareness is more properly postural than gestural, and this difference—and its effect on terminology—must be clarified. Whereas dance theorists such as Warren Lamb and Elizabeth Watson distinguish neatly between the *gestures* of a moving body and the *postures* of a body stilled,[32] there are reasons to assert, as has developmental psychologist Daniel Stern, that kinesthetic awareness is functioning in both.[33] Locked in a cramped or awkward position, we may not be visibly moving, but our neuro-receptors nevertheless pick up the sensation of discomfort and, accordingly, compel us to move. Kinesthesia, in Stern's reading, refers to the feedback the body provides, and to which the subject can choose to listen; kinesthesia thus stands for body awareness in general, with the understanding that the body is never—even while dreaming—entirely in repose.

The degree to which subjects can become aware of the kinesthetic background underlying their existential choices and sense of corporeal bounds is, to be sure, a matter of debate. That debate is one of the central concerns of this book. For some theorists, the body is condemned to move in disciplined ways under a gestural regime it can neither escape nor fully acknowledge; for others, the subject has intermittent awareness of her movements, and can even develop practices to increase that awareness and thereby learn to alter the practices themselves. On one side of the fence, Pierre Bourdieu has argued that gestural routines are so "durably installed" that subjects no longer experience the kinesthetic sensation of performing them.[34] On the other, Deidre Sklar replies that no routine is so durably installed as to prevent kinesthetic awareness and potentially, through that awareness, transformation of the routine.[35] Both perspectives, as opposed as they may seem, take as a given that culture, in order to be "installed," depends on the disciplining of the body through gestural and postural norms. In the course of this book I will take on both sides of the debate, generating a theory in which the kinesthetic knowledge gained through gestural performance both permits the acquisition of these durable norms and introduces the possibility of realizing a potential beyond them.

But what, precisely, do I mean by "gesture" and "gestural routine"? It could be argued, as has Adam Kendon, that the word "gesture" should be reserved exclusively for designating *communicative* gestures, comparable to speech.[36] As a linguist, Kendon is appropriately concerned with how gestures signify, the work they do, rather than how it feels to perform them. And this attitude is almost universal on the part of theorists of gesture, from Quintillian to Giorgio Agamben, from François Delsarte to Jean Baudrillard, regardless of whether they are interested in expressive gestures or bodily techniques such as gait. Yet one theorist of gesture stands out for having recalled the origin of gesture in the *dual* neuromuscular function of the body's organic tools. André Leroi-Gourhan, the subject of Chapter 3, maintains that from an evolutionary perspective, there is no necessary distinction between the instrumental and the expressive gesture; both are *"chaînes opératoires"* that produce kinesthetic experience as part of the recursive loop of correction and refinement over time. Considered abstractly, expressive and instrumental gestures are interchangeable; what makes them *gestures* is that they involve the body in a double process of active displacement (through contraction of the muscles) and information gathering (through the neuro-receptors located along these muscles). To provide a brief example: the movement of striking a stone can produce a tool, a mimed performance of making a tool, or a gestural sign of fury; ultimately, however, on the level of sensation and quality of effort, there is no way to distinguish between an expressive gesture and an instrumental skill. An actor can train herself to smile in a certain way, and then absorb that smile as part of her professional repertory of "I can's." The salient feature of smiles and strikes, of expressive and instrumental gestures, is that both produce kinesthetic experience in the course of being performed. Since it is impossible to determine precisely which motor behaviors are expressive and which ones are instrumental, all motor behaviors, Ingold suggests, may be considered "skill sets," sequences of gestures or gestural routines, that generate kinesthetic feedback as part of their dual function (operational and cognitive, or information-gathering).[37]

By "gesture," then, I mean something like "technique of the body" in Mauss's sense (see Chapter 1): a way of sleeping, standing, running, dancing, or even grimacing that involves small or large muscle movements, consciously or unconsciously executed. Although too broad, perhaps, the term has the advantage of allowing us to name any use of the body that can become a source of kinesthetic feedback, and thus agency. My aim is to construct a theory of how a biologically and/or culturally informed use of the body affords a type of awareness that is "agentic" in the sense that it plays a role in what a subject does and feels. Gestures, of course, interact with other information-gathering processes of the mind and body. They are organs of what I call "distributed agency," mobilizing sensory surfaces to engage "the dynamic mentality of one's neuromusculature" in decision-making processes on many planes.[38] In some cases, the subject *attends* to the clear message, or "dynamic mentality," of the neuromusculature; she becomes "conscious" of the kinesthetic directive (in Daniel Dennett's sense of the term).[39] In other cases, the subject may remain largely unaware of why she has altered or repeated her routine. Either way, the gesture—communicative, instrumental, or aesthetic—draws on a kinesthetic background; in order to move, the subject must rely not only on learned routines and personal or collective desires but also on her engagement, her *embeddedness,* what Martin Heidegger calls her "everyday being-in-the world."[40] As I will repeatedly demonstrate, the term "gesture"—because it evokes the kinetic-kinesthetic loop—belongs to a phenomenological vocabulary just as securely as it does to a linguistic one. Thus, while Kendon's effort to discriminate between types of gestures offers certain advantages in clinical situations, it is the underlying continuity among gestures that I wish to emphasize here.

But there is one more category of gesture that Kendon treats in passing, the "performative gesture," that is central to the thesis of this book. In the strictest sense, the performative gesture is an "operator," Kendon explains; it is a learned shape or sequence that not only indicates but instantiates, embodies, a "request, a plea, an offer, an invitation, a refusal."[41] Similar to verbal performatives, gestures of request, refusal, and so on realize the action they denote. My use of the word "performative" draws from this classical, Austinian understanding of the term, but I expand its meaning in ways suggested by both Michaux and Butler, whose works I examine more closely in Chapters 4 and 5. These writers maintain that it is not only "operators" that are performative, that create something that did not exist without or before them; rather, *all* gestures are performative insofar as they bring into being, through repetition, a body fabricated specifically to accommodate their execution. As in the example with which I began, the limbs and torso of the graffiti writer assume a certain shape, and they produce a particular muscular tension, as a result of sketching and resketching the enlarged letters of the name, that is, as a result of performing a gestural routine. In contrast to verbal performatives, which involve the body on a far smaller scale, gestural performatives in the sense I develop here provide occasions for rich kinesthetic experience. A gesture is a performative—it generates an acculturated body for others—and, at the same time, it is a performance—it engages the moving body in a temporality that is rememorative, present, and anticipatory all at once.

My sense of a performative that is also a performance is very close to Peggy Phelan's understanding of live performance as "representation without reproduction," an event that leaves a nonvisible remainder that is resistant to language.[42] However, I theorize this remainder as salient, productive, and interoceptively available, rather than abject, negative, and out of reach. Performing gestures can generate sensations that are not-yet-marked, not-yet-meaningful. These sensations exact change; they may be productive of new movements, new meanings. Culture is, of course, limitlessly recuperative, and the sensory excess of gesturing is only one part of a recursive loop in which the body is freed only to be, once again, enchained. But if, as Bourdieu has stated, culture's struggle against the individual body has to be "endlessly won and rewon,"[43] and if, as he insists further, a cultural *habitus* must be flexible in order to be sustained (it must accommodate "an infinite number of practices that are relatively unpredictable"),[44] then we owe it to our creative selves to see just where that flexibility, where that infinity, ends.

A final note on the graffiti writer who appears intermittently in my discussion: Although this book is not explicitly about graffiti, the practice of forming large-scale letters with the entire body evokes the duality of gestural practice and serves to illustrate the arguments that I—and others I discuss—have made. The figure of the graffiti writer gathers together the subjects treated: Mauss's "techniques of the body"; Merleau-Ponty's musings on "motor power"; Leroi-Gourhan's theory of the origins of inscription; Michaux's gestural experimentation with mark-making; Butler's notion of the body as sign; and, finally, Derrida's meditations on *"tâtonnement,"* or groping, as a tactile-proprioceptive-kinesthetic exercise related to spacing, or *"différance."* In the last chapter, "Illegible Graffiti," I show that a number of major philosophical texts of the neo-Hegelian tradition harbor a scene in which a graffiti writer, a scribbler, turns back reflexively to ponder the role of the body in forming words. This fascination with the sensuous choreography of graffiti, I suggest in conclusion, might very well be due to the way it dramatizes the functioning of culture. Culture as gesture, producing always more and other than it intends.

CHAPTER ONE

The "Structuring" Body:
Marcel Mauss and Bodily Techniques

EVER SINCE "Les Techniques du corps" (Techniques of the body) first appeared in print in 1935,[1] the name Marcel Mauss has been associated with the establishment of a field devoted to the study of gesture as simultaneously a biological, social, and psychological phenomenon. Mauss's prescient contribution was to recognize that all three factors manifest their influence not only through stated beliefs but, even more fundamentally, through specific movement patterns, some linked to ritual and aesthetic practices, others to the manipulation of tools. Mauss was of course not the first thinker to treat bodily techniques as culturally significant; he inherited a rich tradition culminating in eighteenth-century treatises on perception and body language.[2] By the time Mauss composed "Techniques of the Body," the moving body was garnering attention in many other realms as well, such as modern dance, eurythmics, the Alexander technique, and, soon after, the Feldenkrais method. In the industrial realm, Frederick Winslow Taylor had attempted to render movement more efficient; Etienne Jules Marey's and Eadweard Muybridge's photographs dissected movement into slices of time, and German fascists were struggling to perfect movement for the purposes of hygiene and the promotion of a national ideal. What distinguishes Mauss's approach is that he was not interested in the perfection of the body through corporeal practices, or even in discovering a "natural" body that certain carefully developed corporeal practices might hope to respect (although there are hints of this in his writings). Mauss's project was neither aesthetic (he did not aspire to free and celebrate the body, as did Isadora Duncan) nor instrumental (he was not interested in determining, as were the industrialists, how best to exploit the kinetic energy of human beings). Rather, as an anthropologist, he sought to understand how a physiological given, the human body, becomes a classed, gendered body—to wit, a *social fact*—through the act of gesturing. Mauss may have been influenced by early musings on the role of dance movement in the works of E.°E. Evans-Pritchard and studies by American anthropologists, but the remarkable efflorescence of ethnographies on dance and bodily techniques over the course of the twentieth century can only be attributed to him.[3]

Mauss was part of a wave of cultural relativism that flowed through the *sciences humaines* at the turn of the century. Possessing an erudition and an open mind rarely found together, he proposed that sophisticated bodily techniques of all varieties are developed in every society without exception. He thereby introduced a large dose of skepticism with respect to the Comtian thesis that highly civilized societies all pass through the same three phases of technological achievement, and that therefore societies that do not possess electricity or the steam engine are evolutionarily backward, stuck in an earlier phase. Instead of regarding societies with different technologies and body practices as "primitive" or "barbarous," Mauss and the generation he trained began to entertain the notion that perhaps there is no civilization "that is, on all points, technically superior to another," as André-Georges Haudricourt wrote in 1948. "Progress in one area leads to backwardness elsewhere."[4]

This new cultural relativism facilitated a growing interest in bodily techniques other than those developed in "advanced" Western societies. Paradoxically, however, such cultural relativism also implied an increased sensitivity to the potentially superior ways in which human anatomy could be brought into harmony with instrumental practices in societies other than those previously dubbed "advanced." Mauss and his followers not only presupposed that there is more than one way to do things; they presupposed that there are cultures in which things are done *better*, or, to put it more analytically, cultures in which bodily techniques manage to preserve a wider range of movement possibilities offered by the human kinetic disposition. These cultures, even if lacking in machinic technologies, could be considered more evolved with respect to, at least, kinesthetic concerns. For instance, as Mauss notes in "Techniques of the Body," the bodily techniques composing the French *habitus* are far from the most practical or intelligent with respect to physiology, insofar as they end up foreclosing many of the kinetic possibilities available to a newborn child. For example, he wrote, if French children were encouraged to assume the squatting position so widely practiced in non-Western cultures, they would avoid the restrictions on lower-body movement that result from sitting in chairs.

Insofar as he reframed the context within which the body should be studied, Mauss inaugurated a major paradigm shift in the social sciences, one that has had wide repercussions in the domains of philosophy, literature, art, and performance. Countless critics have explored these repercussions in a variety of realms, but the aspect of the paradigm shift that is most important for my present purposes is both less obvious and more profound. To be sure, Mauss has often been credited with forging "the notion of bodily techniques, which opens up a whole new category," as one critic puts it, thereupon making the body "the very first matter of the social, the site where it is inscribed [*le lieu où il s'inscrit*], where we must learn to decipher it."[5] My own hypothesis, however, is that while drawing attention to the role of the moving body in the perpetuation of cultural regimes, and while recasting the body as the material on which these regimes are first inscribed, Mauss simultaneously discovered the role of kinesthesia in *transforming* these regimes. He did not privilege kinesthetic and other forms of somatic awareness in the same way, or to the same extent, as did his (rough) contemporaries William James and John Dewey. The bulk of his work on techniques of the body focuses on how distinct societies impose specific practices on the body, not on the rich somatic feedback the body produces. Yet he would be a far less interesting (and far less dialectical) thinker if his writings merely led us to conclude that the body is a surface, a materiality, on which culture, through movement practices, stamps its indelible trace. From the very beginning of his investigations into socially elaborated techniques of the body, Mauss is concerned with the meaning-making aspects of motor movements, that is, the way movement experience supports *yet inflects* a culturally legible signification. As a close reading of "Techniques of the Body" demonstrates, hidden in Mauss's Durkheimian sociology, in his conviction that the social precedes and forges the individual, is a radical phenomenology according to which the performance of acquired social practices—involving kinesthetic feedback—may create forms of resistance that no inscription can entirely fix.

Mauss gives only the barest hint that kinesthetic feedback conditions in its turn the conditioning the body receives; it is the task of later ethnographers and movement theorists to adduce a systematic account of how such a recursive process might be understood. What is bracing about Mauss's writings, and the reason they remain an exemplary resource, is that the issue of kinesthetic resistance only arises in the context of a much greater emphasis on the tenacity of social conditioning. That is, Mauss does not celebrate the moving body's interoceptive grasp of itself outside the context either of language (and its influence on how interoceptive experience is constituted) or of social coercion, the organized—as opposed to natural—forces that solicit the body to move in the first place. Mauss's texts provide grounds for the hypothesis that the social production of the body and the body's production of the social are inextricably intertwined rather than chronologically successive. His analysis of body practices in "Techniques of the Body" suggests that the emergence of the individual body as a producer of interoceptive experience and the establishment of society as a forger of individual bodies are in fact simultaneous events, both equally predicated on the body's *animate* form, its capacity to move in space.

Mauss's mature teachings on the body promote two interrelated propositions. First, he argues that social conditioning reaches beyond the ideas in the mind (what Emile Durkheim called "collective representations") to lodge itself in the very tissues of the body. Second, he observes that cultural subjects have a lived experience of such social conditioning, that is, a sensual apprehension, in those tissues, of socially organized kinesis. Although Mauss does not investigate deeply the ways in which kinesthesia, or the felt experience of moving, might inflect the gestural routines a subject executes, his work provides a roadmap for future research, a critical resource for renovating contemporary paradigms of embodiment, performance, and technesis. In contrast with his successor Bourdieu, who tends to see cultural subjects as stamped indelibly with conditioned patterns they cannot change, Mauss allows us to recast the act of gesturing as deeply contradictory in its implications. Gesturing is the visible performance of a sensorimotor body that renders that body at once culturally legible (socially useful) *and interoceptively available to itself.* Mauss sets out an agenda for a truly phenomenological constructivism, one that places gestural performatives, as opposed to discursive performatives, at the center of cultural theories of subjectivation and resistance.

"I must be touched to feel"

Precisely why did Mauss become interested in studying the imprint of culture on the body? What aspects of his training as a historian and sociologist of religion eventually led him to theorize the ways in which the body moves? How, in short, did "Techniques of the Body" come to be written? The function of this chapter is to answer these questions, first through a close reading of "Techniques of the Body" to determine what it actually says, then by means of a historical recontextualization of Mauss and the discourses from which he derived inspiration. My objective is to return to the very roots of Mauss's approach and to draw from them the sustenance necessary to construct a theory of gesture that realizes a potential he did not fully exploit. In this way, I set the stage for the emergence of a phenomenological theory of subject construction that accounts more fully for how meaning is both embodied and displaced by moving human subjects.

The primary argument of Mauss's deceptively modest text, first delivered as a series of lectures and finally published in 1935, is that gesturing is absolutely central to the cultural construction of the body. In making this argument, Mauss successfully shifted the attention of his scholarly community away from what had previously been considered the essential role of representation, myth, or language and toward the equally important function of the moving body as a maker and interpreter of cultural meanings. In "Techniques of the Body" his stated project is to trace the "repercussions and effects" of acquired physical practices not only on the individual psyche and on group dynamics but also on the very physiology of the body.[6] He insists repeatedly that human motility is a subject that cannot be ignored if other aspects of the human social world are to be properly explained. "Techniques of the body," Mauss begins, are organizations of kinetic energy that are plural, differential with respect to the societies in which they evolve, as opposed to natural, necessary, or given with the species. "I mean by this word [technique] the ways in which men, in every society and in a traditional fashion, know how to make use of [se servir de] their bodies" (SA, 365). Following the logic of the verb se servir de, he specifies further that the word "technique" does not necessarily imply the use of a prosthetic tool but refers to the human body itself considered as a type of instrument that one makes use of and thus models to certain purposes (SA, 371–372). The particular ways a body moves, the sequence of gestures it executes (e.g., to eat) or the attitudes it assumes (e.g., to sleep), differ according to culture, era, class, and gender.

Although he wrote "Techniques of the Body" near the end of his career, according to his student André-Georges Haudricourt, Mauss had been building the conceptual groundwork for a study of bodily techniques from very early on. As Haudricourt recounts: "In his courses, Mauss insisted on the necessity of gathering as much information as possible on the use and function of the object collected for the museum. This dynamic conception of technology eventually led him to conceive of a type of technique that produced no material object or instrument: he called these 'techniques of the body.'"[7] For Haudricourt, then, it was the museologist's contemplation of stationary cultural artifacts that instigated an inquiry into how they had been made. But in fact, Mauss arrived at the study of bodily techniques through a wide variety of channels, the most important of which I will examine further on. In the very first pages of "Techniques of the Body" Mauss provides a hint of how diverse these channels were: he indicates that his long-term interest in bodily techniques was awakened not by the contemplation of artifacts and the skilled bodies that made them but rather by his reflections on the movements his *own* body could make. In other words, Mauss initially framed his disciplinary turn toward the moving body with an autobiographical anecdote, suggesting in this way that a two-pronged approach, at once first person and third person, would be the only one appropriate to the odd self-reflexivity involved in capturing the objective creation of an intimate self.

According to his own account, Mauss was inspired to consider the subject of bodily techniques as early as 1898, when he become friendly with a scholar charged with writing an encyclopedia entry on *La Nage* (swimming). "This was a point of departure for me," Mauss explains, "a new object of study. Afterwards—and I realize this now—I began to pay attention to the transformation of swimming techniques over the course my own generation."[8] What Mauss begins to notice is not simply that members of other generations, or other cultures, swim differently than he, but that his own method of propelling himself forward in water is artificial, the product of training rather than necessity. "Formerly," he recalls,

> we were taught to dive, we were taught to close our eyes, then open them under water. Today, the technique is reversed. . . . Further, we have lost the habit [*usage*] of swallowing water and then spitting it out. During my time, swimmers thought of themselves as a kind of steamboat. It was stupid, but actually I still make this gesture [*C'était stupide, mais enfin je fais encore ce geste*]: I don't seem to be able to get rid of my technique. (SA, 367–368)

The advantage of Mauss's first example is that its very marginality (at least in a culture where swimming is not central to survival) permits him to step back from it to witness both its arbitrary quality ("It was stupid") and the tightness of its grip ("but I still make this gesture"). If he had begun with religious ritual gestures, such as making the cross or bowing, or even with a set of gestures related to hygiene, he would have had to struggle against the weight of the belief systems these gestures manifest. His opening is thus strategic, allowing him to model the self-reflexive glance, the recourse to a first person experience of a bodily practice, that he will advocate with respect to the observation and understanding of all gestural routines, even those that seem most "natural" or weighted with meaning. Moving quickly from swimming to shoveling, walking, table manners, and finally the centerpiece of the essay, the training of gender, Mauss introduces the Aristotelian term *habitus* to cover all of these, that is, to designate all techniques of the body that are at once faculties—the "I can's" a subject possesses—and, paradoxically, acquisitions, faculties that do not exist until they are learned. *Habitus* is well chosen, insofar as it captures the odd temporality of the gestural, that sudden ownership of a capacity that is both always virtually one's own (an innate faculty of the moving body) and, paradoxically, something one obtains *only through the intermediary of the other.* Ultimately, it is Merleau-Ponty who turns out to be the theorist of this paradoxical structure; however, it is Mauss first who puts the structure in his way.

After focusing on a swimming technique familiar to him personally, Mauss then shifts to the plane of generalization, arguing that the *habitus* present in any culture is composed of a set of motor responses corresponding to anatomical constraints as well as social exigencies. Invariably satisfying more than just physiological (instinctive or biological) needs, socially generated techniques of the body fall into discrete, graduated degrees of specialization. The first category Mauss identifies are the techniques that have to do with birthing and weaning; such practices may be considered "culturalizing" in the broadest sense, for in most cases (and there are surely exceptions), ways of giving birth, practices associated with the swaddling, comforting, feeding, and carrying of the infant, bring the baby's body into a cultural existence that is not gender specific. Both the gendered-male body and the gendered-female body of an Indian infant birthed in the traditional way (*"accouché debout"* [standing up], according to Mauss) will experience the pull of gravity downward toward the hands waiting below. Of course, very early on in the infant's development, differences in handling according to gender may make themselves felt; male bodies might be handled more roughly, or weaning might take place earlier, although there are bound to be tremendous individual differences even within one social setting or *habitus.* At any event, the body one experiences having varies from culture to culture (and not just from psyche to psyche), even at the earliest developmental stages.

Moving from birthing techniques to carrying techniques, Mauss then describes the advanced physical accomplishment of the infant-toddler who must learn to cling by means of his or her inner thighs to the mother's hip in cultures where mothers are in constant contact with their offspring. In contrast, babies held in a harness or stroller suffer a slight physical retardation in comparison with the babies who move more freely, and thus develop a muscularly molded body at an earlier age. Referring to the technique of the body that the infant slung on the hip acquires, Mauss glosses: "It is a remarkable gymnastique feat [*gymnastique*] for the baby, essential for life. And it is another type of gymnastic feat for the mother who has to carry the baby" (SA, 377). This *"gymnastique"* is formative not only physically but psychologically. The infant who "rides on the hip [*à califourchon sur la hanche*]" has greater physical intimacy with the mother; there are thus psychosexual implications to this fundamentally kinetic event: "It seems as though here"—in the case of the child held at the hip—there are born psychic states buried in our infancy. Genitals and skin make contact, and so on [*Il y des contacts de sexes et de peaux, etc.*]," Mauss's sentence trails off. The implication is that a technique of the body produces as its corollary particular experiences of the body of the other as well; models of intersubjectivity and a sense of one's sexuality could very easily be traced back to techniques of this sort. In short, contact with the other is what establishes our capacity for interoceptive experience in the first place.

In an essay devoted to Merleau-Ponty that sheds considerable light on Mauss as well, Judith Butler has meditated on the way the birth of the self as capable of interoception is predicated by Merleau-Ponty on contact, through touch, with the other. In "Merleau-Ponty and the Touch of Malebranche," Butler explicates Merleau-Ponty's grounding condition for self-hood in the following terms: "it is only on the condition that a body is already exposed to something other than itself, something by which it can be affected, that it becomes possible for a sentient self to emerge"; "I cannot feel if nothing touches me. . . . I must be touched to feel."[9] While the passage from "Techniques of the Body" quoted above certainly associates tactile contact with psychosexual maturation, it is also clear that for Mauss touch is always framed by specific bodily techniques—gestures, ways of ambulating or bearing weight—requiring movement. Mauss, then, is more concrete here than Butler; for him, touch presupposes a specific way of touching. In Mauss's example, the *"contacts de sexes et de peaux"* require a reaction on the muscular level: to maintain contact, the infant must grip. Touch, then, does not occur in a vacuum but establishes (and is the result of) culturally differentiated modes of kinesis. Touch isn't simply touch but soft touch, rough touch, consistent touch, or rhythmic, punctual touch, all of which imply and stimulate specific ways of moving, using the muscles, and then feeling the way these muscle sets have been used. The social, or intersubjective, element of the tactile contact inheres not only in the fact of being touched—a universal precondition for the emergence of subjectivity—but also in the *way* one is touched—a culturally differentiated precondition for the emergence of subjectivity. This is the profound lesson, with respect to the nascent or emergent self, of Mauss's "Techniques of the Body." As Mauss would claim, the social intervenes in the production of the individual not as some abstract, touchable and touching "other" but as a concrete, culturally specific "other" possessing a set of acquired touching "techniques."

By the time Mauss approaches a discussion of gender, it has been well established that movement practices, such as the way one is carried by the mother and the way one responds "gymnastically" to her touch, are crucial to the discovery of one's own body, whether that body is considered to be gendered from birth or not. Although Mauss is clearly a subtle thinker of psychosexual relations, and is thus aware of the potential gendering of the body at any stage, for him, the teaching of gender per se as a set of "techniques of the body" or gestural routines begins in earnest when the child enters adolescence. It is at this point that distinctions between the ways men are supposed to move and the ways women are supposed to move are imposed with full force. Most of the societies Mauss mentions provide formal education to the male children while retaining the women at home. But this does not mean that a rigorous *"dressage"* of women's bodies does not take place. Mauss's most telling example is that of the Maori technique of the body called *"l'onioi,"* a sequence of movements that exaggerates the sway of the hips while walking. The *"onioi"* is taught only to girls (Mauss does not indicate precisely when) through repeated drilling; girls who fail to practice this walk are verbally scolded for "not doing the onioi" (SA, 370).[10] Initiation rituals later provide further occasions for gender distinctions to be imposed through gestural routines inscribed on the bodies that perform them. However, this early interchange between mother and daughter establishes gender as something that is acquired on the level of movement.

Broadening his scope to discuss techniques of the body affecting almost every aspect of adult existence, Mauss then goes on to discuss the acquisition of such seemingly automatic behaviors as positions for sleeping and arrangements for sexual intercourse as well as more aestheticized behaviors such as riding horses, dancing, and the gestural routines required for specific *métiers.* Thus, the physical, but also spiritual and psychic life of an individual is determined by patterns of choreographed behavior. From the moment a child leaves the womb (and perhaps even before), its body is the subject of either unintentional or intentional *"dressage."* Mauss finds it hard, then, to say that there is a "natural" body, although certain types of movement are permitted (by the angle of joints and so on) and others rendered impossible. The closest Mauss comes to identifying a physical act that is not *"monté,"* put together somehow by culture from the anatomical givens, is the squat, or *"accroupissement."* In a passage that has become famous,[11] Mauss observes that *"l'enfant s'accroupit normalement"*— that is, infants *in general,* when left to their own devices, squat (SA, 374).

Some cultures do not set up obstacles to this normative infant behavior, and it becomes the default attitude assumed throughout the entire life of the adult. Other cultures, however, discourage children from squatting on their heels—perhaps because it keeps them nearer to the earth—insisting instead that they sit in chairs, which shortens the hamstrings and produces pain in the sacrum. "In my opinion, the squatting position is one that the infant should be allowed to retain," Mauss concludes in one of the great moments of modernist cultural relativism: "The greatest error is to take it away from him" (SA, 374).

Most interesting in Mauss's treatment is that he considers the squatting position to have physiological consequences, not merely social ones. Those who practice the technique of balancing the hips over the heels actually transform the shape of the limbs and joints involved: "A certain form of the tendons and even of the bones is nothing but the consequence of a certain way of carrying and setting down" (SA, 374). A technique of the body, the practice of which is socially sanctioned and reinforced, can actually shape the material body; the phenomenon of squatting is thus social and physiological at once. But Mauss suggests that the story is even more complicated, for the sociobiological is accompanied by a psychological attitude: sitting in chairs has, for certain Westerners, a symbolic significance, the implication of rising above the earth, not getting oneself dirty, being "civilized." The normal tendency of an infant ("normal" because prefigured by the position a baby necessarily assumes in the tight space of the womb) is overlaid with social and psychological meanings to the point where its reinforcement or inhibition has little to do with what the body itself might require in order to remain healthy or to avoid pain. Mauss calls the techniques civilization concocts, such as sitting in chairs, "efficient" ("efficace") not because they are harmonious with physiological givens (they avoid producing strain or injury) but rather because they fulfill other social requirements, such as ensuring hierarchies or establishing gender distinctions. All techniques of the body have to be "efficient" with respect to one or more demand. For instance, sitting on a chair allows the body to rest and remain relatively immobile; chair-sitting corresponds at least somewhat to a physiological exigency, the need to assume a position that saves energy for the accomplishment of some other task. At the same time, chair-sitting also establishes the maturity of a subject within Western culture; however unhealthy it is for the hamstrings, the *social* advantages of chair-sitting outweigh the physiological disadvantages. As Mauss shows time and again, in the case of shared bodily techniques, those belonging to the *habitus* of an entire community, the psychosocial implications of a practice often take precedence over the physiological ones.

Since the shared bodily techniques of an entire culture are rarely efficient in the practical sense, they must be taught in such a way that their *cultural* efficacy, the fact that they establish and maintain class, gender, and race distinctions, is made resoundingly clear. It must be brought home to the student that an infraction of the shared gestural regime entails serious consequences. Since the act of transmission of a gestural regime is so crucial to maintaining these distinctions, it is often ritualized, itself invested with psychosocial significance. Mauss signals his awareness of the crucial role of gesture transmission when he observes that the acquisition of techniques is dependent not only on the naturally mimetic attitude of infants but also on more organized or intentional forms of indoctrination. He notes that human societies are in fact distinguished from animal societies by their emphasis on the *verbal* transmission of gestural routines. As Mauss demonstrates in the example of the Maori woman scolding her daughter for failing to "do the onioi," techniques of the body are passed on by an authority figure to a subordinate through an apprenticeship that combines language and gesture in a way that, as William Noble and Iain Davidson have argued, has profound evolutionary consequences.[12] In the case of the Maori apprenticeship, the linguistic accompaniment to the gestural training is at once coercive ("you are not doing the onioi [*toi tu ne fais pas l'onioi*]") and commemorative (SA, 370). That is, the verbal phrase itself preserves *and reinforces* the "socially established" meaning of the technique: in this instance, "you are not doing the onioi" means "you are not being a proper woman." "Doing" the set of gestures *("l'acte monté")* is a way of *being* a woman; swaying the hips from side to side in an exaggerated manner is part of what it feels like (and looks like) to be (gendered as) a woman. The verbal instruction and the scolding are necessary to compensate for the discomfort experienced by the anatomically unmotivated, biologically inessential, and thus fundamentally arbitrary exaggeration of the inevitable swaying of the hips. And as the swaying is practiced, repeated over time, the trauma on the knees and feet and lower back will eventually be naturalized as part of what it feels like to be a woman, or to have a woman's body. In some cases, however, these sensations might be noted as uncomfortable, at odds with other bodily needs that perhaps have not yet received a name, but that nonetheless, as we shall see, eventually exert a pressure on the convention and weaken its hold on behavior.

Oral transmission of techniques of the body is an element of what Mauss calls "tradition" (SA, 371). The techniques themselves thus exist on several registers: they are chains of movement performed by individual bodies; they shape the bodies that perform them; and they play a role in a wider system of social organization, transmitting and embodying the laws of cultural tradition. It is in this last sense that techniques of the body may be considered *"efficace"*: they are efficient instruments for creating and enforcing social distinctions between male and female, old and young, and for defining bodies as appropriate for executing certain tasks. Much of the time, techniques of the body are not, in fact, "efficient" in any other way. Doing the *"onioi"* is certainly not a more efficient way to arrive at one's destination, although swimming with alternate breathing may be. On the one hand, then, Mauss can say with some confidence that techniques of the body constitute (and require) a "constant adaptation to a physical, mechanical, or chemical goal (for example, when we drink)" (SA, 372). The many enchained gestures involved in lifting a glass to the mouth and sipping from it serve the purpose of facilitating the ingestion of fluids necessary for survival. On the other, some of those gestures have nothing to do with a physiological goal or purpose: the raising of the English pinky, for instance, is unnecessary and impractical; it is a movement that is only "efficient" insofar as it successfully perpetuates a classist and racist social system without, however, hastening the flow of liquid to the mouth. It is implicit throughout Mauss's account that socially "efficient" techniques of the body must work hard to suture meaning to movement. The name of the act or the verbal instructions used to teach it must somehow convince practitioners that what they are doing really does mean what they are told it means: doing the *"onioi"* makes you a desirable woman; raising the pinky lends you class.

Mauss's anecdotes imply that culture is strong enough, its languages sufficiently persuasive, to divorce the meaning of gestures from the way they make the body feel. A gesture can be semanticized, made to mean something for a particular culture (being a woman), even if executing it means something quite different on the kinesthetic register (being in pain). Perhaps for this reason, the natural movements of the body, the default positions it would most likely assume in order to accomplish a task, appear irretrievable. Mauss's emphasis on the symbolic meaning of movement practices renders problematic the attribution of "naturalness" even to the gestural routines associated with the fulfilment of basic needs. As Mauss comments, "in sum, there simply may not be a 'natural way' for adults to do things" (SA, 370). He states here not that no "natural way" exists but that such a way might be unavailable to *adults,* that is, to subjects whose moving bodies have been thoroughly saturated with acquired techniques and their cultural meanings. At the same time, however, Mauss provides a blueprint for future theorists who wish to distinguish between the earliest, instinctual, or anatomically motivated movement practices of the infant (such as squatting) and the more verbally mediated and gender-specific practices imposed on the prepubescent or pubescent social being. The grip of culture on the body is never completely solid, Mauss implies, because training cannot ensure that earlier, more spontaneous ways of moving will be stamped out. *"Dressage,"* in short, does not always work. It is in fact Mauss himself who reveals a scenario in which the body—as a set of movement possibilities—exerts pressure on the domesticating and discriminating routines favored by culture. His example of the Maori mother teaching her daughter such a basic motor skill as walking is predicated on the *failure* rather than the success of the transmission: "you are not doing the onioi" is, after all, the salient phrase. Not only does Mauss provide evidence that the daughter is not conforming to the technique of the body that her society requires her to perform in order to be gendered "woman" but he also shows us that the Maori language *registers* this nonconformity, it indicates that the *habitus* is not solid, uniformally applied and acquired, but instead vulnerable to resistance of an albeit subtle kind.

The Maori daughter's nonconformity receives no direct explanation in "Techniques of the Body"; yet it is possible to prise one from Mauss's text. While speaking of the traditional context for technique acquisition, he notes that for the subject who is learning how to execute the sequence of gestures, the technique "is felt *(senti)* by the person executing it to be a mechanical, physical, or physico-chemical act" (SA, 372). What Mauss is saying is that most of the time, techniques of the body, or *"actes montés,"* "feel" automatic, inevitable, and natural, because—like a sleeping position or gait—they have been subsumed as a faculty. Our bodies have become sculpted in such a way that the acquired technique now feels more "natural" than what we did before. Blind to the contortions demanded, we no longer sense kinesthetically the impact of our movements on our tendons, ligaments, and bones. However, as the Maori example shows, nonconformity, subversion, and correction undoubtedly exist. Evidence drawn from the evolution of more autonomous athletic or aesthetic techniques, such as swimming or dancing, shows that even within one culture techniques of the body do change over time. And there are subjects who do not manage to master even the most "durably installed" techniques of gender, subjects who continue to thread out of their own kinetic dispositions gestural sequences that do not conform to traditional practices, that do not efficiently support the categories a gestural regime is constructed to maintain. How can such alterations of "traditional" and "efficient" techniques be explained? What resources does Mauss's account offer to help us understand the reluctance of the Maori girl?

Perhaps Mauss's text does not provide us with the answer we require for the very reason that his goal was not to explain resistance but rather the relative lack of it. And yet, even if he does not choose to probe it himself, he does point to a very revealing moment, the fragile period of instruction and apprenticeship when a culturally significant technique of the body is being passed from generation to generation. His example of the Maori girl is more telling than perhaps even he realized, for it signals, for future researchers, a crucial area of investigation: the relation between gesture and language in acts of acquisition and performance.

"Obligatory gestures and signs"

It is now time to turn to the influences that played a role in the composition of "Techniques of the Body," including those that encouraged Mauss to focus on the organic body as a site on which social meanings can be inscribed as well as those that caused him to question whether such inscriptions are as deep as they appear. First, it is important to establish that "Techniques of the Body" did not spring like Athena from the head of Zeus. On the contrary, the essay emerged after a long gestation period; it actually marked the culmination of years of scholarship and teaching while at the same time indicating a new intellectual path that Mauss never lived to pursue.[13] Mauss's decision to investigate the role of the moving body in the maintenance and transmission of belief systems provoked what Bruno Karsenti has called the "first dissonance" with the sociological discourse inherited from Durkheim, a discourse that was dominant during the entire period of Mauss's intellectual formation. This first and crucial dissonance consisted in "anchoring individual representation in the very physiology of the organism," rather than halting, as Durkheim had, the penetration of the social at the layer of the skin.[14] Indeed, Durkheim had gone a long way toward dismantling the boundary between the libidinal life of the individual and the socialized psyche dominated by collectively generated belief systems (or *"représentations collectives"*). To this extent, Durkheim can be seen as providing Mauss with the ammunition to begin questioning disciplinary boundaries (and essentializing categories) of many kinds. However, at the turn of the century, the most seemingly impregnable boundary—that between the social and the organic (and thus between sociology and physiology)—was still solidly in place.[15] Influenced by his mentor, Mauss began as Durkheim had, chipping away at the integrity of the individual psyche to reveal its social conditioning; but he ended up blurring more entrenched distinctions between the organic body and the social form as well.

Karsenti traces the first signs of dissonance with classical Durkheimian sociology back to 1901, the year during which Mauss composed, along with Paul Fauconnet, an entry for *La Grande Encyclopédie* entitled "Sociologie."[16] It is here, according to Karsenti, that Mauss first "tempers" the distinction between "individual representations," the subject's supposedly independent consciousness, and "collective representations," the socially generated images imported into the psyche from his or her milieu. Durkheim had argued earlier in his essay "Individual Representations and Collective Representations" (1898) that psychology, incarnated in this instance in the person of Théodule Ribot, divided the individual's psyche too sharply from the individual's participation in a collective life. To his mind, the mental life of individuals is by no means a direct echo of physiological processes but instead crystallizes and reflects systems of classification shared by the members of a social group. The fault of contemporary psychology, he wrote in 1898, was to "reduce consciousness to no more than an epiphenomenon of physical, organic existence"; the external stimulus, Durkheim insisted, "instead of being discharged immediately as movements, is halted in its progress, submitted to a long development *sui generis,* and a period of varying length elapses before the motor reaction appears."[17] As opposed to Bergson, for whom a freedom, composed of "affects," intervenes in the stimulus-reaction coupling, Durkheim inserts a "collective representation," a structure that would organize, for the human subject, the sensations experienced and provide a socially acceptable action, a motor response.[18]

Mauss's early career was predicated on the principle Durkheim had advocated: that the social intervenes in a crucial way between the organic, material life of the body and the representations that lead that body to act. However, Mauss began to complicate Durkheim's principle by suggesting that the order of the organic itself is not pure and discrete. If the physical body could be influenced in its most seemingly autonomous mechanisms by social pressures, then it made no sense to separate psychology from sociology, or sociology from physiology, for that matter. Sociology, as an approach, could invade the entire spectrum of human sciences, just as the social penetrated every layer of human being. As Mauss argues in "Real and Practical Relations between Psychology and Sociology" ("Rapports réels et pratiques de la psychologie et de la sociologie," 1924), the barriers between the disciplines are artificially constructed, and thus the knowledges they engender are necessarily flawed. The *"paliers"* or "levels" of human existence that sociology, psychology, and physiology were seeking to explicate, Mauss avers, simply cannot be understood in isolation from each other but should be studied simultaneously, as intertwined and mutually constitutive. This approach, which Mauss would refine over the course of a generation, replaced Durkheim's "homo duplex"—a biological versus social man—with an *"homme total."* It is this *"homme total"* that Mauss believed the human sciences, psychology among them, to be slowly unearthing: "what is most interesting to me in these new discoveries in psychology," he writes in 1924,

> is not simply what concerns consciousness, but rather *the relations between consciousness and the body.* In reality, in the way we practice sociology, there is no such thing as a human being divided up into separate faculties. We are always dealing with the corporeal and the mental in their entirety, given once and all at the same time.[19]

In a series of articles composed between 1924 and 1934, Mauss set about analyzing this human being in his/her totality, and, with the same stroke, initiated the process of dismantling the disciplinary boundaries that had prevented the study of the body from entering the purview of sociology. Most notably, in "The Psychic Effects on the Individual of the Idea of Death Suggested by the Collective" ("Effets physiques chez l'individu de l'idée de mort suggérée par la collectivité," 1926), Mauss addresses the problem of psychosomatic disorders, particularly cases of sudden death in individuals for whom a physiological cause cannot be found. Reflecting on events recounted in studies on Australian Aboriginals in particular, Mauss notes that despite their reportedly "startling physical resistance" (SA, 315), they have been known to waste away merely from the psychic depression caused by guilt when accused of transgressing a social contract. How could human subjects succumb so completely to the spell of belief systems to the point where the very health of their bodies could be affected, even ruined, by something as insubstantial as an idea? With at least anecdotal proof at hand, Mauss answers that the power of suggestion, the force of an ethics or belief system (a "collective representation"), is alone powerful enough to produce *physiological* consequences. The organic body is by no means, then, a separate *"palier"* of the human being that can be understood exclusively through the lens provided by the hard sciences.[20] Science is no better than psychology in explaining why, in cases of spontaneous death, the nervous system, respiratory system, and even the circulatory system behave the way they do.

It is in this essay, then, that Mauss begins to insist on the relevance for sociology of that which had previously been the exclusive domain of either psychology or physiology: in the first instance, gestures traditionally believed to express the intimate feelings of an individual (and thus within the purview of psychology) and in the second, movement patterns traditionally believed to manifest the biological reflexes of a species (and thus more appropriately the matter of neurology, anatomy, and physiology). Although

Mauss does not use the phrase "techniques of the body" in either "Real and Practical Relations" or "Psychic Effects," the early essays are clearly a reflection of the material he was concurrently presenting in his courses as well as a prefiguration of the ground-breaking essay he would write eight years later. In "Real and Practical Relations" especially, he highlights the gesturing body as particularly vulnerable to social conditioning and thereby provides a hint of the direction his research would soon take. In his enumeration of socially generated movement practices he includes such aspects of human comportment as facial expressions, habits, skills, ritual movements, chants, and dances. Facial expressions, the first variety of gesture, had traditionally been treated as indices of emotion, the natural and inevitable expressive signs of a personal affective or sentimental disposition. In contrast, habits, rituals, chants, and dances had been conceived as continuous with organic corporeal processes, and thus as falling within the purview of psychophysiology or the study of anatomy. But in "Real and Practical Relations" Mauss implies that the discipline of sociology has much more to say about the motility of human beings than either of its immediate competitors. Movement phenomena, he argues, are constituted as much by social regimes as by biological imperatives or individual intentionalities: "it seems that the layer of individual consciousness is quite thin: laughter, tears, burial lamentations, and ritual phrases are as much physiological reactions as they are obligatory gestures and signs [*des gestes et des signes obligatoires*]" (SA, 289–290). What is left for the psychologist to study, Mauss asks, if even laughter and tears, the most authentic expressions of intimate feelings, turn out to be social configurations, discharges *("réactions physiologiques")* captured in arbitrary signs *("des gestes et des signes obligatoires")?* And what if the movement patterns of dance, apparently so closely linked to the rhythm of respiration, arose as much from social conditioning as from organic drives? [21]

What is ultimately at stake for Mauss in "Real and Practical Relations" is not merely the discipline of sociology, the extent of its range and the nature of its transgressions. More pointedly, he is questioning the very existence of an area of human being that would not already comprise the social, that would not already lie beneath its sign. Is there, he asks, any aspect of an individual's physical comportment—his pulse rate, the dance step supposedly based on that pulse rate, or the feeling of joy that that dance step communicates—that *isn't* affected by socialization? Is there such a thing as an unalloyed feature of organic or psychic life? At bottom, Mauss argues, the body's modes of kinesis previously studied by either physiology or psychology are neither incidental nor ancillary to sociology *but rather its most fruitful terrain of investigation.* For what sociology can reveal by studying gestures of all kinds is that human modes of kinesis are a locus, perhaps the most exemplary locus, where the social, the psychic, and the biological meet. And sociology, for Mauss, is of no interest unless it applies itself to a study of precisely those practices where the social bleeds into other domains and, no less important, where the organic and the individual—the phenomenal body and the subject's experience of it—influence in turn the form the social takes.

"The primacy of the act"

To approach sociology in such a way is, of course, to transform the field entirely, to turn it toward what we now call "anthropology," the study of human beings *tout court* rather than the study of the social, psychological, or organic human in isolation. This vision of an approach that would seize the human as a totality is what Karsenti is referring to when he speaks of the first "dissonance" with respect to a Durkheimian sociology attached to the notion of a distinct stratum dubbed "the social." Karsenti draws our attention to Mauss's conceptual departures from Durkheim, and to this extent his comments are illuminating; however, he is not specifically concerned with Mauss's identification of the gesturing body as a site—and impetus—for these departures, and therefore cannot provide an explanation for why bodily techniques came to have such central importance for Mauss as he developed these conceptual shifts.[22] Other critics have also declined to attribute Mauss's growing interest in bodily techniques to a specific influence or source. "Mauss's interest in techniques and their study," Nathan Schlanger writes, "was in itself a radical thematic departure, which cannot be readily aligned with his prior professional concerns with classification, ritual or religion, or for that matter with his participation in the mapping of the sociological domain at large."[23]

But what neither of these critics acknowledge is that Mauss's increasing interest in the study of bodily techniques was thoroughly in keeping with yet another aspect of his training in Indology, one generally not recalled in studies of his work. Karsenti is attentive to the conceptual shift registered in 1901 in Mauss's essay "Sociologie"; what he does not note (nor have Mauss's other critics) is that the same year "Sociologie" appeared in *La Grande Encyclopédie,* an article entitled "Yoga" also penned by Mauss appeared in the same volume.[24] In this neglected article, Mauss defines "Yoga" primarily through its philosophy; yet, although he attends most closely to yoga's textual incarnations (first and foremost the Yoga Sutras of Patanjali), he also mentions the *"exercices mystiques"* and *"pratiques"* that yogic texts propose as a way of advancing the yogi toward a state of meditational bliss. Mauss shows a precocious grasp of the way yoga conceives of the moving body as continuous with states of mind. Of course, Mauss's perspective is largely that of his generation (and social milieu), which was exposed to yoga exclusively through texts rather than living practitioners.[25] However, even the brief encyclopedia entry testifies to the fact that Mauss had achieved an understanding of yoga as more than mere words: he knew that this religion, as described in the *Yoga Sutras* and Upanishads, involves a belief system transmitted through written texts and verbal formulas (collective representations), and through bodily practices, such as controlled breathing and held postures, capable of harnessing physical energy for spiritual goals.

The impact of Yoga philosophy on Mauss should not be underestimated. I believe that if Durkheim's disciplinary daring encouraged Mauss to seek the social in the organic body, it was yoga that suggested how that organic body could become a form of consciousness that in turn informs psychic and social life. Yoga taught Mauss that ideas and beliefs are, literally, *in the body,* that they can be conveyed and retained in tissues shaped by specific postures and gestural routines. Through the study of yoga, Mauss realized that the ways the body moves are, themselves, a belief system. That is, the process of moving into and through postures is not the corporeal *translation* of a belief or idea; rather, that process *is* the belief or idea as it produces a certain stance toward the world, the self, and the relations linking the two. Mauss realized that in the corporeal practices of yoga, the belief is lived on the order of the body—*as a form of consciousness.* Mauss's research on spontaneous death among Australian Aboriginals certainly revealed to him that the organic body can be penetrated and controlled by an idea or belief; but it was the study of Indian philosophies and religions that introduced the corollary notion that the material body, insofar as it is saturated by consciousness, can take on some of the self-reflexive functions of consciousness as well. Kinesthetic awareness could become a kinesthetic consciousness, reflecting on itself and thus defining—in harmony with social prescriptions or, in rare cases, against them—what a distinct kinesthetic sensation might come to mean.

Mauss did not fall upon Yogic philosophy serendipitously; far from it. He was in fact a student of his generation's leading Sanskrit scholar and historian of Indian religions, Sylvain Lévi.[26] The study of religion as pursued by Durkheim might not have provided Mauss with the tools necessary to create, out of whole cloth, a theory of bodily techniques; it might not have inspired him to pursue what Lévi-Strauss has called "an archeology of corporeal habits."[27] But the study of religion as pursued by Sanskrit scholars very likely did. Such, at least, is the conviction of Camille Tarot, who argues in *De Durkheim à Mauss* that it was specifically Mauss's "full formation as a Sanskrit scholar" that gave him access to the original views on the body he professes in lectures and essays from 1920 on.[28] Lévi, Mauss's teacher, was himself formed by two of the most prominent Indologists of the nineteenth century: Emile Burnouf, a specialist in Buddhism, and Abel Bergaigne, who analyzed Vedic chants and rituals from a philological and anthropological perspective. The influence of Bergaigne on Mauss's evolution is especially clear: while reviewing one scholarly tome after another on Indian religions for *Année sociologique,* publishing no less than fifteen essays on Indology between 1897 and 1903 alone, Mauss absorbed the assumption that grounded all French work in Indology in the lineage of Bergaigne: that the "mythology of the Aryan vedics is intimately related to the *practice* of their religion, and these two aspects *must be studied simultaneously.*"[29] Bergaigne was the first scholar Mauss came in contact with who married philology, the study of the textual forms of cultural transmission, with ethnology, a study of the *corporeal* practices through which that culture is embodied on individual animate forms. Encouraged to study yoga by the discipline in which he was trained, Mauss also derived from yoga a new perspective on the organic body as a place where culture is lived and revised.

We can discern what Bergaigne's assumption might have meant for Mauss by returning briefly to his writings of 1898–1899, texts that served as preparatory research notes for his more accomplished "Essay on the Nature and Function of Sacrifice" ("Essai sur la nature et la fonction du sacrifice," 1899) coauthored with Henri Hubert. In essays such as "Funerary Rites in India" ("Les rites funéraires dans l'Inde ancienne") and "Vedic Ritual Literature" ("Littérature rituelle védique") Mauss responds with enthusiasm to accounts of the Vedic texts. The discipline of Indology, he believes, benefits from a more robust documentation of the culture under consideration; Vedas, Brahmanas, and Sutras contain detailed descriptions not only of beliefs, myths, and prayers but also of ritual *acts,* the sequences of enchained gestures accompanying the verbal forms. In "Funerary Rites," for instance, Mauss is especially attentive to how a performed gesture replaces—or supports—an abstraction. He describes here a ritual sacrifice in which the "sacrifiant," the subject who will commit the sacrifice, undergoes a purification ritual. At one point, words no longer suffice to communicate the import of the event, and the subject must roll himself up into and ambulate in the foetal position in order to dramatize, through gesture, the tense state of gestation. Mauss himself describes the pertinent scene: "the embryo in his wrappings has his fist closed"; "he must come and go around a central foyer just as a fetus moves in the womb."[30]

It is likely that Mauss chose to focus on this scene because it suggests the crucial function of gestural performance, the physical embodiment of abstract ideas in the transmission of cultural values. Although there is no way to be certain, I suspect that Mauss's understanding of the nature of gesture dawns here, at the moment when he learns not only how the fetal position provides the *"sacrifiant"* with the kinesthetic experience of closing and reopening—interpreted through the symbolic system as death and rebirth—but also how the members of the audience are offered the same profound physical experience through kinesthetic empathy. [31] Arguably, by observing the subject roll up into a ball, members of the audience are able to achieve a mild sensation, through kinesthetic memory, of the same movement and are invited to associate it with a symbolic meaning provided by the dharma, the teachings of the religion. Perhaps while reading about and then later recording the episode Mauss even experienced the sensation of fetal folding in his own body; perhaps it was this kinesthetic participation in the social process of an ancient, foreign culture that taught him the importance of gestures in the acquisition and preservation of beliefs.

Be that as it may, it is clear from Mauss's account that the gestural quality of the ritual is what guarantees its success and allows it to compel attention. Mauss appears to realize here that gestural performances secure belief systems in a way that no recitation of myth, no chant alone, can. Performed gestures engage both the subject undergoing the ritual and the audience observing it. To be sure, the ritual depends on "collective representations," preformed ideas shared by the entire community through which they filter their kinesthetic experience of the fetal position. But the spectacle also addresses this experience more directly. It demands that both *"sacrifiant"* and community revive a kinesthetic memory and it sets that memory into a narrative, a chain of events, through which it becomes significant in a new way. What makes the ritual so compelling, and the belief system incarnated in it so strong, is that it mobilizes the mnemonic and kinesthetic force of one of the most universal default positions in human experience: that which is assumed, of necessity, in the womb. The fetal position is not simply associated with death and rebirth because a society assigns it—arbitrarily—this semiotic function; the fetal position triggers all sorts of memories—of safety, of vulnerability, of beginning and end—that are as rooted in anatomical realities as they are in social codes.

This potent example of gestural behavior may very well have suggested to Mauss the crucial role of bodily techniques in securing the longevity and tenacity of religious (and, more generally, cultural) beliefs. His familiarity with Vedic and Brahmanic texts undoubtedly influenced his development as a scholar, allowing him to make connections that his training as a Durkheimian sociologist could not, on its own, have anticipated. He learned to approach the gesturing body as a site where the semiotic functions of culture work on a material that is at once pliant and resistant, culturally underdetermined and anatomically overdetermined, a surface on which to inscribe and a source of sensations potentially in tension with social drives. In "Funerary Rites," Mauss studies a gestural routine (the assumption of the fetal position) that successfully sutures a socially established meaning to a performed but also interoceptively experienced act. In "Techniques of the Body," however, he alludes to a case in which kinesthetic sensation is incompletely sutured to cultural meaning, and thus likely to lead to acts of resistance that reveal the gap between the corporeal experience of gesturing and the verbal accompaniment designed to frame it. As the example of the Maori girl implies, the consciousness of the body and its own motor intentions might enter into conflict with the socially mandated meanings of gestural routines. Mauss's anecdote illustrates that despite all efforts at cultural suturing, there can emerge in the course of performance a discrepancy between the words or instructions recited and the sensations felt. The project of culture might be to marry modes of kinesis to specific meanings, but as embodied signifiers, gestures are more vulnerable to dehiscence (less fixed by convention to their signifieds) than scriptural signs. The fetal position or the seductive *"onioi"* gait are embodied as opposed to disembodied signs; they may be manipulated and framed by ritual or convention, but they can take on other meanings as well, meanings generated by a kinesthetic feedback in contradiction with the meaning previously assigned.

In these early essays on Indology, we witness Mauss in the act of working out the theories he will present later in "Psychic Effects," "Real and Practical Relations," and "Techniques of the Body" concerning the role of the body in anchoring collective representations in individual psyches. Indology clearly revealed to Mauss "the primacy of the act with respect to the representation" *("le primat de l'acte sur la représentation"),*[32] the huge importance of corporeal performance in the maintenance, transmission, and evolution of cultural meanings.[33] It was this precept, that acts trouble their meanings, that Mauss bequeathed to his students at the Institut d'Ethnographie: Marcel Granet, Curt Sachs, Michel Leiris, and Alfred Métraux. All four would follow in Mauss's footsteps, drawing out the implications of his lectures in ways that have only begun to attract attention. Granet's monumental work on Chinese legends and inscriptions, *Danses et légendes de la Chine ancienne,* takes as its grounding assumption that ritual dances—and gesturing bodies—are at the origin of the verbal and visual arts as well as the belief systems they inscribe,[34] while Sachs argues even more emphatically in *A World History of Dance* that prior to the existence of writing, singing, or words, there was dance: "Before all spiritualization was the clearly felt need of traversing and modeling space with the body."[35] Leiris and Métraux, too, turned to the danced rituals of, respectively, the "possessed" women of Ethiopia and practitioners of Haitian *vaudou* in order to explain how the will to move could be harnessed to social and, in some cases, subversive ends.[36]

"The effect in each conscience and each body"

The priority accorded to movement, to "traversing and modeling space with the body," had many implications, not only for Mauss and dance ethnography but also for the development of French phenomenology and cultural theory in general. The example of Indology suggested to Mauss that moving bodies are the surface on which culture inscribes its values; yet it became clearer and clearer—if not to Mauss then certainly to Merleau-Ponty and the philosophers in his wake—that insofar as cultural subjects *are* moving bodies, they also produce a tension in the very culture whose inscriptions they bear. What Mauss's work implies is that if a shared belief is borne by an individual body, this kinetically realized belief will necessarily produce a set of sensations in the body of that bearer, sensations that might eventually cause the subject to question the belief the gesture is supposed to incarnate. The sensations experienced by the body that bears the social meaning are not always experienced in the same way by each individual body. And it is to the individual's situated experience of bearing social meanings, that is, to the individual's sensory experience of the cultural sign, that the logic of Mauss's anthropology finally, ineluctably, leads us.

But what could be the status of the individual subject (and therefore of an individual subject's interoceptive experience) in a corpus dedicated to demonstrating the penetration of social categories into every layer of human being? Wouldn't the subject performing the ritual act be invited, even coerced by the verbal accompaniment to interpret his sensations in a socially predetermined way? Wouldn't the Maori girl, repeatedly told that being a woman consists in "doing the 'onioi,'" eventually fail to recognize her own sensations of discomfort, having subordinated the register of experience to the register of the sign? I would wager that Mauss's response would be "Not necessarily," for his anecdotes repeatedly remind us that the lived experience of performing a gesture can threaten to produce a kinesthetic excess with respect to the predetermined social meanings it is intended to bear. Mauss's awareness of this danger—or rather, this promise—is never explicitly addressed in his works, although it is implied frequently enough to produce a productive tension within his stated project. He shows himself to be surprisingly sensitive to those moments in which a discrepancy occurs between an individual's somatic experience and the structures of meaning a culture imposes. Mauss thereby makes it possible for later scholars to insist on the hermeneutical value of an individual's interoceptive experience, if only to mark the existence of a register not entirely coincident with the social languages designed to encompass it. As Karsenti and Merleau-Ponty both take occasion to observe, even when the anthropologist is making his strongest argument for the predominance of the social over the psychophysiological, or the collective over the individual, Mauss remains committed to the category of individual experience as crucial to the portrait of how culture evolves. That is, "even when the mind of the individual is entirely invaded by a representation or a collective emotion," he observes in "Real and Practical Relations," "even when his activity is entirely devoted to a collective effort [*une oeuvre collective*], such as hailing a boat, fighting, advancing or fleeing in battle, even then, we have to agree, *the individual is the source of particular actions and particular impressions [impressions particulières]*" (SA, 290; added emphasis).

Note that Mauss's examples of acts guided by collective efforts all involve gestural chains: hailing a boat, fighting, advancing, or escaping a battle. He could easily add "rolling up into a fetal position" or "doing the 'onioi.'" His point is that during the course of executing a set of prescribed movements, an individual intentionality is nonetheless engaged and an individual experience *("impression particulière")* achieved. The assertion of this *"impression particulière"* seems to go against the grain of the argument Mauss has been pursuing up to this point. But as we witness here, Mauss's move away from the Durkheimian orthodoxy is complicated and self-contradictory, involving not just one step but two. First, by leaving the "homo duplex" behind, Mauss locates the impress of the social structure not simply on the individual psyche but also on the organic body; second, he locates within this organic body a source of subjectivity, namely, the kinesthetic experience that emerges *as a result* of executing the socially mandated act *("l'oeuvre collective")*. In mature Maussian anthropology, a tension is therefore maintained between two structuring forces, the social body and the individual body. For this reason, "to explain in sociological terms [*expliquer en sociologie*]," as one critic has concluded, "will no longer be to explain the social fact [*le fait social*] insofar as it transcends all individual consciousness, erecting itself as a kind of external constraint. . . . Instead, to explain in sociological terms will involve evaluating *the effect on each individual consciousness, on each individual body* of procedures of socialization that nonetheless link all individuals together."[37] In other words, Mauss teaches that although the subject is governed almost entirely by directives received from the larger social network of which he is a part (the *"contrainte extérieure"*), it is nonetheless the subject's singular body that must perform these actions, the singular body that feels the physical strain of executing them. Through his study of habitual, ritual, skilled, and aesthetic acts, Mauss helps us to unearth a striking paradox: *culture, once embodied, produces challenges to itself.* His work reveals that culture requires individual moving persons to act out its imperatives, but that by acting out these cultural imperatives, individuals reproduce culture in distinctive and potentially subversive ways.

"Let us learn to know the body as a 'structuring' principle"

The intervention of Mauss remains pertinent to contemporary critical theory not simply because he challenged sociologists who adopted Durkheim's terms and concerns (that would make him significant only in a local, historical sense) but further because his work anticipates larger debates within structuralism and poststructuralism that have not yet been resolved. "Mauss's legacy," Karsenti has written, "provokes a discussion that goes considerably beyond the boundaries of sociology and its methodologies. The interpretation of his works is at the heart of a debate between structuralism and phenomenology, a debate that traverses French thought after the war, and which still seems to resonate with the great conflict between an approach that attempts to *seize meaning"*—the meaning of a ritual or social form—"and an approach that seeks to identify formal structures, that is, between comprehension and explication."[38] The cleavage Karsenti discerns between a method that seeks a meaningful grasp of social practices, the raison d'être they are accorded by their practitioners *("compréhension"),* and one that privileges a strict analysis of the hidden structures underlying these practices *("explication")* can, as Karsenti himself observes, be seen to characterize the debates between phenomenology and the structuralist method growing out of Lévi-Straussian anthropology, Saussurian linguistics, and Lacanian psychoanalysis.[39] To the extent that Mauss attempts to "seize the meaning" of the *fait social* he studies, he is a precursor of phenomenology as it was developed by Merleau-Ponty, a philosophy that, according to Karsenti, seeks meaning insofar as it is "meaning for a consciousness."[40] As Jean-François Lyotard has also noted, Mauss prefigures Merleau-Ponty precisely because he mingles a first person account with a third person account, exposing himself to the accusation of "subjectivism," that is, of locating the motor for social action in individual experience rather than "collective representations" (Durkheim), unconscious drives (Freud), or linguistic structures (the protodeconstructive model emerging out of Jean Starobinski's and Jacques Lacan's reading of Saussure).[41]

Both Karsenti and Lyotard presuppose that, had they lived longer, neither Mauss nor Merleau-Ponty (even in his latest phase) would have embraced wholeheartedly the linguistic turn of the 1970s—or, for that matter, the constructivist turn based on the earlier linguistic model. To some extent, it is precisely this resistance to the primacy of the linguistic that has kept both thinkers out of the academic limelight. As Michael Taussig trenchantly observes in *Mimesis and Alterity: A Particular History of the Senses,* critical theory has reserved its highest praise for theorists who argue that immediate experience is a construction, even an ideological fabrication, based either on language, power structures, or systems of socialization, while turning its back on any theory that advances the possibility of a "genuine," "authentic," or "subjective" experience.[42] The problematics of immediacy traverse the work of the Frankfurt School as well, shaping the debate that divided, intermittently, Adorno from Benjamin.[43] However, a careful reading of Mauss's work shows that it contains the seeds of both structuralist and phenomenological approaches; capable of a searing objectivism as well as an equally revealing subjectivism, Mauss introduces in nascent form the tensions still animating critical theory today.

Scholars within anthropology (and in other fields as well) have been quick to celebrate many of Mauss's contributions, including the inauguration of a field of study aimed specifically at the impact of socialization on the moving body. But they have also found weakness in his tendency to adopt the explanatory terms of the societies he describes, practicing the type of subjectivism for which phenomenology has often been criticized. In what is perhaps the most important assessment of Mauss's legacy, "Introduction to the Work of Marcel Mauss" ("Introduction à l'oeuvre de Marcel Mauss"), Claude Lévi-Strauss begins by praising his predecessor for affirming "the crucial value, for the human sciences, of a study of the way each society imposes on the individual a rigorously determined use of his body."[44] However, in a second section, Lévi-Strauss goes on to chide Mauss for failing to transcend the order of description (and thus the order of meaning participants attribute to their acts) so as to achieve an objective analysis of the phenomena concerned. Taking *The Gift (Essai sur le don)* as his primary instance, a work that does not concern bodily techniques per se but instead focuses on systems of exchange enacted in a variety of ways, Lévi-Strauss claims that Mauss invests too much explanatory power in the indigenous terms *mana* and *hau* used to designate these exchanges. In doing so, Lévi-Strauss warns, the anthropologist presents the force of exchange, the force of the social itself, one might say, as "a purely phenomenological given," whereas the anthropologist should search for the unconscious structure that has produced that *"donné."*[45] By employing the term forged by the *"indigène,"* Mauss is guilty of according weight to a "conscious" representation instead of seeking the "unconscious mental structure" that subtended and necessitated its invention: "After identifying the indigenous concept, Mauss should have reduced this concept by means of objective critique to get to its underlying reality [*atteindre la réalité sous-jacente*]" (SA, xxxix).

Somewhat paradoxically, however, Lévi-Strauss accompanies his charge of subjectivism against Mauss with the assertion that any account of a cultural practice is incomplete *without a consideration of the subjective experience of the participant.* Sounding a note that resonates throughout Merleau-Ponty's work as well, Lévi-Strauss concludes that even after the objective analysis has occurred, even after indigenous reality has been reduced to its underlying structures, "we can never be entirely sure to have ascertained the sense and function of an institution if we have not managed to grasp [*revivre*] its impact [*son incidence*] on an individual consciousness" (SA, xxvi). Lévi-Strauss's phrasing invites precisely the kind of investigation Mauss pursues in "Techniques of the Body." But it is Merleau-Ponty, not Lévi-Strauss, who will identify the fruitful intersection in Mauss's work of objective analysis and, for lack of a better term, subjective reimagining. How, indeed, can the anthropologist hope to grasp (or *"revivre,"* to relive) the event of social performance (the *"incidence"* of an *"institution"* on a *"conscience individuelle"*) without taking seriously the terms in which the participant describes this event? How is an individual consciousness to be probed? How is the experience of bearing social meanings on the body to be gleaned?[46]

In "The Philosopher and Sociology," Merleau-Ponty supplies a partial answer. In the eyes of the phenomenologist, ethnography's task is to provide a full account of a participant's experience through recourse to the observer's own experience. The philosopher thus takes up Lévi-Strauss's critique of Mauss but turns it on its head, transforming Mauss's "weakness"— his tendency to accord value to subjective experience—into a strength. Merleau-Ponty makes his point, moreover, with explicit reference to "Techniques of the Body" in terms that should arrest us here. For it is at this point that Merleau-Ponty underscores the true significance of Mauss's contribution to a phenomenological theory of gesture: his insistence on the centrality of interoceptive, kinesthetic experience—both that of the subject observed and that of the subject observing—for understanding how objective, meaning-making structures work, how they can take root in the body but also how they can be changed.

Musing on the objectivity to which the social sciences in general aspire, Merleau-Ponty notes that such a goal is misguided as well as impossible to attain. If the sociologist (an appellation that, in this case, appears to include Durkheim, Lévi-Strauss, and even Freud) wishes to analyze a foreign culture's way of rendering the world significant, he must first attempt to understand the way his own culture has invested familiar practices with meaning. For instance, with respect to kinship relations, Merleau-Ponty writes, structuralist formulae mean nothing "if we have not managed to install ourselves [*nous installer*] in the institution concerned, if we have not understood the style of kinship we are referring to . . . if we have not seized the personal and interpersonal structure at the very base."[47] In what may very well constitute Merleau-Ponty's most severe critique of structuralism à la Lévi-Strauss (and his greatest praise for the protophenomenology he discerns in Mauss) the philosopher then contends that the analyst's structures are merely third person abstractions that have to be realized in first person ways. A grasp of what kinship might mean to someone in a culture not one's own is only available through an analysis of one's own experience of kinship. We cannot grasp the rationale for particular arrangements until we have understood "in which sense certain subjects perceive other subjects of their generation to be kin." Merleau-Ponty is not particularly interested in what an objective analysis of kinship structures can tell us about patterns that seem, initially, strange to us; the goal of a truly phenomenological anthropology would be to bring out the strangeness *within every cultural practice,* a strangeness due to the distance between a set of givens (coitus, reproduction), the way these givens are structured by society (kinship relations), and the way these structures become meaningful, how they are embodied in performance and invested with value. The "meaning" of a Polynesian ritual, then, is not the unconscious conflicts it is intended to resolve (*pace* Lévi-Strauss) but rather the work of em-bodiment, placing meaning in/on the body, that must occur if an arbitrary system is to address something as inexhaustible as sex.

The sociologist can thus only pretend to approach the *fait social* as if it were entirely foreign to him *("il feindra donc d'aborder le fait social comme s'il lui était étranger");* in actuality, meaningful analysis relies on the observer's ability to recognize a process of simultaneous objectivation (the transformation of the intimate body into a socially meaningful surface) and subjectivation (the inflection of a social meaning through its individual embodiment) inherent in all *faits sociaux,* including the ones with which he is most familiar. To access this process, which involves the making flesh of a collective ritual, the suturing of movement patterns to words, the observer turns to his own experience as a "social subject, a subject of intersubjectivity."[48] Sociology is made with such lived experience *("faite avec cette expérience vécue");* an understanding of the subjective experience of a collective ritual or practice can only emerge from a self-reflexive examination of one's own experience of embodying social meanings, an experience that necessitates movement and produces kinesthetic sensations subject to recursive reflection.

In an effort to clarify his point, Merleau-Ponty offers an example drawn from a rather different domain: Freudian psychoanalysis and its parsing of the libidinal body into significant units. This example is particularly relevant with respect to Mauss and the twist he brings to the Freudian analysis of the body. According to Merleau-Ponty, no matter how universally applicable the Freudian paradigm might be (and remember, during this period Merleau-Ponty is reading challenges to Freud's libidinal cartography offered by Ruth Benedict and Margaret Mead), the paradigm is meaningless unless the student of culture can develop an awareness of how he lives in his *own* libidinal body. Freud's paradigm, writes Merleau-Ponty, offers a "schema of all the possible ways of accentuating the bodily orifices of the infant," a kind of general blueprint of the regions of the body and the various ways they receive *"accentuation."* Those that are "realized by our cultural system and described by the Freudians" are no more than *"variantes singulières,"* singular possibilities "among a great number of possibilities, some of which are probably actualized in civilizations still unknown to us."[49] Merleau-Ponty does not reject the Freudian rendering of the body's orifices as significant loci of libidinal investment; he merely states that the way these orifices receive a heightened charge of significance *("accentuation"),* the way they become or interact with a sign, is only one way in which they could receive significance. Studying how orifices receive conditioning in another culture is precisely how one comes to recognize the arbitrariness of the system one's own culture offers. Merleau-Ponty then goes on to state that the "schema" itself, that is, the map of charged, erogenous zones of the body, "cannot tell us anything about relations with the other and with nature, the very relations that define cultural types, as long as we do not refer back to the psychological signification *in our own lived experience* of the mouth, the anus, or the genitals. Only this way can we see, in the different uses cultures make of bodies [*dans les usages différents qu'en font différentes cultures*], the varieties of ways in which the initial polymorphism of the body is crystallized by culture into a vehicle for being-in-the-world."[50]

This last sentence describes much of what happens, as analytic method, in "Techniques of the Body," and in fact, Merleau-Ponty has supplied *in nuce* a reading of this essay. However, the degree to which Merleau-Ponty is depending on Mauss to establish the grounds for a phenomenological anthropology becomes clear only later on, when Merleau-Ponty insists that it is by meditating on the *practices* in which bodily regions are involved *("les usages différents qu'en font différentes cultures")* that it is possible to intuit how they obtain their specific meanings. Freud's sketch of erogenous zones and their related *"usages,"* Merleau-Ponty concludes, "is only an invitation to imagine, based on the experience of our own body, *other bodily techniques [d'autres techniques du corps]*" (added emphasis). What is required of the observer, then, is a double process, a simultaneous *"décentration et recentration"* in which our own subjective "intimate experience of life with others" becomes the source of a self-reflexive, objectifying analysis. In this case, a resumé of another culture's techniques takes us outside of ourselves *("décentration"),* only to plunge us into a heightened awareness of the techniques in which our own bodies are engaged *("recentration").* This cycle becomes recursive when reflection on one's own techniques then triggers the realization that they, too, are artificial, that the body one *is* is not entirely one's own. This telescoping and magnifying of perspective throws into relief one's own peculiar ways of using and making meanings of the body, such that one has virtual access if not to the ways others move, then at least to the ways others make meanings of how they move. A continual *va-et-vient* between first and third person accounts (practiced, as many have noted, in *Phenomenology of Perception*) is the method privileged by Merleau-Ponty, one that promises a grasp not only of the different meaning-making systems but also of the urge toward meaning that characterizes and underlies them all.

That certain regions of the body almost invariably acquire a libidinal charge is not at issue in "The Philosopher and Sociology." Instead, Merleau-Ponty is concerned with showing that such regions are libidinal due to the nature of the practices—the *"techniques"*—mobilizing these regions, techniques that place them into relations of contact and exchange with other bodies. Mauss's "Techniques of the Body" is a crucial work for Merleau-Ponty specifically because it shows that even the deepest, most private interoceptive experience cannot be considered a solipsistic event. That the development of kinesthetic self-awareness is the result of a social process—

such as gripping the mother's waist with the inner thighs—is a belief that Mauss and Merleau-Ponty share. Merleau-Ponty in fact identifies in "Techniques of the Body" one of its most innovative moments, namely the way it predicates kinesthesia—the interoceptive experience of one's own moving body—on intersubjective relations involving a tactile, aural, or visual contact with the body of another.

Merleau-Ponty seems to be suggesting in "The Philosopher and Sociology" that Freud fails where Mauss succeeds. Or, to put it less conflictually, that Mauss's emphasis on bodily techniques, on *"usages,"* promises to reveal more about how the body becomes significant, marked by a particular sexuality, than the insistence by the "Freudians" on a universal subject whose body comes into the world already charged with meanings that owe little or nothing to culturally specific bodily practices. Merleau-Ponty's argument is that body parts are not simply elements of raw anatomy; zones and orifices do not exist for us *until they are used in practices,* and thus inserted into cultural patternings of behavior through interaction with another. One can only experience one's *"polymorphisme initial"*—the virtual, precodified but not predifferentiated—body through the exercise of the very techniques that have codified one's body. The technique of the body "that is actualized in us," Merleau-Ponty concludes, "is never merely one possibility among others, because it is on the evidence of this privileged experience, in which we learn to apprehend the body as a 'structuring' principle [*où nous apprenons à connaître le corps comme principe 'structurant'*], that we are able to glimpse [*que nous entrevoyons*] the other 'possibilities,' no matter how different they are from our own."[51] He concludes by reasserting his commitment to a phenomenology of experience, a first person account of third person structures: "It is vital that sociological research never be cut off from our experience as social beings."[52] Indeed, Merleau-Ponty's marked preference for "Techniques of the Body" over *The Gift* may be due, precisely, to the former's recourse to the author's own experience (here, of swimming), the fact that Mauss's starting point for theory is his own habitual, acquired way of taking in water at every other stroke.

As I stated earlier, that the body has differentiated regions is not at issue, and Merleau-Ponty accepts Freud's identification of these different regions as a way of discriminating body parts that indeed serve discrete biological functions. What *is* at issue is the access the sociologist has to the cultural difference of the other if he depends entirely on the abstract map or interpretive grid. A moment of self-reflexivity is therefore in order, not simply because an element of prejudice must be admitted but, equally important, because the sociologist's lived experience of cultural meanings is precisely what will give him insight into the cultural meanings of the other. Merleau-Ponty proposes self-reflection in the midst of movement as a means of seizing one's own body as "structuring *('structurant')*" as well as structured. A singular, first person experience of a shared, conventionalized set of bodily techniques provides, paradoxically, access to the body as a *"principe 'structurant,'"* an active principle or force that contributes to *making* structures.[53] Importantly, Merleau-Ponty does not depict this prepersonal body in static terms but rather as an energetic power to impose structure. That is, he pictures the body as possessing a structuring force of its own, one that might counter the structuring power of a cultural regime. To know the body as *structuring* as well as *structured* is to arrive at a position from which other possible ways of becoming structured *("les autres 'possibles'")* can be glimpsed. Although Merleau-Ponty employs the verb *"entrevoir" ("nous entrevoyons les autres possibles"),* a word derived from an optical vocabulary, such "glimpsing" is actually performed by the kinesthetic sense. Merleau-Ponty's hypothesis is that a kinesthetic focus on the body provides, under certain conditions, a "glimpse" of the body as a structuring force.

"In the body's tow"

Merleau-Ponty's position assumes that kinesthetic experience of the body is immediate, and that a structuring principle peculiar to that body can be sensed beneath, through, and despite physical conditioning. But the question we must ask is whether such a position makes sense for a contemporary theory of gesture: Does the individual have such immediate access to kinesthetic experience? Can the observing subject "glimpse" through self-reflective interoception the alternatives *("les autres 'possibles'")* residing beyond her cultural limits but within her kinetic range?

At the time Mauss was writing, it was generally acknowledged within the psychological community that individuals could experience a "particular impression" while at the same time communicating a social meaning; in other words, sensations contingent on performance could be "glimpsed." More precisely, Charles Blondel, an important psychologist and contemporary of Mauss, proposed in 1927 that a vague malaise in the body could make itself felt; the technical term at the time for this malaise or general discomfort was *"cénesthésie"* (or *"coénesthésie"*) from the Greek *koinos,* "common," and *aisthesis,* "sensation." Blondel argued in *Introduction to Collective Psychology (Introduction à la psychologie collective),* a work influential for Mauss, that organic processes exert pressure on consciousness, signaling in a vague way the existence of a body in need of attention, whether culture took notice or not. Blondel writes suggestively that consciousness can be "in the body's tow" ("à la remorque du corps"), "tugged" by sensation as if by a tugboat ("remorque") toward the body's shore.[54] If affects and perceptions are deeply shaped by psychic preoccupations and social conditioning, Blondel avers, in contrast, cenesthetic impressions remain "the only domain of sensation that is exclusively our own [le seul domain sensitif qui nous soit exclusivement propre]."[55]

Mauss does not go as far as Blondel, for he believes—as his turn from the "homo duplex" to the "homme total" is meant to underscore—that no domain of human existence remains truly "our own." At the same time, however, Mauss adds a nuance to Blondel's understanding of "cénesthésie," a general ("common") bundle of undifferentiated sensations. As we saw earlier, he states that "the individual is the source of particular actions and particular impressions" while performing the general and shared techniques of a habitus (SA, 290). "Impressions" is as vague a term as "cénesthésie," but when coupled with "particular" it takes on greater force. Every shared technique (such as "hailing" or "advancing in battle") is performed slightly differently by each individual body; at first, we experience the sensations a particular movement produces as private, their implications specific to our body alone. If encouraged or compelled, we can attend to these particular impressions, strive to name them with the terms available, or engage in linguistic bricolage. However, despite our experience, these impressions are not "our own," insofar as social and psychic conditioning inflect them with specific associations and, in some cases, deafen us to their noise.

Mauss's anecdote at the beginning of "Techniques of the Body" about the way he learned to swim is the ideal passage to revisit before concluding. Here, he admits that the technique he acquired at an early age forces him to swallow an unnecessarily large quantity of water. One must presume that he experienced this fault in the practice not objectively or empirically, not by measuring his intake of water against the intake of water by a child who has learned to breathe a different way. Observation of another swimmer might have first made him conscious of his discomfort, but even before that, he would probably have sensed that he was swallowing too much water through sensations of imminent suffocation, nausea, and constriction in his lungs. These differentiated sensations of discomfort can lie close to the surface of consciousness, engendering affects like panic even if it is difficult to identify why.

Again, Mauss's example is distinctive because it points to a domain of practices within culture, what I would call specialized or aesthetic practices, that allow for and often encourage a heightened sensitivity to the body. Swimming in late nineteenth-century French athletic culture does not bear the moral weight of gender-identified behaviors, which must reinforce the fundamental distinctions on which a culture's institutions depend. Thus, it is relatively safe for Mauss to acknowledge consciously and publicly the discomfort associated with an (outdated) stroke. But imagine the case of the Maori girl, for whom a great deal rides on assimilating (or not assimilating) the gendered gait. We can think of similar examples in our own lives, conventional and acquired techniques for moving or remaining stationary that we can only examine critically at our own risk. (Attentive to my own discomfort, I have opted to squat at faculty meetings or stand and sway back and forth during conference presentations; my departures from convention have not, as far as I know, been rewarded with greater respect.) The point is that societies offer opportunities for some techniques to be examined critically while others are enforced by means of disciplinary mechanisms that are as ubiquitous as they are difficult to pin down. Merleau-Ponty is therefore profoundly radical when, in Mauss's wake, he champions a form of inquiry that would demand analytical distance from the most fundamental and unquestioned corporeal practices of our own culture, such as the sexual practices involving the orifices that he references in "The Philosopher and Sociology." It is heartening that Merleau-Ponty believes we can analyze the lived experience of the body in this way; but unfortunately, his conviction is not supported methodologically by his brief account.

Tools exist, however, for thinking through the possibility of analyzing our lived experience and the critique of socialization that such an analysis would imply. Mabel Elsworth Todd, writing during the same time as Mauss, develops a theory of "kinesthetic consciousness," by which she designates both the "particular impressions" that might rise to awareness and those that continue to provide feedback to our nervous system without our awareness. "We are unconscious of most of the small movements involved in posture and locomotion," she claims in *The Thinking Body* (1937); "Usually we are not aware of the initial sensation that starts the reflex or of the movement that completes it."[56] Admitting that some sensations involved in the guidance and control of movements inform the motor body without ever reaching "the seat of consciousness in the upper brain, or cerebrum," she simultaneously enlarges the range of sensations that lie on the border of consciousness and thus are available to scrutiny under certain conditions.[57] To be sure, most vestibular sensations inform choices only at a presubjective level; however, a wealth of kinesthetic sensations generated by an initial movement can become the object of conscious awareness, and therefore constitute an agentic force in the subject's selection of how next to behave. Kinesthetic sensations that were once the object of consciousness can recede into the background or, alternatively, be brought back to consciousness through what Thomas J. Csordas has called "somatic modes of attention," therapeutic retraining, or the simple act of self-interrogation that occurs by chance or as a result of a change in the subject's environment or goals.[58] "A vast number of movements are habitual, that is automatic," Todd asserts, "though they may have been evident to consciousness at some period, as when learning to walk, to use a special tool or acquire a motor skill. However, it is possible to bring the organic impressions and resulting movements into consciousness and thus to control the adjustments. This fact underlies the learning process in purposive movement and conditions any improvement."[59]

Gregory Bateson offers support for Todd's argument in *Steps to an Ecology of Mind,* proposing that the functioning of kinesthesia reveals the barrier between conscious and unconscious to be more porous than one might think. In the process of habit formation, for instance, there is a "sinking of knowledge down to less conscious and more archaic levels"; for that reason, the word "know," he states, "is not merely ambiguous in covering both *connaître* (to know through the senses, to recognize or perceive) and *savoir* (to know in the mind)," but further, the word "varies— actively shifts—in meaning for basic systemic reasons. That which we know through the senses can *become* knowledge in the mind."[60] In other words, kinesthetic sensations are part of an economy of conditioning; we could not function if we had to rehearse consciously all the gestures (and reexperience all the associated sensations) every time we exhibited a certain skill; but we could not improve or adapt our skills if we could not allow that which we "know through the senses" to become, once again, "knowledge in the mind." Like Todd, Bateson considers the period of skill acquisition to be paramount; during this period, the nervous system can mobilize kinesthesia or compartmentalize it for purposes of efficiency. Expanding on Bateson's and Todd's insights in "Genre and Embodiment: From Brazilian Capoeira to the Ethnology of Human Movement," J. Lowell Lewis posits an "intermediate mode," familiar to dancers and athletes, in which the subject enjoys a heightened awareness of kinesthetic feedback while simultaneously depending on skills deeply embedded in unconscious memory structures.[61] Performers in particular must be able to engage their knowledge on both levels, since they instrumentalize their bodies (constitute them as visible surfaces) and, at least intermittently, sense their bodies, monitoring interoceptive sensations to be sure they can sustain, extend, and repeat the actions they display.

The period of skill acquisition usually takes place in infancy and early adolescence; few of us are required to learn new gestural vocabularies or techniques on a regular basis throughout our lives. Most individuals learn the basic and most enduring gestural routines of the *habitus* (such as walking, running, and often swimming) at an age when our neural networks and anatomies are particularly sensitive to cultural molding and therefore far less vulnerable to later alteration. But de-skilling, the process whereby we become conscious of old habits and attempt to change them, is a more common experience for adults. How deeply we can "glimpse" the worlds of sensation that old habits generate is a question that cannot be answered in any uniform way; how effectively we can mobilize kinesthetic self-awareness for the purpose of agentic innovation or resistance is, again, a matter of individual talent, training, aspiration, and design.

What is clear, at least to Mauss and the introspective phenomenologists he inspires, is that an attempt to apply consciousness to sensation is by no means an act of narcissism, as some critics have implied. For Jean Starobinski, to give just one instance, any attention paid to kinesthetic sensations takes away "from my investments in the *other*," replacing worldly concerns with "an instinctual satisfaction" and exhibiting a narcissism that is symptomatic of "contemporary Western culture."[62] At the antipodes of Starobinski's position, Merleau-Ponty claims that attention to one's bodily techniques and the sensations they engender can be the basis of a philosophical and ethnographic method, one that posits sensory self-reflexivity as the conduit to greater understanding *of the other*. Merleau-Ponty and Mauss might agree to some extent with Starobinski that "what I devote to an awareness of my body I subtract from my presence in the world"; however, for them, awareness of the body and a momentary detachment from the world do not necessarily constitute a "regressive or narcissistic libidinal investment" in the self.[63] Obviously, such a conclusion contrasts sharply with that drawn by Merleau-Ponty—and it is here, at precisely this point, that the chasm between phenomenology and poststructuralism yawns wider. For the phenomenologist, focusing inward, or *"recentration,"* is far from an act of narcissism; rather, it is a way of rediscovering in one's own experience the basis for an empathetic encounter with the other. Finally, Mauss and Merleau-Ponty coincide in their estimation that the body's ability—its *faculty*, at once innate and acquired—to exercise a kinesthetic sense constitutes one of the richest resources of the *habitus* itself. Insofar as culture provides paths to self-awareness, it allows individuals to assume *a critical distance from culture*, a distance that can liberate if not the body then at least thought. After all, when Mauss manages to recognize the absurdity of his swimming technique, he is not suddenly, miraculously, relieved of the habit. The liberation that occurs when the mind considers movement as gestural routine does not ineluctably lead to the abandonment of the gestural routine (although it can). To view the moving body as a "'structuring' principle" is not to call for a return to a natural body, defined for once and for all. Instead, it is to approach the body as agentic kinesis, a kinesis that parses anatomical possibilities into distinct gestures available for *but not equivalent to* social meanings. No gesture is ever entirely relieved of social meaning; however, by focusing on the sensations produced by acts of gesturing, the subject momentarily detaches movement from meaning, thereby recognizing that movement and meaning might be coupled in different ways.

CHAPTER TWO

Gestural Meaning:
Maurice Merleau-Ponty, Bill Viola,
and the Primacy of Movement

URING THE LAST fifteen years of his life, roughly from 1945 *(Phenomenology of Perception)* to 1958–1961 (the "Nature" lectures), Maurice Merleau-Ponty developed a theory of the gestural that has provided fruitful new directions for continental philosophy to pursue.[1] By combining a unique set of commitments—to Husserlian phenomenology, Heideggerian epistemology, Gestalt psychology, Marxist materialism, and Maussian anthropology—Merleau-Ponty inaugurated a school of thought that associates human understanding not with cogitation but with *embodied* cogitation. He was interested in the body's implication in what the mind thinks it knows. Indeed, it has become almost banal to claim that Merleau-Ponty is the philosopher par excellence of embodiment. What has been far less frequently acknowledged is the degree to which he conceives that embodiment in terms of the gestures the human form can execute, the routine movements by means of which the whole person explores the world.[2]

Phenomenology of Perception is, almost from the first page to the last, a meditation on the role of the gestural in acts of embodied perception and cognition. Gestures clearly hold a privileged place in Merleau-Ponty's philosophical and aesthetic writings; however, what he means by the term is not always easy to discern. In *Phenomenology of Perception, The Structure of Behavior,* and the lectures collected in *Nature: Lectures and Course Notes,* "gestures" *("gestes")* cover roughly the same ground as Mauss's "techniques of the body," especially when treated in the context of the acquisition of habit. Elsewhere, though, *"un geste"* appears as a rather amorphous type of sign, a smile, for instance, but also a way of clenching the brows, scratching an itch, playing a keyboard, or applying paint.[3] It would seem that gesturing, for Merleau-Ponty, is the inescapable medium in which animate forms navigate environments and enact intentions. Gestures are therefore, for him, the link between a naturally given body and an existential/cultural situation. Neither produced entirely by culture nor imposed inevitably by nature, gestures are a culture's distinctive conjugation of what Merleau-Ponty called the body's "general power," a social manifestation of its biologically driven "prepersonal cleaving" to being (PP, 92).

It is perhaps due to this crucial, intermediary position of the gestural that it has become an important category for contemporary theorists of the body, especially those who are interested, as was Merleau-Ponty, in examining how cultural, organic, and technological forces interact to give birth to embodied meanings. Nowhere has this interest been more pronounced than in the area of new media theory. In fact, new media theory has become a locus for a renewal of interest in Merleau-Ponty's writings, just as the aesthetic objects privileged by new media theorists frequently thematize, register, and even dissect the gestural dimension. Although performance studies and dance ethnography have made headway in championing Merleau-Ponty's contributions, it is arguably in the area of new media theory that his insights have been most fruitfully explored. Mark Hansen, José Gil, Brian Massumi, Brian Rotman, and Sha Xin Wei have each argued persuasively that phenomenology's approach to embodiment promises to correct a technological determinism that in the past has neglected to consider the role of situated performance in humanity's commerce with machines. One of the most provocative thinkers of the gestural, however, is the video artist Bill Viola, whose works have, not incidentally, been at the center of a number of studies by new media theorists (although how "new" video now appears is a matter of debate). Viola's concern with exploring the gestural is similar to Merleau-Ponty's insofar as both strive to locate within the performance of gestures a key to how socialized beings manage to convey spontaneous, unscripted meanings through sedimented forms. The first part of this chapter will therefore sound the resonances of the gestural in Merleau-Ponty's writings; the second part will reach forward to explore how the category of the gestural can renovate paradigms of embodiment currently employed in critical theory, in particular, the critical theory that has emerged from analyses of new media's artistic forms. I also turn to recent findings in neuroscience that appear to support Merleau-Ponty's approach to the gesturing body as a negotiation between the given and the forged. Studies by contemporary phenomenologists such as the experimental psychologist Daniel Stern and the neuroscientists Francisco

Varela and Alain Berthoz suggest new readings of Viola and Merleau-Ponty alike.

"A figurative significance"

As opposed to Mauss, who studied gestures primarily with respect to the belief systems they embody and the cultural subjects they construct, Merleau-Ponty sought a global theory of the gestural capable of embracing not simply "techniques of the body" but also reflex and communicative gestures. Although in *Phenomenology of Perception* he ultimately ends up gathering all gestures under the same umbrella, the organization of the book divides gestures into three distinct types: chapter 1, "The Body as Object and Mechanistic Physiology," treats reflex gestures; chapter 3, "The Spatiality of One's Own Body and Motility," is concerned with habit and skill acquisition; and finally chapter 6, "The Body as Expression, and Speech," theorizes expressive and communicative gestures as elements of a signifying system that he compares to spoken language. Most radical about his approach is his rejection of the traditional separation between the conventional and the natural, and thus the arbitrary and the motivated, inherited from the eighteenth-century philosophical tradition. For Merleau-Ponty, even reflex gestures are not simple genetic inscriptions inevitably attached to expressive, libidinal, or survivalist functions. Instead, reflexes are "interpretations" of an environment, "proto-significations" rather than purely indexical, automatic responses. As he writes in "The Body as Object and Mechanistic Physiology," "reflexes themselves are never blind processes: they adjust themselves to a 'direction' of the situation, and express our orientation towards a 'behavioral setting'" (PP, 91). On this reading, even reflex movements can be seen as "modalities of a preobjective view" (PP, 92); when performed, they tint with a situational coloring both the objective stimuli of the physical world and the behavior of the responding body, each of which comes into legible existence in the moment the reflex is performed. The order of the "preobjective" antedates individuation; yet this anonymous life force is never instantiated as such but is embodied in movements calibrated to adapt to a specific setting. Insofar as reflex movements open themselves to "the 'direction' of a situation," insofar as they adapt to a specific setting, they are "modalities" of instinct, oriented and therefore *gestural*.

Years later, Merleau-Ponty would return to the problem of the reflex gesture in his lectures at the Sorbonne entitled "The Concept of Nature," buttressing his premise with new empirical data derived from experiments conducted by E. S. Russell, Adolf Portmann, and Konrad Lorenz. In these lectures, delivered during the same years when he was composing *The Visible and the Invisible,* Merleau-Ponty argues that situational contingencies inflect reflex movements *("les comportements inférieurs"),* rendering them subject to neither mechanical repetition nor the force of entelechy. Instead of unfolding themselves in an inevitable fashion, regardless of geographical and cultural circumstances, reflexes, or "instinctive" actions, emerge as part of a *relation.* The reflex appears in an intersubjective context; it therefore instantiates a kind of "presignification."[4] Merleau-Ponty offers the example of the behavior of the female pigeon, whose involuntary, periodic ovulation is influenced by the presence (or lack thereof) of a male. In this instance, a presumably automatic function of the prepersonal animal body "adjusts itself to the 'direction' of a situation" (PP, 91). Granted, ovulating is not a reflex "gesture," but it exhibits the same tendency to occur more or less frequently (and in modified ways) depending on the interanimal and environmental context. Citing further evidence from Lorenz, Merleau-Ponty insists that reflexes, or "instinctual movements," must be understood not as mechanical responses to objective stimuli but as "styles of spontaneous behavior that anticipate an aspect of the world or of a partner."[5] Instincts are "substitutions . . . that not only superpose themselves on fundamental biological acts (such as copulation), but actually displace them, transfigure them, submitting them to conditions of *display.*"[6] Borrowing evidence from Portmann, Merleau-Ponty concludes that animals displaying mating behavior do so not in a preprogrammed, blindly instinctive manner, but always with an eye toward the "interanimal" situation in which that behavior is to be instantiated. Thus, there are no two reflexes entirely alike; each display—say, of brightly colored tail plumage—brings a slightly different body into being. Apparently, "styles of comportment" exist even among birds, suggesting that gestural sequences derived from particular socialities ("interanimal" behaviors linked to a certain terrain, climate, and population) select from movements genetically available to a specific anatomical (here, aviary) form.

Insofar as *Phenomenology of Perception* is an elaboration of the earlier *Structure of Behavior,* it treats motor behaviors as primordial. (This will become important shortly when we turn to Bergson and Deleuze.) Evincing his debt to Gestalt approaches, Merleau-Ponty argues that such behaviors sketch out a first "form or structure" for an environment that would otherwise remain amorphous and disorganized, alien to use or transformation (PP, 132).[7] Whether intentionally or unintentionally produced, even reflex gestures are "condemned to meaning," as Merleau-Ponty puts it dramatically in the *Phenomenology* (altering Sartre's phrase "condemned

to freedom"). Performed with reference to the existential, they lend a social interpretation to an indifferent natural world. Embodied reflexive behaviors *("comportement inférieurs")* thus constitute a modulated response
to a contingent set of conditions. However, such behaviors, or instinctive
"displays," are only *"pre*-significations" rather than full-blown signifiers;
they have not yet achieved the status of convention, often remaining dependent on what Blondel called *"modifications organiques."*

Because reflexes are fundamentally genetic, preprogrammed reactions
that are only slightly modified to address the particularity of the situation
they confront, their relationship to a consistent, predictable, empirical
body is relatively clear. When we squint and knit our brows in a reflexive
effort to protect our eyes from the sun, we can only do so in a limited number of ways because of the structure of our orbital muscles. Our responses
may vary—we might, for instance, force the eyes to remain fully open—
but this is usually due to a strong social or pharmaceutical intervention,
as when we have been exposed to punitive instruction or influenced by
hallucinogenic drugs. In sum, innate reflexes can "adjust themselves to a
'direction' of the situation" *only so far.* At the same time, however, they
can be seized and integrated into a network of social meanings in which
they become signs for something they did not initially reference. A gesture
such as clenching the eyebrows can be distanced from its initial meaning;
it can become, for instance, a sign of concentration rather than simply a
reflexive response to bright light. Yet, because gestures are movement
phenomena, and produce, physiologically, a circumscribed set of kinesthetic sensations, they always retain a vestige of their initial relation to
the body's processes, the *body's* intentionality, distinct from that of the
socialized individual. Clenching the brows, whether it abets squinting or
signifies concentration, requires a muscle contraction and, as such, possesses an effort quality that remains relatively consistent. Although various
emotions become associated with the contraction (since affects are always
integrated into movement vocabularies in contingent ways), the range
of emotions correlated to that contraction will be limited by the type of
attitude (tense anticipation or repose) that muscle contraction physically
engenders.

Merleau-Ponty describes the process whereby a reflex gesture (a "protosignification") becomes a full-fledged corporeal sign in the following lines:

> For example, the knitting of the brows intended, according to Darwin, to
> protect the eye from the sun, or the narrowing of the eyes to enable one to
> see sharply, become component parts of the human act of meditation, and
> convey this to an observer. . . . A certain way of bringing the body into play

suddenly allows itself to be invested with a *figurative significance* which is conveyed outside us. (PP, 225; original emphasis)

Drawing on Darwin's *The Expression of the Emotions in Man and Animals* (1872), Merleau-Ponty implies that gestures such as knitting the brows or narrowing the eyes maintain a particularly strong—motivated—connection between the kinesthetic experience of performing the gesture (e.g., tension or constriction) and the figurative meaning the gesture conveys. Thus, although the muscular phenomenon of knitting the brows might have a different figurative meaning in each culture, due to its movement quality it is likely to be associated with a semantic kernel synonymous with constriction rather than release, focus rather than dispersal. To this extent, then, expressive gestures derived from reflexive "proto-significations" never become utterly arbitrary with respect to the kinesthetic experience of performing them.

In contrast to expressive gestures such as knitting the brows, habitual behaviors possess a far more attenuated relationship to physiological invariables. Varying dramatically from culture to culture, instrumental motor habits acquired after birth seem to stray further from that which might be seized as their biological meaning. However, it is absolutely vital to Merleau-Ponty's argument that he manage to preserve the link between the modality of the reflex and the modality of the acquired, the habitual, and the skilled. He insists repeatedly that gestures of *all* types are simultaneously open to social manipulation and anchored in a presocial, animal order of existence; they all possess a kinesthetic value, an effort quality, as well as a differential (cultural) meaning. By the end of *Phenomenology of Perception,* he asks us to accept that even the gestures of speech (what he calls *"gesticulations verbales"*) are rooted in a prepersonal motor body.[8] The strength and the weakness of Merleau-Ponty's approach to the gestural lies precisely here, in his desire to reduce all three varieties of gestures to a common ground:

> It is impossible to superimpose on man a lower layer of behavior which one chooses to call "natural," followed by a manufactured cultural or spiritual world. Everything is both manufactured and natural in man, as it were, in the sense that *there is not a word, not a form of behavior which does not owe something to purely biological being*—and which at the same time does not elude the simplicity of animal life, and cause forms of vital behavior to deviate from their pre-ordained direction. (PP 220; added emphasis)

On the one hand, Merleau-Ponty's refusal to distinguish neatly between nature and culture, the instinctive and the socialized, or the indexical (necessary) and the conventional (arbitrary), is what lends his theory its *souplesse,* its richness as a vehicle for thinking about the nature of the gestural today. On the other hand, the crucial differences between distinct types of gesture tend to become blurred, inviting a kind of metaphorical traffic between registers that supplants logical argumentation and ultimately fails to convince. To my mind, Merleau-Ponty's most significant intervention is in the area of habitual gestures, a category that does not overlap completely with Mauss's category of bodily techniques. Interestingly, in the *Phenomenology,* habitual gestures include not only skill sets but also facial expressions and body language, from smiling to executing a salute. For instance, for Merleau-Ponty, a way of figuring dismay or shock with the muscles of the face is as socially constructed as a way of sewing or using a keyboard, although it may be acquired far earlier and in a different way. The expression of an emotion, then, is figurative (conventional) insofar as social forces provide it with meaning and indexical (necessary) insofar as a biological motivation inspires its performance and links it to a particular quality of kinesis. In support of this view, Merleau-Ponty writes: "It would be legitimate to speak of 'natural sign' only if the anatomical organization of our body produced a correspondence between specific gestures and given 'states of mind'"; but, at least according to Merleau-Ponty, "the angry Japanese smiles, the westerner goes red and stamps his foot or else goes pale and hisses his word" (PP, 219).

Significant here is not whether the cultural differences Merleau-Ponty identifies are accurate; from a theoretical standpoint, what matters is his insistence in this passage that *culture makes of anatomy an arbitrary sign,* placing it into a differential system that will alter (although, to his mind, never sever) its relationship to a biologically driven indexical movement. He is in fact attempting here a balancing act between a biologism that aspires to retrieve the necessary relation between muscle and meaning on the one hand and on the other a cultural constructivism that understands that meaning to have entered a network of signifying relations evolving independently of its putative indexical origins. Despite his assertion that "there is not . . . a form of behavior which does not owe something to purely biological being," he goes on to emphasize the degree to which facial expressions are acquired through *social interaction* rather than biological disposition; accordingly, he finds that the relation of facial expressions to the affects they are intended to express and the kinesthetic experiences they engender is neither necessary nor consistent. The kinesthetic experience of tension resulting from clenching the cheek muscles might very well signify a heightened emotional state in all cultures, but in one it comes to be associated with pleasure and in another with rage. Following theorists of expression such as Gabriel de Tarde and Charles Blondel,[9] Merleau-Ponty also concludes that it is social conditioning, occurring largely through mime, that sutures a particular facial expression to a particular social (figurative) meaning. Further, social conditioning not only sutures, it also selects: infants might be capable of any number of facial contortions, but their adult interlocutors volunteer a limited set of gestures that only partially and imperfectly map the full terrain of movements and movement experiences available to the human being. Yet Merleau-Ponty, once again attempting to reinstate the delicate balance, refuses to sever these volunteered gestures from the experience of their motivation in sensation. Imperfect as they may be, these socially volunteered gestures are valuable tools, socially acquired "I can's" that can self-modify—in the same way reflexes do—when adjusting to the " 'direction' of a situation." Merleau-Ponty's most compelling insight with regard to facial gestures is that, similar to reflexes and learned skills, they too are at once biologically given on the level of the species, socially encoded on the level of the group, and contingently forged on the level of the individual. We thus have to approach a smile, for instance, from three different angles: (1) as an example of motor behavior, an attempt to solve a problem, to do something in the world (a physiological "I can"); (2) as a "figure," a conventional and culturally specific sign for pleasure and approval, or, alternatively, anger and frustration; and finally (3) as a set of kinesthetic experiences, such as clenching (of the cheek muscles and jaw), stretching (of the lips and chin), and exposure (of the teeth and gums). Merleau-Ponty's treatment of gesture is provocative because it suggests that interaction among these three levels is constant and, under certain circumstances, *available to reflection.* Gestures are the site of a complex negotiation of forces without which situated meanings would never appear and the history of such meanings would never evolve.

"The 'direction' of a situation"

Phenomenology of Perception leaves us with many enigmas, and my efforts to explicate some of the more vague passages have probably only raised additional questions. A longer exposition and a closer reading might clarify Merleau-Ponty's argumentation; but instead of following his argumentation further, I prefer to explore his ideas through their application—and thus transmutation—in works created in his wake. This provides an opportunity not only to test the salience of his ideas but also to witness how they have been buttressed, modified, or betrayed by recent theorists similarly concerned with relations between biological imperative, social construction, and individual feeling.

The analyses I will generate here of the works of contemporary video artist Bill Viola and, through them, the ideas of Merleau-Ponty go somewhat against the grain of current scholarship. By focusing my gaze on the gestural, I remain close to Merleau-Ponty's own texts; at the same time, however, I distance myself from a strong trend in new media theory that associates embodiment not with shaped motility, as does Merleau-Ponty, but with a far more mysterious entity known as "affect." Throwing the spotlight on the category of affect in his *Image-Mouvement* (1983), Gilles Deleuze inaugurated this trend, which led a generation of young scholars back to texts by Henri Bergson (and to a lesser extent William James) that emphasize the mind's debt to the body understood largely in terms of sensation.[10] Due to the influence of Deleuze, "movement" also emerged as an important term, but always in its abstract form, associated with change and passage, something the body does in time but subordinated nonetheless to affect. As a consequence of this priority accorded to affect, some new media theorists have credited affectivity—divorced from specific motor sequences—with the capacity to lend human subjects independence from the species-related response mechanisms and social conditioning so central to Merleau-Ponty's own speculations.

However, in Bergson's work, to which Merleau-Ponty is also indebted, not only are affectivity and motility profoundly intertwined but motility is accorded ontological priority with respect to affectivity (understood as emotion). In a passage from *Matter and Memory* that has become a kind of touchstone of new media theory, Bergson establishes the role of bodily affects in the process of perception, arguing that the body's interoceptive sensations mediate its interaction with external stimuli in a process later theorists have called "self-affection." Waves of affect, he writes, "interpose themselves between the excitations that I receive from without and the movements I am about to execute." The body is a source of sensory feedback that intervenes between the external world and the internal world either to filter out or focus on certain elements of the exciting environment. In passages far less frequently cited, however, Bergson insists on "the utilitarian character of our mental functions, which are essentially turned toward action"; he states further that "perception as a whole has its true and final explanation in the tendency of the body to movement" and that perception must always be seen as "an elementary question [posed] to my *motor activity*." In most cases, the nervous system formulates a response over time; it requires an "interval," which becomes, in Bergson's language, "a center of indetermination."[11] During this interval the motor body seeks the appropriate way to respond; in Merleau-Ponty's terms, the body "adjusts" itself to the "'direction' of a situation" (PP, 91). There is certainly an experience of qualitative, affective states; however, far more crucially for Bergson, there is also an experience of "nascent muscular sensations" (MM, 111), arcs of movement, or "tendencies," proposed by a body attempting to choose which habit, which embedded motor memory, will best serve the demands of the present moment. Affects—or what Bergson calls "attitudes" (MM, 131)—may indeed be responsible for modulating what would otherwise be a more reflexive response. But they do not work in a vacuum. To be expressed, they must rely on the movement possibilities retained by the nervous system. Humans do not execute automatic reactions, precisely because, although "turned toward action," they mediate their actions through another layer of experience that Deleuze associates with affect, Bergson with the memory of past actions, and Merleau-Ponty with what he calls a kinesthetic "background" *("fond")* that includes skills and the kinesthetic memory of performing them.[12] It is these kinesthetic memories that allow behaviors to become "gestural" in Merleau-Ponty's sense, that is, to take cognizance through sensory feedback of both the resemblance and the alterity of the present situation and to produce a nonreflexive, nonmechanical response. In doing so, the subject also renders the movement "figurative," or culturally meaningful, since that movement now embodies the entire intersubjective situation in its calibrated performance.

It is important to underline that when Bergson introduces the category of the affect (or what he calls "the affection" or the "affect image," to distinguish it, for instance, from other types of images, such as the perceptual or the mnemonic), this category is not equivalent to the category of emotion but includes what we would consider somatic sensations as well. Elaborating on the concept for the first time, Bergson actually associates the "affect image" with the cutaneous experience of pain: "There is hardly any perception which may not, by the increase of the action of its object upon our body, become an affection, and, more particularly, pain. Thus we pass insensibly from the contact with a pin [a tactile perception] to its prick" (MM, 53). The affect-image, or "prick," is itself a "source of positive action . . . , nothing but the effort of the damaged element to set things right—a kind of motor tendency in a sensory nerve" (MM, 54; 55–56). The choice of response "is likely to be inspired by past [motor] experience, and the reaction does not take place without an appeal to the memories which analogous situations may have left behind them" (MM, 65).

Deleuze is largely faithful to Bergson with respect to his account of affectivity as a filter on action, but, significantly, he neglects the philosopher's emphasis on motor memory as part of the interoceptive feedback that shapes the action the subject will ultimately take.[13] Deleuze privileges instead the role of an emotional attitude and attributes to it—instead of the motor memories—the capacity to produce, on its own, the action that is "unpredictable" and "new" *("quelque chose d'imprévisible et de nouveau")*.[14] Deleuze goes so far as to identify the human face (as opposed to the pin-prick on the skin) as the locus of affection, the site where it is active and displayed. By identifying affection with the cinematic close-up, Deleuze makes it seem as though affect were entirely an affair of large-screen emotions, and that it is these emotions that ultimately govern the way a subject will respond. However, Bergson himself makes it clear that while affections (not just pain but also pleasure and fear) play a role in producing an attitude toward virtual action, and thus help determine the choice a subject will ultimately make, it is motor memories of past actions that capture and filter the perceptual information in the first place and continue, throughout the interval, to offer their skilled answers to the question of pain.

When Bergson formulated the theories in *Matter and Memory* that would become significant to subsequent scholars he was drawing on a number of important discoveries that had been made during the course of nineteenth century but remain relevant today. These discoveries reveal what one might call the *intelligence* of the motor body, the meaningful quality of its choices. Once it was established by the physiologists Charles Bell and François Magendie in the 1820s that muscles do not merely react to messages transmitted from the brain but also *inform* the brain of what the body should be doing, the importance of sensory nerves embedded in muscles, tendons, and joints became increasingly clear. By the end of the century, John Dewey and William James and, in parallel universes, William Wundt, C. S. Sherrington, and later Henry Head (the latter especially important to Merleau-Ponty) were stressing that human agency, as defined by action, could not exist without the input of the kinesthetic sensations produced by movement. Head's work and that of Gestalt psychologists Kurt Goldstein and Adhémar Gelb allowed Merleau-Ponty to conclude that the sensorimotor nerves are activated during the act of perception and that these nerves, through their kinesthetic and proprioceptive receptors, relay feedback to the brain, constantly correcting and refining its first reactive impulses so that they conform to the unique present. Previous patterns and sequences of movement learned and sedimented in memory are then rendered available as "nascent" possibilities to be sorted through and selected during the pregnant interval central to Bergson. It is not that these motor memories are entirely lacking in affective tonality, or that emotions do not play a role in the process of movement selection; rather, what early twentieth-century neuroscience revealed was that the lived past ensures us an unknown future through the conduit of kinesthetic sensation. Affections, Bergson asserts, are what differentiate for consciousness our body from other bodies and inanimate things (MM, 234). During the crucial interval of *self*-affection (the self's dialogue with the self), kinesthetic impressions provide our body with an "ideo-motor present" (MM, 68), not to impose, mechanically, actions from the past, but to select and re-shape past actions so that we might successfully negotiate the next step. By choosing to accentuate action-oriented kinesis ("the ideo-*motor* present'), Bergson implies that self-reflexivity and its existential correlate, "freedom" (MM, 249), are ultimately predicated on the existence of a kinesthetic sense. This sense exerts a variety of agency that is neither en-tirely coincident with, nor utterly divorced from, the conscious intention-ality of a self-present subject. As opposed to self-affection understood as a transparent dialogue between two identical sources, kinesthetic feed-back is a rejoinder emanating from our *em-bodiment;* it speaks in a lan-guage we cannot always translate and provides sensations we cannot always name. In short, the moving body is another self within the self that informs the next move we make.

Opening up the spaces between

In the wake of Bergson, Merleau-Ponty develops to a far greater degree what his predecessor assumed as a given: that human subjects are prima-rily engaged in answering a *motor* question with a motor response. One of the advantages of Merleau-Ponty's approach is that by attending to the affective register associated specifically with kinesthetic memory and kinetic potential, he reintroduces the sociohistorical dimension of individuated motor response. Often accused of lacking a historical sense (by Sartre, among others), Merleau-Ponty actually locates history at a very profound level, at the site of the nervous system understood as a repertoire of his-torically contingent and culturally specific "I can's." After all, the motor patterns available to a subject at any given time—those rehearsed during the Bergsonian interval—are *acquired* routines and not simply universal human possibilities of movement. It is salutary to approach works in new media previously treated in Deleuzian terms in such a way as to recall Bergson's and Merleau-Ponty's emphasis on "motor tendencies," elements of affect's intervention that are too frequently forgotten in the reduction of affect to an overflow of feeling. This can be attempted even in the case of new media artists famous for heightening our awareness of the emotion-affect supposedly recorded on the screen. For instance, although many theorists have treated Bill Viola as an artist concerned with the *emotional* intensity communicated via the screen to the viewer, it can be shown that he is equally interested in the gestures that frame the emotions his filmed subjects perform. In my analyses of Viola's *The Passions,* a series of digi-talized video installations first exhibited in 2003, I will reinstate the sig-nificance of motor memory in the productive moment of indetermination by focusing on the relation between gesture and emotion-affect, rather than on emotion-affect alone. In doing so, I aim to restore animation to the notion of embodiment that new media theory has borrowed from Bergson and Merleau-Ponty. Whereas in the previous chapter I sought to correct a constructivist approach that suppresses the kinesthetic, intero-ceptive element in performance, insisting on kinesthesia (the body's sen-sation of its own movements) as a resistant force, here I strike out in the opposite direction, attempting to balance a celebration of affect as au-tonomous resistance to sedimentation by revealing affect's reliance on the habitual *and socially generated* muscular articulations Merleau-Ponty calls "I can's." In my readings, embodiment will be seen as a dynamic of self-affection inflected by social patterning and thus impossible to theo-rize without reference to gestural routines.

Bill Viola's *The Passions* series, first exhibited in its entirety at the J. P. Getty Museum, consists of twenty-one video installations, almost all in color, mounted on various types of liquid crystal display (LCD) and plasma screens.[15] According to the artist, *The Quintet of the Astonished* (Figure 2.1) was the first piece composed (in 1998), the first installation from which the others were generated. The inspiration for the composition came from a painting Viola saw at the National Gallery in London, Hieronymous Bosch's *Christ Mocked* (Figure 2.2). Imitating the compositional grouping (but not the verticality) of Bosch's painting (c. 1490–1500), Viola placed five actors into a tight arrangement in which they could dramatically change their postures over time without invading one another's intimate emotional

Figure 2.1   Bill Viola, *The Quintet of the Astonished,* 2000. Color video rear projection on screen mounted on wall in dark room. Photo: Kira Perov.

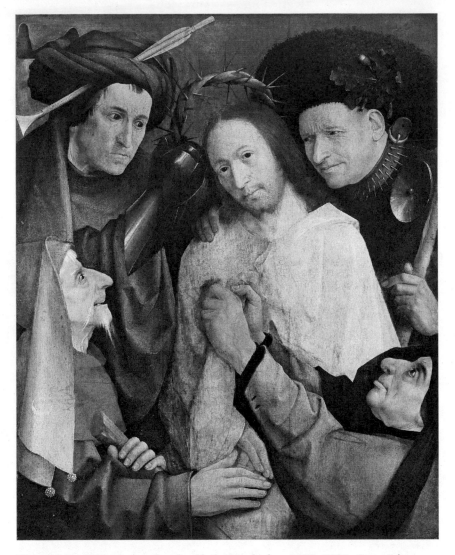

Figure 2.2   Hieronymus Bosch, *Christ Mocked*, c. 1490–1500. Copyright National Gallery, Picture Library, Washington, D.C.

space.[16] The four men and one woman in *The Quintet of the Astonished* are a transposition of the four darkly clad tormentors and the one fair Christ-figure in the Bosch painting. Viola filmed the five actors with high-speed 35-millimeter film (with frame rates of up to 384 frames per second, as opposed to the normal 24), which he then transferred to video, thus creating a sixteen-minute video strip out of approximately one minute of real-time performance. Traces of the influence of *Christ Mocked* can be seen in Viola's choice of colors, lighting, and the framing of the screen, which was recessed in space, evoking a small chapel in a cathedral.

Similar in this regard to the other three "Quintets" that would eventually emerge from the same inspiration (*The Quintet of Remembrance, The Quintet of the Unseen, The Quintet of the Silent*), *The Quintet of the Astonished* portrays only the upper half of the body of each actor (pelvis to head), with a special emphasis—as in the painting—on the hands. Indeed, as can be witnessed by observing the short clip available on the Getty Museum website,[17] the hands of the actors attract the attention of the viewer as much as, if not more than, the facial gesticulations. At one point during the sixteen-minutes that compose *The Quintet of the Astonished,* a hand with four fingers spread wide occupies the center of the screen; if we compare the composition with that of *Christ Mocked,* we see that this hand has been placed at the location in the Bosch painting where we find the corresponding four folded fingers that rest on Christ's shoulder. A visual echo of these folded fingers can also be found on the left-hand side of the frame, where a male figure rests his hand on the shoulder of the pale, Christ-like female figure. In the video, the outstretched fingers in the center of the frame remain immobile for a long time, but the two hands of the figure on the right-hand side and one hand of the figure in the right-hand corner next to him sway back and forth in a distracting manner, evoking the intensity of the posture assumed by the figure in the lower right-hand corner of the Bosch canvas.

In his preparatory notes to *The Quintet of the Astonished,* Viola writes that he hoped to capture "a compressed range of conflicting emotions from laughing to crying"; the emotions were to "come and go so gradually" that it would be "hard to tell where one begins and the other leaves off."[18] In a later interview, Viola explains further that he was less interested in a dramatic portrayal of the emotions per se than in the transitions from one emotion to the next. He asked his actors to move fluidly and gradually through sorrow, pain, anger, fear, and rapture in such a way as to "ope[n] up the spaces *between* the emotions."[19] In order to achieve this effect, Viola gave his actors two sets of instructions: they could either "work from the outside in," as in the technique analyzed by movement theorist Paul Ekman, "or from the inside out," as in Method acting.[20] The first choice would involve putting the body "in a place that will engender emotion," and the second, creating "an emotional life within that is then expressed outwardly."[21] Although the two approaches to the connection between (externally observable) bodily movement and (internally felt) emotion derive from two different theories of acting, they both presuppose a causal relation: what happens on the level of emotion finds its correlate on the level of kinesis. According to Viola's own account, his directorial style emphasized the inner-toward-outer Method approach, for he refrained from choreographing the actors in any way and simply gave them an emotion to express. Actors "were free to invent whatever gestures and expressions suited their individual tasks," one observer recounts.[22] This statement is belied, however, by the placement of the actor's hands, which intentionally (one cannot help assuming) evoke the hand positions of the figures in the Bosch painting.

Although Viola was clearly interested in the physicality—almost athleticism—of the exercise, no accounts I have yet found attend with anything like thoroughness to the pelvis-to-head embodiment of the labeled emotions. For instance, Mark Hansen's readings of *The Passions* in his article "The Time of Affect" and in *New Philosophy for New Media* concentrate exclusively on the facial gestures and the transitory phases between them, phases that reveal, according to Hansen (following Deleuze), "the unpredictable and the new."[23] Viola locates a space of freedom in the excess of affect over categorical emotion, that is, in the fuller "field of intentionalities" that the transitional phases captured on the screen reveal. But what does Hansen mean by "intentionalities"? In his readings, Hansen relies faithfully on Bergson's concept of a self-affecting organism, but Hansen strips this self-affection of its relation to "the movements [the subject is] about to execute," and thus to the "motor intentionalities" identified by Merleau-Ponty. To some extent, Hansen is able to do so because he considers only the facial gesticulations, which correspond more neatly, at least according to some, to distinct categorical emotions (and thus disclose, under deceleration, their ambiguous "in betweens"). Ignoring the physical manifestations of feelings (or, rather, performed feelings) in the shoulders, hands, and sternums of the actors, Hansen presumes that the strong emotions Viola seeks to capture, such as joy ("laughing") and sorrow ("crying"), are registered and communicated by means of the facial features alone.[24] The face, according to Hansen, displays a kind of semiotics of emotion, and it is in between these facial signs that we should locate the emergence of the unpredictable and the new. In Hansen's account, the larger body gestures, such as the waving of the hands back and forth in the right-hand corner of the frame, do not appear to maintain the same tight relation to expressive values (such as joy or grief), nor do they seem to have the potential to release the unscripted "in betweens."

If we were to watch the actors' performance at real-time speed, we would see a rapid succession of emotions expressed in what would probably appear to be exaggerated grimaces, a kind of facial typology or catalogue of stereotyped emotional expressions. But we would also observe violent and rapid upper body movements and be made far more aware of the actors' choreographic blocking.[25] The slowing down of the frame speed has the effect of revealing the in-between facial gesticulations, but it also discloses the enchained movements, and the ambiguous pauses between enchained movements that the body makes as it moves toward the expression of a violent emotion. Specifically what the viewer believes to have witnessed while observing these transitional, in-between states may in fact depend a good deal on the training the viewer has received. For instance, as a scholar of digitalized video, Hansen's focus is primarily on the facial expressions of the actors, what he terms their "affective tonality."[26] For him, it is the surface of the face that reveals the untapped potential of the feeling body. In contrast, when a phenomenologist trained in the tradition of Merleau-Ponty observes the actors, the *muscular tonicity* of the gesticulating bodies is more likely to catch the eye. In my own case, the facial gesticulations appear in the context of the larger body movements the subjects are executing. Trained as a dancer, I am struck by the changes in posture, the shifts in weight, the strange angles at which a head is carried, the degree of tension in hunched shoulders, the compositional play of arm positions, the vectors created by a finger, as well as the dynamics of facial muscle tone. Further, as a former performer myself, I view these figures bringing the Bosch painting to life *as performers,* not as subjects engaged in spontaneous emotional release. Studying them closely, I attempt to imitate their blocking: I learn their roles, copying the large body movements such as shoulder crumpling, hand lifting, and mouth contorting. Yet, try as I might, I cannot produce through sheer will power the twitch of a facial muscle or the trembling of a cheek. In that regard, Hansen is correct when he insists that new media technologies are able to expose to sight elements of aliveness (he says "affectivity," I say "motility") that are performed without volition.

It could be argued that what we witness when we observe Viola's videos is not a performance that actually took place and that therefore it is incorrect to designate his subjects as "performers." From this perspective, the bodies we see on the screen are not real bodies but only digital photographic reproductions of real bodies manipulated by postproduction technologies to appear in guises otherwise not exposed to view. Yet, however distorted the images may seem, they have not been digitally transformed. That is, the bodies filmed did indeed execute the twitches, tremblings, and contractions that are only visible to the observer when the execution of their movements has been slowed down. In short, a trained actor's body has actually executed the movements that radical deceleration allows us to see. Furthermore, it is to those bodies and their movements that we, as spectators, kinesthetically respond. True, many of the actor's facial gesticulations and upper-body movements have not been voluntarily produced and are therefore not "performed" in the sense of constructed as part of an intention to express a particular categorical emotion. But these movements are nonetheless *human* movements available as potentials belonging to the human kinetic disposition. They cannot be considered skills per se, but they are the building blocks of skills. They are decidedly not products of digital remediation, pure manipulations of playback that no human body would be capable of performing.

I would insist in addition that these involuntary facial gesticulations escaping both categorization and real-time perception occur—and on some level are experienced by the subjects—as tension in the jaw or as the sudden release of constriction in the brow; that is, they are experienced as kinesthetic sensations (and not simply "affects" in the sense of emotions). These facial gesticulations are thus kinesthetically available while remaining for the moment culturally meaningless (asemiotic). This distinction is an important one, for in some cases the in-between gesticulations *can* be felt by the body performing them even if they do not fall within the parameters of voluntary gestures invested with meaning. Although I stated earlier that it is not within the muscular capacities of human beings to reproduce voluntarily twitchings and tremblings, there are reasons to believe that even these types of movement are not entirely beyond the purview of trained actors.[27] Some varieties of twitch or tremble can in fact be reproduced by the trained actor or mime. An observant and skilled performer will be able to train herself to imitate, for instance, those involuntary contortions of the face that a human subject makes on awaking from sleep; the acquisition and willed reproduction of such normally involuntary forms of motility is a large part of an actor's *métier*. I am not claiming that Viola's actors are in control of or experiencing on a conscious level the finer shifts in their musculature during the in-between phases the video exposes, but rather that such shifts are experienced somatically and remain accessible, under certain conditions, as movement material from which performances—and even cultural signifiers—can later be made.

"On the basis of the animal's embodied history"

To return to Merleau-Ponty, the muscular dynamics I perceive could be seen to belong to what he calls the "autonomous" body, the "prepersonal" body that "gears itself" or "cleaves to" the world, even before the subject assumes a perceptual, cognitive, sexual, or emotional attitude toward it.[28] They might be associated with the instinctive, presignifying motility that Merleau-Ponty claims always underlies our signifying forms (there is not a single "form of behavior which does not owe something to purely biological being," he states [PP, 220]). For Merleau-Ponty, as for Bergson, there is always a crucial connection between affect (that which is felt) and move-

ment (that which is simulated or performed), that is, between the anticipatory, protentive attitudes and the nascent motor actions that the body,
cleaving to the world, prepares to make. Thus our view must be double:
The clenching of the brow and the twitching of the cheek are potentially
expressions of an emotion, but they are also elements of a nascent motor
project, one that contributes to the realization of intentions on the order of
the kinetic. The body's sensations of itself (its "self-affections") may indeed,
as Hansen states, provide a constant flow casting itself forward before the
actual initiation of activity (in the protentive moment); however, the body
also has its own intentionality, which is constrained (and enabled) by more
than emotional attitudes. This motor intentionality relies for its execution
on already acquired skills, the "I can's" a situated, socialized body is capable
of performing. For Merleau-Ponty, the moving body has a prior claim on
the world, or rather, the world demands movement of the body, and this incontrovertible exigency draws on and produces movement patterns that
will determine—as actualized gesture in the present but also as history of
gesturing in the past—the production of the unpredictable motor response.

Recent research in cognitive psychology and neurobiology has tended
to support Merleau-Ponty's account, which ultimately subordinates all varieties of intention to that of the sensorimotor body. An important pio-
neer in the field, the neuroscientist Francisco J. Varela, asserts forcefully in
an essay of 1991 that *"The fundamental logic of the nervous system is that
of coupling movements with a stream of sensory modulations in a circular
fashion."*[29] Varela takes it as axiomatic that "cognition depends on the
kinds of experience that come from having a body with various sensorimotor capacities . . . themselves embedded in a more encompassing biological
and cultural context."[30] This context is composed of the kinetic dispositions
of the animate body (the biological context) combined with the history of
its realized movements (the social or existential context). Protention, on the
neural level, he expands, is "incoherent or chaotic activity in fast oscilla-
tions . . . until the cortex settles into a global electrical pattern . . . selec-
tively binding a set of neurons in transcient aggregate . . . a creative form
of enacting significance *on the basis of the animal's embodied history.*"[31]

Alain Berthoz has arrived at similar conclusions through research on kinesthetic and proprioceptive functions. However, the neuronal activity does
not appear to him chaotic but rather organized by synergies or schemas of
previously inscribed behaviors. Berthoz's view is thus closer to Bergson's,
for he supports a conception of the brain as "a repertoire of sensorimotor
schemas that are just so many possible actions and that organize perception even before sensory stimuli are processed."[32] As in Bergson's paradigm, a perception is simultaneously a set of sensations, a call to rehearse

and select from a "repertoire" of "sensorimotor schemas," *and* an attitude or affective stance. In an interval that is surprisingly brief, potential strategies of response "can be anticipated, selected, and internally simulated [on the neuronal level] before being executed, using the same neural structures as those of the action itself."[33] On the one hand, the "*pleasure* taken in looking at something, or the *fear* of what might be seen" influence which movement patterns will be evoked in advance of the actual perception, and to that extent affect enters into the choice of schemas the subject will rehearse.[34] On the other, the repertoire from which those rehearsed, projected movements are drawn can only contain the schemas that the life history of the organism has previously provided. Berthoz draws on Bourdieu in order to argue that although affective attitudes toward the stimulus might be directing the choice of virtual (projected) or actualized motor response, the repertoire of responses is itself constrained by the contents of the *habitus,* the gestures and gestural routines a socialized individual has acquired. Quoting from Bourdieu's *The Logic of Practice,* Berthoz reiterates that "'in practice' stimuli do not exist solely as objective truth; they operate only as conditional and conventional triggers, dependent on encountering agents that are conditioned to receive them. The *habitus* can only produce the response written objectively in its 'formula. . . .' To my mind," Berthoz concludes, "this text [Bourdieu's] is fundamental."[35]

Thus, Berthoz and Varela both find that the sensorimotor capacities of the body are not entirely free and unpredictable but are underwritten ("written objectively") by neural circuits laid down by past actions ("the animal's embodied history," in Varela's terms, the "library" in Berthoz's). At the same time, however, they agree that there is clearly an element of creativity at work—otherwise the animal's embodied history would overdetermine every action that the animal could ever take. Berthoz, while acknowledging the existence of variation, reserves judgment with respect to its origin: "How the rigidity of [the] repertoire"—which he compares to a "library"—"is compensated by the plasticity of the rearrangements . . . is still unclear."[36] Varela ventures further than Berthoz, attempting to account for a plasticity inherent to the sensorimotor system. Varela hypothesizes that when the subject is confronted with a new situation that does not appear to conform to a previous one (and that therefore might not be resolved by rehearsing verbatim past actions), the neural circuits suffer what he calls a "microbreakdown." During this "microbreakdown," or neural reorganization, the system hesitates, searches among a "myriad of possibilities," multiple ways of creating new aggregates, connections, circuits, and eventually, behaviors. What is called on here, though, is a creativity that is partial and responsive, still constrained by the kinetic dispositions and realized gestural routines (the "embodied history") of the organism itself. Neuronal connections are not made in a vacuum, Varela asserts, but instead with reference to the organism's physiological possibilities for flexion and its acquired "I can's." Thus, when Viola asks "Is it possible to express emotions without the movement of the face?" he is asserting, as is Varela, what one contemporary philosopher has called "the primacy of movement."[37] The way the face moves, the way it *can* move given both biological inheritance and acquired *habitus,* is ultimately at the root of all emotional response. To this extent, Viola adds his voice to a growing chorus of cognitive scientists, such as Varela and Berthoz, and developmental psychologists, such as Daniel Stern, who have actively sought to extend and corroborate experimentally the tradition of phenomenology inaugurated by Husserl and Merleau-Ponty.

But let us return to the images from *The Passions* series and look once again at the "in-between" gesticulations on the faces of Viola's actors that inspired this detour into scientific models of motor response. To what extent are these gesticulations "new" and "unpredictable"? What "embodied history" of the human animal are they drawing from? How are innate kinetic dispositions and socially acquired "I can's" interacting to produce something beyond the legible, categorical gesture we recognize?

The salient feature of these gesticulations is that they do not appear to belong entirely to the fully achieved, categorizable emotions that Viola asked his actors to display. While moving from joy to dejection in *The Quintet of the Astonished,* for instance, the actor's facial features execute movements that are not recognizable gestures, not inscriptions in the "library" of our culture's expressive habits. This is not to say that they are entirely incapable of conveying meaning in another situation, within another *habitus.* Just because they are not inscribed in our culture ("written objectively in its 'formula'") does not mean that they are not inscribed somewhere else. As varieties of muscular contraction or release, these gesticulations possess and transmit an "effort quality," as Laban would say, or, alternatively, a "vitality affect," to evoke the terms of Daniel Stern. Stern's distinction between "vitality affects" and "categorical affects" is especially pertinent here, for it allows us to understand better what Viola is trying to show: not the named emotion (the categorical affect) such as the anger or the sorrow the actor has been asked to perform but rather the in-between gesticulation, the trembling, clenching, or stretching motions that I have been relating to a motor order of action.[38] It is to these not-yet-signifying, not-yet-"written" motions that I now wish to turn.

Stern is a child development psychologist, and thus his research focuses primarily on the sensorimotor existence of the infant. However, his observations are also relevant to the case of adults, for even fully socialized adults (if such a thing were possible) constantly gain intimations of—and are influenced by—this vaster and more nuanced region of affective experience. In *The Interpersonal World of the Infant,* Stern claims that the first sensations an infant experiences (both in and then outside the womb) are not affects in the sense of anger, fear, or rapture but rather "vitality affects," interoceptive sensations related to qualities of movement, touch, sound, and so on. These affects, to be distinguished from the more culturally inflected "categorical emotions" identified by Darwin,[39] involve kinesthetic distinctions such as jerky versus smooth, taut versus relaxed, distinctions that correspond precisely to the clenching and releasing movements I pointed out in *The Quintet of the Astonished.*[40] According to Stern, these kinesthetic discriminations are the true "background feeling" of both cognition and affective (in the sense of emotional) experience. In *The Interpersonal World of the Infant* Stern proposes that "all mental acts . . . are accompanied by input from the body, including, importantly, internal sensations. . . . *The body is never doing nothing.*" "Envision Rodin's Thinker," he proposes:

> He sits immobile, posing his head on his hand and an elbow on his knee. True, he is not moving, but there is extraordinary tension in his posture, suggesting active, intense proprioceptive feedback from almost every muscle group. This feedback, along with the thinker's presumably heightened arousal, provides the background feeling against which his specific thoughts are etched.[41]

For Stern, then, the "background feeling" is produced by "intense proprioceptive feedback" and kinesthetic sensation ("extraordinary tension"), not necessarily *emotional* tone. Stern's kinesthetic and proprioceptive "background" can be productively compared to what Merleau-Ponty calls *praktognosia,* or kinesthetic "background," a nonverbal understanding composed of signals the body receives all the time and from the beginning of (the subject's) time. These body signals are received in the womb, in the crib, seated in a chair. They issue from what Stern calls an "as-yet-unspecified self"; they are the "background music of an autonomous body that, under certain circumstances, can become louder and enter our awareness."[42] If one of Viola's actors were to become aware of the tension in her shoulders (even while concentrating on the emotion the tension accompanied), she would be accessing the normally muted "background feeling" underlying her thoughts and emotions. (And it is only by focusing her attention on such a kinetic arousal or "vitality affect" that she might develop the capacity to repeat the movement voluntarily.) Although vitality affects eventually become linked to specific emotions, the tension in the shoulders could conceivably be experienced as just that: a rapprochement of the shoulder blades at a particular spot on the upper back. As Stern points out, our movements, before we attach meanings to them (or, more accurately, before meanings are attached to our movements in an intersubjective milieu), are indeed capable of providing us with a rich somatic awareness of executing them. Executing movements, then, can allow us not only to feel emotions but also to feel ourselves in the act of performing them.

It is important to note that for Stern, almost from birth, the movements the human body performs and the vitality affects with which these movements are associated undergo some degree of cultural organization. Vitality affects are the earliest and most primitive cultural organization of the sensorimotor apparatus. They are "cultural" because each culture privileges some sensory experiences over others (a good deal of touching versus very little, or tight swaddling that prevents certain movements and thus access to certain kinesthetic sensations); and these affects are "primitive" because they remain closest to an innate and probably survivalist function of the organism (recoil from toxins, for instance, or attraction to warm, gentle touch). In contrast to Bourdieu, Stern contends that our kinesthetic background (composed of "vitality affects") is not permanently absented, returning only under distorted, culturally constructed forms. Under certain conditions, Stern insists, we may become aware of "elusive qualities" such as "surging," "fleeting," and "fading away,"[43] or turn our attention to the tightening of the muscles between the eyes as we read this page. As movement practitioners affirm every day, layers of sensorimotor organization that are normally inaccessible ("prereflexive") can at times become the matter of a reflexive consciousness. Attending to this "background" might make us sensitive to the intentionalities of the motor body (rather than the psyche), the "nascent muscular sensations" and kinetic "tendencies" that Bergson once described (MM, 111). My hypothesis, which I test in the next section, is that lying behind—and continuously supporting—the categorical gestures Viola's actors were told to display are sets of evolving "vitality affects" related specifically to the effort qualities required to move from one gesture to the next. It is this background of proto-signifying movement matter that Viola's digitalized videos expose to view.

Groping through the space of the present

If we now turn to *Anima,* another installation from *The Passions* (Figure 2.3), we see how Viola addresses, artistically, Stern's distinction between the categorical and the vital, emotions and the matter of movement itself. In this color video triptych, three actors adjust their gestures to achieve the

Figure 2.3
Bill Viola, *Anima*,
2000. Color video
triptych on three
LCD flat panels
mounted on wall.
Photo: Kira Perov.

expression of four categorical emotions—joy, sorrow, anger, and fear—but at a technologically decelerated pace that reveals the "in-between" gesticulations, the constant movements linking one to the next.[44] Recorded in a single take, *Anima* originally lasted one minute; extended through digital manipulation, the finished piece consists of over eighty-one minutes of playback time. Strangely, the name *Anima* evokes the categorical, fixed posture rather than the vital, or the forever-in-continuous-motion. At first glance, *Anima* would seem to be referring either to the word "soul" or else to an equally transcendent register, that of Carl Jung's archetypal female. At the same time, however, *Anima* strongly suggests the word "animation." The tension in the title between *Anima* as archetypal fixity and *Anima* as pure mobility is reflected in the piece itself, which involves a set of emoting (rather than talking) heads.

As Hansen has observed in "The Time of Affect," the faces in *Anima* appear to be "registering an overabundance of affective information."[45] But while these faces may indeed be supersaturated with emotion, engaged in displaying "interstitial microstages of affectivity," it should be noted that they are also unveiling a surprising diversity of movement possibilities available to the human face. These briefly glimpsed movement possibilities are involved, however, in a signifying project. Each one is, in Stern's terms, an *emergent* signification, a motility in the process of being shaped by the cultural (expressive) weight it will soon bear and toward which it is ineluctably moving. To give an example from *Anima,* the play of rippling muscles on an actor's cheeks or the increasing arch of the brow might not be immediately equivalent to (or even a constitutive element of) any one of the categorical emotions the actors were asked to reproduce. However, these (as yet) nontaxonomized microgestures, these in-between phases through which the muscles pass, are nevertheless already directed toward, *moving toward,* the legible gestures between which they fall ("the 'direction' of the situation"). To that extent, they remain elements of skilled practice, points on a movement continuum that the gesture, as sign, splits into parts.

It is entirely plausible that during the performance of a gesture such as a pout or a grin, that is, during the in-between phases we witness in *Anima,* any number of microbreakdowns occur, moments when the muscles hesitate among options and the features of the face could depart on alternative paths. The execution of the gesture could thus be seen in Husserl's terms as a layered instant composed of both retentions—the body's grasp on that which was previously performed—and protentions—the body's grasping for that which it could enact in the future. Merleau-Ponty's contribution to the phenomenology of embodiment could be said to lie precisely here, in the application of Husserl's paradigm of time consciousness to motor, rather than cognitive, intentionalities. Merleau-Ponty, Bergson, and the neuroscientists who follow in their path understand movement, like thought, to be shot through with retentive patterning, the sedimentation of previously executed gestural routines, and at the same time future-oriented, groping through the space of the present in search of the movements that will best address the demands of the next lived moment. Given this structural resemblance between consciousness and the motor function, their shared protentive and retentive deferral of the present, we can think of the sensorimotor body as intelligent, involved in a ratiocination as nuanced as that we associate with the mind.

Ultimately, what we witness in *Anima* is the pull of two forces, each of which contributes to the uniqueness yet repeatability of the gesture. Linked together in decelerated video images are the vital and the categorical: on the one hand the protosignifying in-between movement such as a pinched mouth about to open and on the other a fully legible signification, an iterable, acquired gesture such as a beaming grin. My own viewing of the installations reveals not a body freed from "I can's," not a mass of "vitality as such," but rather a motor body in the process of recalling and anticipating its possibilities, organizing itself within an intersubjective situation to play the role to which it has been assigned. After all, what we are looking at in *Anima* is a troupe of actors who were told to imitate a given set of nameable emotions. The things their faces do may not always be subject to classification, but their in-between muscle movements are nonetheless part of the body's directedness toward the performance of a certain task: here, the emoting of nameable emotions according to established (aestheticized, perhaps even commercialized) modes of communicating them.

If we insist on calling the "in-between" gesticulations perceptible to viewers of *Anima* "microstages of *affectivity*," that is, if we emphasize affect over kinesis, then we imply that at every moment the filmed subjects move they are expressing rather than *doing* something with their bodies. But what if we were to pull our focus out of the affectivity we think we see as we regard Viola's images and retrain that focus on the gesticulations themselves? Could the lived present then be treated as primarily a movement phenomenon, as I believe Merleau-Ponty wished it to be, a phenomenon to which movement analysis should be applied? How would this change in emphasis influence our approach to Viola's performing bodies? What other works would have to fall within our purview if we were to take this analytical turn, and how else might we want to look at them?

It is noteworthy that the installation in *The Passions* series that has received the least critical attention is *Four Hands* of 2001 (Figure 2.4). Here,

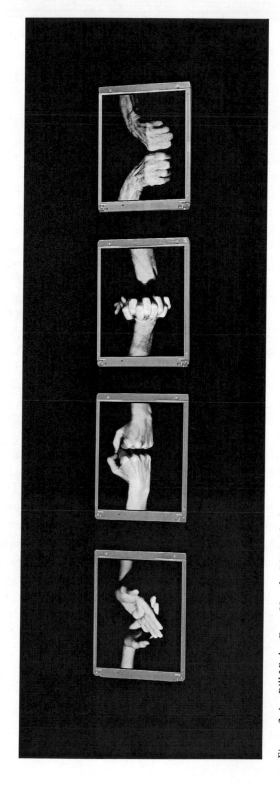

Figure 2.4 Bill Viola, *Four Hands*, 2001. Black-and-white video polyptych on four LCD flat panels mounted on shelf. Photo: Kira Perov.

Viola mounts four small LCD flat-panel display screens on a shelf (the dimensions are 9 by 51 by 8 inches). On each screen Viola projects moving images of a pair of hands: those of Viola's son, his wife, his own hands, and the hands of an elderly actress named Lois Stark (intended, perhaps, to evoke his mother who had recently passed away). The Getty catalogue informs us that *Four Hands* was shot with a black-and-white low-light camera. In the frame, we see only the subdued iridescence of taut or creased skin as it moves over the spiny bones of the hands. Peter Sellars describes the scene beautifully in "Bodies of Light," one of the critical essays included in the Getty catalogue: a "series of gestures," he writes, "are shared across the 'four hands'"—really, four *pairs* of hands—"in sequencing that remains slightly elusive. Sometimes a gesture initiated by a son is taken up by the mother; sometimes the mother is teaching and leading her son."[46]

Although in the finished work the emphasis is clearly on the transmission of symbolic gestures from one generation to the next, Viola tells us that his initial inspiration came from images of isolated individuals in the act of gesturing, such as *The Annunciation* (c. 1450–55) by Dieric Bouts of the Netherlands (Figure 2.5); the seventeenth-century English chirogrammatic tables of John Bulwer in which images of hands are cropped and placed into grids (Figure 2.6); and paintings of Hindu and Buddhist mudras. Viola's account of his sources has somewhat misled his critics into believing that the sharing of gestures in *Four Hands* underscores their universal quality, as opposed to what Sellars clearly grasps: the passing down of a gestural *habitus* from mother to son.[47] In *Four Hands* Viola's claim that the meaning of performed gestures is universal and innate is undercut by the scenes of generational transmission the video registers. Embedded in the sequential structure of the piece is the implication that such gestures are transmitted and acquired in an intersubjective setting, as a result of acculturation, miming, apprenticeship, and dialogic response. The mother and son, especially, appear to be miming each other's hand gestures, communicating in a motor language that develops through exchange, performance, appropriation, and variation. The unison of the two hands is broken by responsive differing, just as in intersubjective situations two subjects might perform the same gestures but in slightly modified ways, qualitatively contrasting with, replying to, the dynamics, velocity, and tonicity of the other's performance. The transmission scene of *Four Hands* implies that gestural vocabularies are at least partially acquired (rather than received at birth) and derive at least some of their meaning from the context in which they are performed. At the exhibition, easily discernible orange cables connected one screen to the next like an umbilical cord, thereby foregrounding the *interdependence* of the subjects and their gestural responses. Would the son make the same gestures as the mother if they were not linked by apprenticeship, furnished with occasions for the teaching and learning of expressive means?

The architecture of *Four Hands* is ambiguous, allowing both readings their due: the performed gestures can be seen as universal and innate or, alternatively, conventional and acquired. But what *Four Hands* demonstrates

Figure 2.5   Dieric Bouts, *The Annunciation*, c. 1450–1455. The Getty Museum, Los Angeles. 85.PA.24.

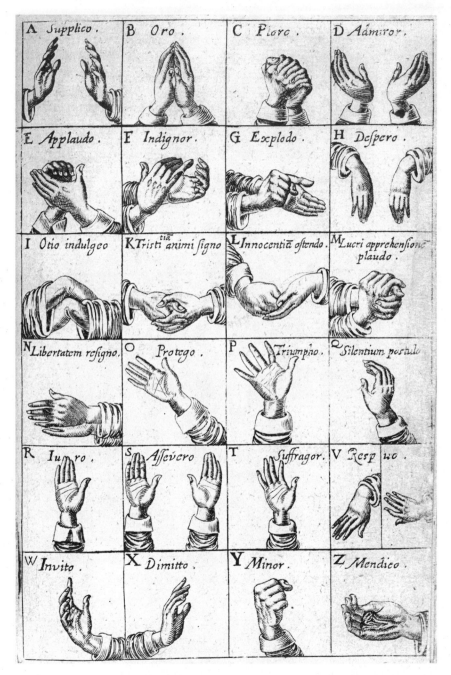

Figure 2.6 John Bulwer, engraving, in *Chirologia, or the Naturall Language of the Hand,* 1644. Copyright British Library Board. All Rights Reserved. 959.a.14.

unequivocally is that the in-between microgestures, displayed during the interval and captured by the eye, are not undirected "waves of affect" or "emotional flows." In contrast with the highly dramatic—even melodramatic—facial and upper-body gesticulations of the actors in *Anima,* the quieter, monochromatic hand gestures performed in *Four Hands* announce far more clearly their approaching conformity to the categorical and the legible gestures of established gestural sign languages or mudras. Thus it is more difficult to claim that the "in-between" movements are fully free of cultural conditioning, an illustration of protention inventing movement without any recourse to the sedimented past. When we watch the hands moving in and out of defined, chiseled forms, we become aware of the activity of hands not as they search freely in a limitless continuum for the next pose but rather as they move through a catalogue of nascent motor actions *toward* the categorical, legible pose. In *Four Hands* Viola reveals motility in its dialectical essence, at once a recursive, selective feedback mechanism attentive to presignifying sensations and a set of conditioned gestures that must signify in an intersubjective milieu. He captures the body as it creatively explores "nascent movement sensations" and samples kinetic "tendencies" (MM, 111) before veering toward the codified expression of a culturally established, arbitrary, and conventional meaning.

More than any other work in the exhibition, then, *Four Hands* exacerbates the tension between legibility and the ambiguous qualities of kinesis that exceed codified gestural forms. Because we are looking at hands, not faces, we tend not to experience an intense affective identification with the image but instead engage in a detached, aesthetic contemplation of the architecture created by muscle, flesh, and bone. In *Four Hands,* the potential for a deanthropomorphizing gaze is exponentially increased because the hands stand alone; they have been cropped from the expressive faces that, as Deleuze has argued, prove to be such a strong magnet for human affect. Once affect is not the theme and intense affective engagement is no longer the solicited response, Viola's works reveal indetermination to be a kinetic-kinesthetic dynamic that engages vitality affects as well as emotion-affects, building on (rather than departing from) an evolutionary, cultural, and embodied past.

For Merleau-Ponty, it is not possible to imagine—and certainly not to view—a movement utterly divorced from the determinations of the past, whether that past is conceived as biological (a vocabulary of reflexes we inherit) or existential (the neuronal pathways laid down in the course of our lives). Nor, however, is it the case that the past reveals itself without modification, without an inflection to suit the demands of the present.[48]

Such is the ultimately paradoxical nature of our performative instantiation. On the one hand, we are destined to reiterate a certain number of primary dispositions, kinetic "I can's" with which an organism "gears itself" to an environment. Without this initial set of motor capacities establishing our proprioceptive and kinesthetic being-in-space, the world around us would lack meaning, our senses could never be organized, and we would not even be able to estimate distances in space. On the other, these initial dispositions are the very matter on which society works, redirecting, pruning, and modifying tendencies so that we can belong to a particular time and place. Thus, we are only "open" to the unpredictable arrangement of circumstances because we have autonomous bodily functions—such as breathing, focusing the eyes, and grasping with the hands—that "gear" us to an environment, that project schemas for understanding that environment in advance. And we are only "open" to responding differently (despite our socialization) because our biology gives us "I can's" that are flexible or varied enough to enable us to wrap ourselves around the situation at hand. This paradox, which structures our "freedom" all the way down the line, is central to a rigorous, dialectical phenomenology, the paradox that we are only "free" because we are capable of being enchained, that we can only see because anatomy, training, and personal experience cause us to see in a certain way (PP, 139).

In a passage I quoted earlier (but emphasized differently), Merleau-Ponty asserts that there exists no "form of behavior which does not owe something to purely biological being—and which at the same time does not *elude* the simplicity of animal life, and cause forms of vital behavior to *deviate* from their pre-ordained direction" (PP, 220; added emphasis). My change in emphasis (from "biological being" to the verbs "elude" and "deviate") is meant to draw attention to the way the contingencies of the situation inflect a "vital" behavior, making it unlikely to be performed in a mechanical way. However, without a sensitivity to social contingencies, to the dense particularities of the situation, we would be unable to curve the innate dispositions that are our primary resource for embodiment. But where does such sensitivity come from? How is it developed? Merleau-Ponty seems to suggest that our body's incorporation of the social in the form of a body *hexis* (neural pathways inscribed through imitation and training) provides a sort of "library," a choice of responses, that we can draw from to "deviate" the given and "elude" the automatic. That which would, from another perspective, hem us in and potentially crush us (our social construction) instead contributes to forming an "embodied history" of gestural possibilities that ensure our (albeit limited) freedom from unreflected action. And these possibilities, although sometimes available to consciousness, are not the mind's but the body's: they belong to a motor *intelligence* that has learned to recognize social cues.[49] Possessing "I can's," then, is not a sufficient condition to produce the "responsive differing" I referred to previously in connection with *Four Hands*. Motor intelligence must involve an ability to engage "intense proprioceptive feedback" (Stern, xvii). This feedback, a nonverbal self in dialogue with the self, must function to interpret context, to offer, combine, and select, if contingent gestural meanings are to be made from sedimented gestural signs.

The rewarded destinations of the face

In conclusion, I want to return to the question raised at the beginning of this chapter concerning the source of the unpredictable and the new. If, as I have been arguing, the freedom afforded by the interval of self-affection is both triggered and hemmed in by the culturally specific gestures we rely on when we act, then to what process or force can we attribute innovation, resistance, and the emergence of the previously unknown? If not affect, then what?

Merleau-Ponty indicates a partial answer when he turns to the issue of gestural conditioning (the acquisition of a *habitus*) in the chapter entitled "The Body as Expression, and Speech." Here he offers the example of the infant's smile as one of the earliest instances in which the given, autonomous body confronts the pressure of cultural norms. When the smile is proffered, he notes, it is merely one gestural possibility among others emerging from the bone and muscular structure of the human face. But in an intersubjective setting, this movement possibility takes on a specific meaning; under normal conditions, the infant who repeats the now meaningful smile will receive reinforcement from surrounding adults: "a contraction of the throat, a sibilant emission of air between the tongue and teeth, a certain way of bringing the body into play suddenly allows itself to be invested with a *figurative* [cultural rather than biological] *significance* which is conveyed outside us" (PP, 225). In other words, an experience of a vitality affect (the *rushing* air as it passes through the larynx), a tactile sensation (the *wetness* and *roughness* of the tongue as it strokes the palate), and even an effort quality (the *contraction* of the labia or nostrils) is suddenly invested with another meaning for the infant. As a corollary, the "way of bringing the body into play" foregrounded earlier may recede into the background once the infant begins to privilege the figurative significance of the movements performed over the sensations experienced in performance.

Merleau-Ponty is identifying in this passage a social dynamic that has been confirmed in more recent studies, such as those conducted by the child developmental psychologist Andrew Meltzoff. In tests conducted with new-borns, Meltzoff recounts, researchers found that starting around twelve days after birth, infants shift from sticking out their tongues in self-absorbed play to regularly protruding the tongue "in imitation of an adult model."[50] Meltzoff claims that sticking out the tongue is something infants simply do from birth; it is one of their earliest "I can's," detached from an assigned meaning, the closest thing we know to a precultural reflex. Sticking out the tongue first appears to the infant as a feeling of movement (the sliding of tongue on lips) and only later takes on cultural meaning as infants find their behavior repeated on the faces of their caregivers. Infants even begin a few days later to correct their ways of protruding the tongue; if at first they protrude the tongue in order to explore the tongue's dimensions and sensations for their own sake, soon they will be seeking to approximate more exactly the behaviors they observe in others around them. Importantly, self-correcting efforts inspired by the observation of others have the secondary effect of reducing the number of other gesticulations performed, or postures assumed; socially motivated self-correction causes the muscles of the face (or body) to *tend toward* the execution of only a certain, culturally specific, even family-specific vocabulary of gestures. From very early on, then, the in-between gesticulations are not entirely free of cultural inflection; once even minimally socialized, the infant is less likely to engage in playful exploration of a fuller range of movement possibilities, because only some of these possibilities have been experienced as culturally significant; only some have become the rewarded destinations of the face. However, that does not mean that on the way to these destinations, the body has not passed through, or will not continue to pass through, many culturally non-invested gesticulations that could become, under the right circumstances, the movement matter of other types of performance. The process of correction that Meltzoff identifies implies that the body is born with a very extensive "motor power," as Merleau-Ponty has put it, a motor power capable of generating a host of gestures that will eventually have meanings *and a host of gestures that will not.* Further, and most important, every gesture that will be granted meaning in a cultural milieu will also remain another movement possibility, providing an experience of kinesis, a gestural materiality, on which "figurative significance" has contingently come to rest.

Finally, Merleau-Ponty's discussion of infant language acquisition provides a telling illustration of the way kinesis, rather than simply emotion-affect alone, offers the possibility for gesticulatory innovations beyond the gestures that any one cultural system prescribes. In "Indirect Language and the Voices of Silence," Merleau-Ponty depicts language acquisition as a process of continual self-reduction, defining the "self" here as the vocal apparatus and its physiological, we might almost say material, possibilities of manipulation. "The important point," Merleau-Ponty stresses, "is that the phonemes are from the beginning variations of a unique speech apparatus, and that with them the child seems to have 'caught' the principle of a mutual differentiation of signs and at the same time to have acquired *the meaning of the sign*."[51] If the child can grasp the difference, in an intersubjective setting, between "babbling" and sounds that bear intersubjective meaning, then the child knows *on a kinesthetic level* how to do more than she will be, by any one given culture, required to do. The "principle" the child discovers is that a sound gains its meaning not purely from what it is, or purely from what it feels like to produce it, but rather from the way it differs from another sound. As well as learning the differential, conventional meaning of the phonemic clusters, then, the child also feels the not-yet-classified or rewarded sensations produced by pronouncing these clusters, the qualitative continuum of movement she has been forced to segment into communicative or operational units. She has felt something that cultural representations do not allow her to store as perceptual image (or nameable, categorical emotion). These unclassified sensations will be retained instead as motor memory, part of a "kinesthetic background" from which the future—as protentive projection—will later emerge. Physiological potentialities of the lips, throat, tongue, and vocal chords will be "repressed" (Merleau-Ponty's word) but will remain *as prior inscription* on the level of motor experience, that is, on the level of kinesthetic memory of past action. The child can draw on these lived "I can's" belonging not to culture *but to the apparatus,* if given the opportunity to do so.

Perhaps inspired by Merleau-Ponty's comments, Julia Kristeva also turns to infant language acquisition for a key to the acculturated body's gesticulatory, expressive, and affective excess over its cultural self. In a clinical research experiment recorded in "Contraintes rythmiques et langage poétique," Kristeva studies the sounds produced by infants four to six months old.[52] At this point, infants are engaged in a process of self-correction similar to that observed in Meltzoff's study on sticking out the tongue, only here they are working to shape (and parse) a continuum of unintelligible vocalizations into the significant phonemes of a single human language. With the aid of analog audiotape, Kristeva trains her ear to hear the sounds *in between* the phonemes of French, or, alternatively, Chinese (the cultural backgrounds of her clinical subjects). The sounds she hears in between recognizable phonemes belong to the extensive "motor power" of the human vocal apparatus, the physiology of which offers a range of sound-making movements capable of being conjugated into any one of the existing six thousand languages humans use—or even other languages not yet invented. And it is important to preserve this space of the *not-yet-invented,* the to-be-organized-into-culture, for, as Merleau-Ponty observes time and again, we do not know what nature beyond culture is. We do not even know what our own anatomy allows. "The psychophysiological equipment," he emphasizes, "leaves a great variety of possibilities open, and there is no . . . human nature finally and immutably given" (PP, 220). On this reading, a human being's past, or "the animal's embodied history," as Varela puts it, includes culturally specific gestures acquired in infancy and skills learned later on but also movements sketched out perhaps only once, available to the apparatus, the "equipment" with which we are born.[53] The individual's motor repertory is thus not limitless, but it is certainly richer than any single culture can encode. We are each a self-disclosing motility, the parameters of which undoubtedly exist but remain unknown.

Perhaps what makes us capable of spontaneity is not the limitless capacity of the neuronal system to create new movements but rather the limitless capacity of the neuronal system to connect the movements that human anatomy allows, to enchain human possibilities of kinesis in new ways. The "freedom" to innovate, to produce "the unpredictable" and "the new," then, should be seen to derive not from a projection of "emotional tone" ahead of bodily performance and beyond learned response; instead, such "freedom" should be attributed to the untapped movement potentials of the human animate form, potentials that are always emerging, in the course of being explored. The subject's motor body does not contain limitless new ways of moving; rather, the motor body contains new ways of moving *that have not yet been parsed and organized by a single culture.* In short, the subject's body knows more about movement, both as kinetic possibility and kinesthetic experience, than any one cultural *habitus* allows the subject to name. These ways of moving (and the neuronal connections that underlie them) might not be inscribed in a *habitus,* not filed in a "library" (Berthoz, 164), but they are nonetheless inscribed on a deeper, phylogenetic level, on the level of the kinetic dispositions of bipedal anatomy. This in no way implies an ahistorical biological determinism, for as Merleau-Ponty repeatedly states in his late lectures in *Nature,* the explicit limits of bipedal anatomy remain unknown and subject to continuing exfoliation in an intersubjective milieu.

It is thus arguable that the nascent motor actions never fulfilled (but fleetingly proposed) are precisely what we witness in *Anima* and *The Quintet of the Astonished* at the moment when the actors pass from one emotional expression to the next. That is, these actors are drawing on a kinesthetic background, a continuum of motility—say, between the Chinese and the French—that could eventually be parsed, differentiated into gestures we recognize as fully meaningful in a shared cultural context (as in Creole or dialect). Viola's camera recovers the consciousness of a process that the subjects themselves may or may not have, a consciousness of a process through which the body discovers within itself a movement possibility, a virtual "I can," that is not immediately exploited but that could eventually be bent to the service of a meaningful cultural performance.

But a final question remains: To what extent can the emergent self or infant body play a role in creating new forms of motility once the *habitus* has left its mark? Can we become aware of our own kinesthetic background? Can we reflect on the prereflexive self? Some scholars have answered in the negative; Bourdieu, for one, asserts that gestures learned early on influence in seemingly inescapable ways the body's motor being. Yet evidence accrues that later training and observation can eventually allow us access to alternative movement capacities, options that will themselves be limited by the personal history of the singular body, its injuries and the peculiar shape of its bones. Many of those movement possibilities exist as virtual pathways, movement logics that could be pursued, even within the gestural routines we already possess. Most of the time, as Drew Leder has remarked, the subject remains ignorant of kinesthetic feedback and therefore of the alternative logics the body might pursue.[54] However,—and here lies a crucial objection to Bourdieu—bodily awareness is not eradicated by its "absenting"; instead, this awareness merely recedes into the "background," potentially available to be called up again.[55]

Merleau-Ponty maintains that we indeed have numerous opportunities to return to and sensorily recapture the "vitality affects" or kinesthetic background that invests our socially legible gestures with situated meaning. We can shift our attention from the meanings we are making to the kinesthetic sensation of making them, thereby revealing an alternative approach to the body as "protosignification," a materiality on which meanings will be inscribed. Merleau-Ponty refers to these moments as "dropping away," as periods of extended attention to performance, when the semantic value of a word, for instance, recedes into the background and instead the "verbal gesticulation" is perceived as "a certain use made of my phonatory equipment."[56] If we can manage to separate ourselves momentarily from our semantic projects, not only do we hear the noise of the sound-clusters we call words but, more important, we seize the cultural organization of sound *at the level of what it feels like, qualitatively, to produce it.* Extending Merleau-Ponty's insight, the anthropologist Thomas J. Csordas has proposed that every culture offers its own set of "somatic modes of attention," skilled practices that encourage subjects to access this kinesthetic layer of knowledge and experience. "Somatic modes of attention," he writes, "are culturally elaborated ways of attending to and with one's body in surroundings that include the embodied presence of others."[57] (His examples range from yoga and meditation to love-making, charismatic healing, and learning to dance.) What Merleau-Ponty dubs "the tacit *cogito,* myself experienced by myself," is available through culture's own technologies of self-monitoring, somatic modes of attention that are themselves, of course, limited by the languages in which they are couched.

Perhaps there is ultimately no complete escape from acculturation, no blissful "dropping away" from acquired routines. Paradoxically, however, each culture provides routines to counter routines, a set of procedures to reveal the gap in another set. Through slow-motion technologies or somatic techniques that make us more aware of the continuum from which gestures have been cut, it is possible to increase one's sensitivity to the gap, to lie in wait for the emergence of that short but pregnant interval, that the next step on the chain both renders possible and leaves behind. Our freedom to innovate, our plasticity, should be seen to derive from our rich mnemonic store (our "library") of socially acquired "I can's" as well as the proto-signifying resources of bipedal anatomy. In *The Passions* Viola displays these not-yet exhausted resources, these kinetic possibilities in the course of being kinesthetically explored, either to be pressed into the service of already established gestural vocabularies or, in privileged cases such as choreography, to be expanded into a logic of their own.

CHAPTER THREE

Inscription and Embodiment:
André Leroi-Gourhan and the Body as Tool

L'outil n'est réellement que dans le geste qui le rend
techniquement efficace.

    —André Leroi-Gourhan, *Le Geste et la parole,* 2 (1964)

I T IS DIFFICULT to imagine a theory of gesture that did not take
the contributions of the paleoethnographer André Leroi-Gourhan
into account. He was the first to treat gesture explicitly as a discipline (through which society imprints itself on the body) and a conduit of
agency (through which the subject innovates and departs from the script).
Yet, as significant as his work clearly is, his legacy has proved to be a con-
tested one. On the one hand, Leroi-Gourhan's chronology of prehistoric
material culture has been falsified by the emergence of new evidence since
his death in 1986; the account of prehistoric styles and their aesthetic evolution offered in *Treasures of Prehistoric Art* of 1965 has been judged in-
accurate; and his structuralist interpretation of paired signs has been
rejected as acontextual and anachronistic. On the other, scholars in art history and archeology continue to refer to him as "the greatest of prehistorians"[1] while insisting that his contributions to the study of Paleolithic art
have never been surpassed.[2] What, precisely, is so "prescient" and "original" in his work?[3] What can a study of Leroi-Gourhan—especially his theory of gesture—lend to a contemporary understanding of the moving body
and its role in the making and remaking of culture?

Aside from the impact Leroi-Gourhan has had on prehistoric archeology, he has also exerted a considerable influence on the development of
many related fields, including the history of writing, the philosophy of deconstruction, and the burgeoning discipline of new media theory. At the
end of the 1960s (the period of Leroi-Gourhan's most stunning advances),
Derrida made a first and important attempt to lead the paleontologist
out of the disciplinary envelope in which he had been confined. *De la*

grammatologie (1967) advances a strong argument in favor of composing a general science of the human based on Leroi-Gourhan's theories as
adumbrated in *Le Geste et la parole*, his two-volume study of human evolution (translated into English as *Gesture and Speech* in 1993). Following
Derrida's lead, Bernard Stiegler has published a five-volume work on humanity's technological destiny, *Le Technique et le temps*, in which Leroi-
Gourhan also plays a central role. In Stiegler's words, *Gesture and Speech*
represents "the last word on paleoanthropological thinking—and undoubtedly this heritage still remains to be assumed today, either by paleoan-
thropology or by philosophy."[4] From the perspective of both Derrida and
Stiegler, Leroi-Gourhan's crucial contribution consists in having refused
to envision a human nature, a human *physis*, outside of its constitutive
relation to *technè*, or prosthetic tools. For Leroi-Gourhan, they argue,
humans come to have the bodies they have, are embodied in a specific way,
through formative interaction with these prosthetic tools. Thus, the most
urgent question Leroi-Gourhan raises—the one that preoccupies not only
Derrida and Stiegler but the current generation of new media theorists as
well—is whether humans, through their development of increasingly sophisticated tools, eventually render their current form of embodied existence obsolete. At what point does the machine (in Stiegler's terms, the
"*what*") begin to define the human subject (the "*who*") with whom it is
inextricably intertwined? If, as Stiegler proposes, "Technics is inventive
as well as invented," is it possible that the human, gesturing body will
be—or has already been—subsumed by another form of embodiment,
one dependent on and wholly "invented by" technics itself?[5]

   In seeking to respond to these questions, Derrida and Stiegler at once
respect and distort the weighty corpus of Leroi-Gourhan's works. They
fruitfully draw attention to the emphasis he placed on tools as constitutive of human embodiment, but they tend to neglect his equally forceful
emphasis on the gestures manipulating those tools, and thus on the lived,
somatic-kinesthetic experience of being a human body engaged in interaction with them. An important context for reading Leroi-Gourhan's work
is thereby lost: he possessed both a Marxist apprehension of the importance of material conditions in constituting human consciousness (which
Stiegler most explicitly recalls) *and* a phenomenological appreciation of the
body's sensual engagement with these conditions (which Derrida ends up
acknowledging far more than Stiegler). Without doubt, Leroi-Gourhan
understood that, as Stiegler states succinctly, "the appearance of the human is the appearance of the technical . . . the human invents itself in the
technical by inventing the tool."[6] However, Leroi-Gourhan adds three
important caveats, each of which will occupy me in this chapter: (1) that

tools are nothing without the gestures that manipulate them and that in fact make them into tools; (2) that gesturing is evaluative, a form of perception, adaptation, and creation, as well as a programmed routine, an operating chain; and (3) that tools and machines, techniques and technologies, are not entirely the same thing and therefore theories of the gestural destiny of humans have to take these differences into account. I agree fully with Stiegler that Leroi-Gourhan's "heritage still remains to be assumed today"; but in contrast to Stiegler, I would argue that it is in the domain, paradoxically, of advanced inscriptive technologies that the work of assuming Leroi-Gourhan's legacy has really begun. In this chapter I conduct a close reading of *Gesture and Speech,* taking into account the careful analyses Derrida and Stiegler have already offered. But I also test Leroi-Gourhan's prophecies against the evidence of contemporary digital poetry, seeking the persistence of the phenomenal gesture in one of the most technologically mediated forms of "speech." My goal is to reveal in Leroi-Gourhan's writings the foundations for a theory of gesture that emphasizes the role of performed movement in understanding how humans forge themselves through interaction with tools.

Retrieving the animal body

A fact rarely mentioned in treatments of Leroi-Gourhan's work is that he studied with not only Marcel Mauss but also Marcel Granet, a scholar of dance and ritual performance for whom movement practices were clearly at the root of verbal and scribal activities.[7] Almost without exception, critics have ignored the legacy of Granet and Mauss in *Gesture and Speech*, preferring instead to accentuate Leroi-Gourhan's debt to Lévi-Strauss and a structuralist-linguistic approach to cultural phenomena.[8] But the legacy of movement-based analysis is easy to identify in Leroi-Gourhan's work on the material remains of Paleolithic and Neolithic peoples. In *Gesture and Speech*, he is not interested in taxonomizing these remains or speculating on the belief systems they supported; rather, he regards spearheads and other flint tools as mirror images of what Mauss called *"montages physio-psycho-sociologiques de séries d'actes,"*[9] or, more simply, "techniques of the body." The major thrust of *Gesture and Speech* is to resituate tools in the context of movement routines facilitated by the anatomical developments that define—at least for physical anthropologists—the human species. Leroi-Gourhan approaches prehistoric material culture as the outgrowth of diverse *physical* practices, each of which corresponds to a unique cultural *habitus*, a geographically and ethnically discrete human society with its own articulated modes of conditioned movement.

Although much has been made of Leroi-Gourhan's reading of cave art (almost a caricature, it is true, of structuralist binarism as applied to iconography), he was arguably more innovative in the domain of methodology than interpretation. Mentored by the early twentieth-century prehistorian Henri Breuil, Leroi-Gourhan had, until the 1950s, followed Breuil's stratigraphic procedure of excavation, making a vertical cut into the earth layers in order to trace the evolution from one stage—or layer—to the next.[10] When he began his series of revolutionary excavations at Pincevent, France, in 1964, he perfected the planographic method, which consisted of making a horizontal cut in order to study the fossil remains of one time period alone. By replacing a comparative method with one that isolated a single layer of remains, he triggered a paradigmatic shift in the approach that archeologists would take to prehistoric materials from that moment on. Of course, this methodological shift presupposed and fortified a hermeneutic one: Of importance to Leroi-Gourhan and his followers was less the determination of a chronology for layered sets of remains than a deepened understanding of the interrelations among the remains found at one level and situated within one temporal frame. Leroi-Gourhan's "privileging of synchronic over diachronic in relational analysis of cultural texts" does indeed characterize the Saussure-inflected structuralist enterprise, as Annette Michelson has noted.[11] But this synchronic, relational attitude produced far more than a stereotypical structuralist reading of visual "texts"; it also gave birth to "paleoethnography," a method for interpreting prehistoric artifacts and traces that emphasizes not only internal, pictorial or syntactic relations but also the techniques—and the gestural routines of human bodies—that must have been employed in order to forge them.

Leroi-Gourhan distinguished himself first and foremost from Breuil and his colleagues by recontextualizing remains (bones and tools but also cave art and decorative objects) in the spaces and arrangements in which they were found.[12] Hypotheses concerning the beliefs and values of prehistoric *homo sapiens* were fragile and speculative, he felt, whereas data gathered from the evidence of spearheads, carved stones, and wall paintings told a credible story about the technical (rather than spiritual) capacities of humans who lived thirty thousand years ago. He wrote in 1964 that although the interdependence and "continuity between the two faces of group existence"—a technoeconomic base and a superstructure of beliefs, practices and rites—had been grasped by Durkheimian sociologists, they had nonetheless tended to accord more importance to the social (superstructural) than the material (base) in their accounts. In contrast, Leroi-Gourhan's stated goal was to see the social and the material *"comme un courant à double sens"*—a current flowing both ways—but one whose most profound impulse derived from the force of the material (*"dont l'im-*

pulsion profonde est celle du matériel").[13] His twist on the materialist, base/superstructure paradigm, however, was to see even this *"impulsion profonde"* of the material as itself a reflection of a zoological condition. That is, he was convinced that the humanization of material resources could only occur because of even more profound changes in primate anatomy. Trained as a prehistoric archeologist, an ethnologist, and a physical anthropologist, Leroi-Gourhan realized the extent to which the characteristics Durkheimians called "human" had to do with a biological reality: the development in an *animal* of particular features that allowed the species to do things that, in retrospect, appear human. The technoeconomic infrastructure to which he refers in *Gesture and Speech* would thus be derived from an even deeper base: the anatomical, physiological, and neurological composition of the human animal. The superstructural results of this technoeconomic base, such as tools, art objects, funerary rituals, and so on, had to be linked back to this deeper biological (or, as he liked to put it, "zoological") layer.

To look at the material products, techniques, and behaviors of humans as a reflection of their anatomical specificity is to treat humans first and foremost as a type of animal belonging to the zoological kingdom. Species-specific features pertaining to the bones as well as the brain would in this case be held responsible for the movement chains developed as well as the traces in matter these chains leave behind. If Marx displaced the motor of history from consciousness (the mind) onto the material conditions of production that generate consciousness, Leroi-Gourhan displaced this motor once more from material conditions of production (tools and the relations of humans among one another via tools) onto the kinetic-anatomical features of the animal *body* that made it feasible to have tools—and thus tool-mediated relations—in the first place. Again, this shift introduced humans as possessing a moving body belonging to the zoological kingdom and thus in continuity with other animals in that kingdom. A cat, Leroi-Gourhan suggests at one point in *Gesture and Speech*, has in its anatomical framework a faculty for the construction of a tool that is simply a weaker version of a similar animal faculty that is built into the kinetic disposition of *homo sapiens*. He notes that in the prehensile carnivores, for instance, manual activity is already quite developed, with a complementary density of fibres in the "sensorimotor zones of the cortex": "The cat in particular shows a high degree of separation [between face and paws], which is reflected in the use it makes of its front paw in a large number of operations. . . . Unlike the walkers, all the graspers [*les préhenseurs*]—even those a long way from the human end point of the evolutionary process—possess the basic potential for technicity [*les virtualités fondamentales de la technicité*]" (GP I, 115–116; GS, 80). The presence of a virtual technicity in the paws of a feline, for Leroi-Gourhan, is sufficient "to suggest how far back in the animal kingdom we can locate the fundamental instruments of human technicity" (GP I, 116).

Leroi-Gourhan still refers to a "human technicity," but given the link he discerns between lower carnivores and humans, he could just as easily have spoken of an "animal technicity," consistent throughout many species but more developed in the case of humans. He implies, in fact, that tool-making should be seen as fundamentally an animal activity before being analyzed as a human one. To some extent, his critics have been alert to this nuance; Stiegler, for instance, acknowledges Leroi-Gourhan's repositioning of "man" within a zoological continuum when he writes that "what is in question [in *Gesture and Speech*] is not emptying the human of all specificity but radically challenging the border between the animal and the human."[14] However, there are implications of this repositioning that Stiegler and Leroi-Gourhan's critics in general fail to explore: that (1) if tool-making and manipulation are neither coincident with nor exclusive to human beings, then there is no special purchase to the argument that the human and the technical come into being simultaneously (through a process of transduction peculiar to humanity), and (2) if tool-making and manipulation are available to animals and humans alike, it is because their bodies are themselves *sensate* tools. The hand that touches is also the hand that is touched—to recall Husserl's famous image—and thus the first tool is also a gesture that produces kinesthetic, proprioceptive, and haptic knowledge.[15] Leroi-Gourhan is quite clear about the role of sensation in making the body into a prehensile tool: the "basic potential for technicity" must be located in the paw, in the faculty of vision, and in the faculty of proprioception, *before* they are realized in an external, prosthetic tool. By approaching the human from a zoological perspective, and by relating the development of *technè* to kinetic dispositions, Leroi-Gourhan places on center stage the fact of being an animal body, a sensate body that hears, feels, sees, tastes, smells, and—most important for my purposes—moves. As we shall see, the tendency to ignore the larger implications of Leroi-Gourhan's account of fundamental technicity is one of the reasons Stiegler's and Derrida's analyses remain incomplete, leaving a good part of Leroi-Gourhan's theoretical ore unmined.

Humans first appear in *Gesture and Speech*, then, as a certain kind of body possessing a very particular kinetic disposition, or way of walking, manipulating, focusing, handling, and so on. By making this claim for the primacy of anatomo-physiological developments, Leroi-Gourhan was in fact going against the grain of a strong and tenacious tradition of scholarship in paleontology that associated the emergence of "Man" not with ambulatory or manipulative potential but rather with the acquisition of an enlarged brain. For many years scholars had been puzzled by the presence at prehistoric sites of—simultaneously (and for them, paradoxically)— the small skulls associated with primate bodies and the types of hearths and tools consistent with the activity of bipedal, hominid bodies. But discoveries over the course of the 1930s made it evident that human-like techniques and forms of locomotion were being practiced by creatures that did not possess the cerebral volume of contemporary *homo sapiens sapiens*. The unearthing in 1959 of a hominid dubbed Zinjanthropian leant further support for the bipedalism-first scenario. Leroi-Gourhan's conclusion was that although "it is difficult to assign pre-eminence to any particular characteristic, since in the development of species everything is interlinked," there could be "no doubt that to some extent cerebral development is a secondary criterion. . . . a correlative of erect posture and not, as was thought for a long time, primordial" (GP I, 33; GS, 19). For him, the root of all additional developments in human history was "upright carriage" *("la station verticale"),* which presupposes a specific form of ambulation and, no less significant, a greater and more complex participation of the muscles of the hands and face. Particular modes of mobility and gesturing could thus be taken as defining features of the human itself.[16]

But precisely what role did bipedalism and the liberation of the hand play in determining the *technological* destiny of humans? Did anatomy alone determine this destiny, or, to Leroi-Gourhan's mind, was there another factor that should be taken into account? The philosopher Maxine Sheets-Johnstone has attempted to respond to these questions by engaging the argument Leroi-Gourhan advanced in 1964–1965 and testing it against research published by more recent paleontologists. Referring to Leroi-Gourhan's first insight, Sheets-Johnstone asserts in *The Primacy of Movement* that archeological research of the 1980s and 1990s provides ample evidence supporting the hypothesis that creatures with significantly different skull shapes yet with a mode of locomotion and hand shape similar to that of *homo sapiens sapiens* were indeed able to accomplish tasks we still persist in defining as "human," such as building complex habitations, carving ornaments, and shaping stones.[17] Yet, she continues, these findings do not suggest that "anatomy is destiny," as Freud famously wrote; the kinetic dispositions of an animal are only that: *dispositions,* a set of possible directions to be taken, the promise of certain orientations in space facilitated by the degree of flexion in the joints and ligaments, the length and shape of bones, the angle at which the head is carried, an opposable thumb, and so on. Even these orientations might be subtly altered by a host of environmental and, most important, cultural contingencies. In

Sheets-Johnstone's words, "the mere possession of an anatomical part does not guarantee any particular behavior."[18] What the acquisition of an upright posture *does* ensure, however, "are certain movement possibilities and not others. To identify and describe these kinetic possibilities is ultimately to delineate a particular kinetic domain of dispositions," a "repertoire of I can's."[19]

Turning back to *Gesture and Speech*, we see this approach rehearsed in Leroi-Gourhan's own. When he first introduces the notion of "program" (*"programme"*) at the beginning of volume 2, it is as a *product*, not as a cause: A program emerges from the contact between the nervous system of an individual organism and the contingent stimuli of a specific environment. "In short, the nervous system is a machine not for fabricating instincts [*une machine à fabriquer de l'instinct*] but for responding to internal and external solicitations by *constructing* programs [*en construisant des programmes*]" (GP II, 13; my emphasis). "The only fact that emerges from experimental study of animal behavior," he concludes, "is the *plasticity* of an individual animal's behavior in relation to its specific means. This must be interpreted as a liberation, not from instinct, but from the fixed sequences established at the confluence of the individual's internal biological environment and the exterior" (GP II, 13; GS, 221; added emphasis). There is thus no originary and inescapable program laid down by genetic code, because programs are "constructed" en route, so to speak, in the existential process of confronting situations and actualizing a "disposition" under conditions that cannot be envisioned in advance. In other words, living bodies are equipped with an apparatus that is primed to construct programs, not with the programs themselves. Anatomy certainly plays a large role, and, to be sure, an inherited, species-specific potential for enchaining movements within a certain range already exists. However, it is culturally framed experience—which Leroi-Gourhan names *"tâtonnement,"* or "groping"—that will provide opportunities for some operating chains, but not others, to emerge.

"Par tâtonnements successifs"

The neuroanatomy of the animal body is thus clearly not a code to be translated systematically into preprogrammed movements but instead a set of possibilities for the generation of any number of gestural routines. This point will take on greater importance when we turn to Derrida, who interprets Leroi-Gourhan as positing the existence of a neuroanatomical blueprint of behavior (a "program") similar to a cybernetic code (also called by Derrida a "program"). But we can already see that Leroi-Gourhan's visionary contribution consists precisely in resisting the assimilation of pro-gram to code; he approaches the biological organism as an invariant, a limited set of resources that nonetheless can be realized in an inestimable number of unpredictable ways by each individual culture, even by each individual member of a culture. In short, there is no algorithm that can account synchronically for that which can only unfold diachronically. Leroi-Gourhan thereby strikes a balance between a biological determinism (in which all cultural developments are predicated on inborn racial charac-teristics) and a cultural constructivism in which the material attributes of an organism result from symbolic systems (culture) alone. Often ignored in the account of Leroi-Gourhan's vision of neoroanatomy is the degree to which he recognizes the role of environment and culture in lending phe-nomenological heft to capacities that might not have existed *in any form whatsoever* before being actualized in performance. In this respect, his ap-proach is consistent with that advanced by the contemporary anthropolo-gist Tim Ingold, who extends the subtle premises of *Gesture and Speech* in fruitful ways. In *The Perception of the Environment: Essays in Livelihood, Dwelling, and Skill,* a study of hunter-gatherer societies and map-making skills, Ingold defines human kinesis—its anatomical, neurological, and sen-sory components—as a "developmental system," a potential for becoming, not a "formal genetic 'endowment'" that programs behavior in advance.[20] For both Leroi-Gourhan and Ingold, the skills a creature acquires, the forms it takes, are not "received by the organism-to-be at the point of con-ception, but generated within the dynamic functioning of developmental systems."[21] This means that the gestures involved in walking, talking, or writing—gestures we insist on identifying with human bodies—are far from biologically innate; rather, they constitute, as Ingold has written, "em-bodied skill[s], incorporated into the human organism through a process of development."[22]

Interestingly, it is Leroi-Gourhan's (and Ingold's) understanding of the dialectical generation of animate bodies that ends up ushering *gestures* into the limelight. Gestures become the site of increased scrutiny not only because they are so various—and thus illustrate the "plasticity" of human behaviors with respect to anatomical and neurological invariants—but also because they are the very matter of "programs" in Leroi-Gourhan's sense. The "dynamic functioning of developmental systems" takes place at the moment when the body's movements are realized in the form of gestures (that is, as culturally inflected, iterable techniques). Gestures *are* that dy-namism; their performance is the means by which programs take hold on the body (through what Alain Berthoz calls "synergies and schemas" of neural networks connecting the muscles and the mind).[23] In volume 1 of

Gesture and Speech Leroi-Gourhan refers to gestures and gestural sequences as "operating chains," thereby emphasizing the fact that gestures are at the root of the tool-making and tool-manipulating practices that define "the human" in paleoethnographic terms. In volume 2, however, he renames operating chains "programs," underlining in this way the power of gestures both to *generate* (as opposed to reflect) actions and to shape the muscular structure of bodies modeled over time to execute these actions. The retentive and protentive duality of programs should be recalled at all times. Resulting from the nervous system's confrontation with "internal and external solicitations," programs are an *effect,* not merely a generator, of performance. A program will eventually become anticipatory, suggesting a way of responding to a future stimulus that resembles the one for which it was forged; but the program is first and foremost recuperative, an imprint or record of a previous movement. The question remains, then, if the program is belated and recuperative, then how does the initial movement come to be? What force shapes the first movement before it becomes inscribed as a repeatable routine?

According to Leroi-Gourhan, movements are actualized as potentially repeatable gestural programs through a variety of processes: apprenticeship through mime; verbal instruction; and experiment, or what he terms *"tâtonnement."* Since human beings are always born into a social milieu, their responses to "internal and external solicitations" will be to a large extent governed by responses previously realized (and handed down) by other human beings inhabiting the same space. Closely following Mauss's emphasis on early socialization, Leroi-Gourhan concurs that "The acquisition of elementary operating chains," or programs, "takes place during the first few years of life" (GP II, 29). Leroi-Gourhan is speaking here about technical skills, not expressive facial expressions, but even these are acquired by modeling motor energy to mirror gestures executed by others, that is, through unconscious mimicry. As the child ages, the learning of programs occurs through other channels, such as conscious imitation and apprenticeship of described or labeled actions. However, as I have indicated, Leroi-Gourhan adds a third and vital form of program acquisition, one that threatens to unsettle the purely mimetic nature of the former two. He adds that along with acquiring the *habitus* through "training by means of imitation [*dressage par imitation*]" and verbal communication [*la communication verbale*], humans also *contribute* to the *habitus* "by means of experiential groping [*l'expérience par tâtonnement*]" (GP II, 29). The role of the social, then, while certainly dominant, is neither exclusive nor total. Presumably, at every point in the subject's maturation, the subject is able to engage in the practice of "groping" *(tâtonnement);* the experience such groping provides will qualify, correct, improve, or even contest the knowledges the subject has acquired through observation and copying. In fact, innovation could not occur without the potential to "grope": "acts accomplished for the first time by groping gestures [*par tâtonnements successifs*] inscribe themselves as programs in a sequence of different memories . . . afterward, the play of these different memories [*le jeu de ces différentes mémoires*] allows for the accomplishment of more complex operating chains, leading even to the alteration [*l'incurvation*] of behaviors in the course of their performance [*au cours du déroulement des chaînes*]" (GP II, 18).

What Leroi-Gourhan affirms is that a certain amount of groping activity, approximate but also often random, intervenes in or initiates the acquisition of gestural routines and their incorporation as programs stored in the nervous system, muscles, and bones. There are two developmental phases at which this activity might be said to occur: during infancy or during adolescent-adult apprenticeship. If we imagine *"tâtonnement"* as occurring early on, say at the moment when the infant first tries to bring the hand to the mouth in order to insert a finger, then *"tâtonnement"* can refer to the earliest untrained movements, those that possess *no initial mimetic component* but that, through empirical testing (practice) and mimetic self-correction over time, eventually lead to skilled (socialized) behaviors. (We should recall here the tongue-protruding behavior of the infants studied by Meltzer and treated in the previous chapter.) Leroi-Gourhan's point in this instance would be that groping movements—"the acts accomplished for the first time by groping gestures"—can only issue from presocial kinetic-anatomical potentials of the species. But if we imagine *"tâtonnement"* as occurring at a later date, say, when the adolescent tries to learn to make a flint spearhead, then the groping activity might very well be based on earlier learned routines or programs (such as striking an object to create a rhythm) and thus manifest a social inscription (as opposed to an inborn kinetic disposition) as it is applied to a new task. The many approximate gestures produced during the period of groping (as the adolescent alters an old routine to achieve the new) would also leave behind memory traces, or, in Leroi-Gourhan's terms, "inscribe themselves as programs in a sequence of different memories." These mnemonic traces of movement—stored as proposed connections between nerves in the muscles and the cerebral cortex—would arguably remain available for later use in unpredictable ways: "afterward, the play of these different memories"—programs constructed through *"tâtonnement"*—would allow "for the accomplishment of more complex operating chains, leading even to the alteration [*l'incurvation*] of behaviors in the course of their performance."

The salient point is not to determine when the period of *"tâtonne-ment"* is to be developmentally located, for allusions throughout *Gesture and Speech* indicate that it can occur both early and late. Neither do we necessarily have to decide whether a given gesture emerges from a biological potential untouched by socialization or whether it is a variant of an already established routine (part of the *habitus*). Whether a variant of modeling or blind groping, the swerve away from established programs of movement—as well as the subsequent integration of some of these swerves into new routines—does occur, perhaps more than we recognize. And Leroi-Gourhan produces a convincing account of why it does, although not in *Gesture and Speech* but in the two volumes of *Évolution et techniques,* in which he attempts to identify the origins of technological innovation, or swerves away from the norm. In this work, he turns directly to the issue of nonprogrammed, unforeseeable behavior, asking how it is that invention occurs, by what process—individual *"génie"* or chance—innovative techniques come into existence. Although he concludes that it is impossible to measure with accuracy the role of individual genius in the technological history of specific communities, he nonetheless develops a theory of agency through *"tâtonnement"* (rather than haphazard discovery) that lends greater resonance to the term as it is found in *Gesture and Speech.*[24] In a section of the first volume entitled "L'Intention Technique" (Technical intentionality), he reflects that even though an adult member of a community is saturated by a shared *habitus,* even though her body is governed by programs, or gestural routines, a "technical intentionality" can nevertheless produce alterations in the way her body moves. This is because a "technical intentionality" always seeks, according to Leroi-Gourhan, not to imitate what was done before but to do it better, or perhaps by new means—to achieve what Hubert Dreyfus has called "maximum grip."[25] The primary focus of a technical intentionality, Leroi-Gourhan says, is to produce "contact" between the subject and the matter soliciting attention: "in technical intentionality we see that the desired action is always conceived by the worker as a type of contact"; the question the worker invariably asks is "How to make contact? [*Comment prendre contact?*]"[26]

What this means is that manipulative or instrumental gestures will, when governed by a technical (and not simply operational) intentionality, also double as exploratory, knowledge-seeking gestures: "in almost all cases technical acts seek contact, seek touch [*la recherche du contact, du toucher*]."[27] Stronger than the need to repeat, then, is the desire to alter one's movements and one's tools in order to gear the body's actions more completely to the world. Thus, even in the midst of all the social and environmental constraints placed on the individual worker, she will continue to strive for a more efficacious contact with the material, or perhaps do so without placing her body in harm's way. In the process, she improves her access to tactile knowledge, orienting her body in such a way as to gain a proprioceptive, haptic, evaluative grip on the object and/or the tool. Recasting what he avers in *Gesture and Speech* concerning the *"incurvation"* or altering of programs through *"tâtonnements,"* Leroi-Gourhan writes in *Évolution et techniques* that it is specifically from the "confrontation" between the acquired technical skill of the worker and a "desire for contact" that, *"par tâtonnements,"* the newly invented tool, the newly invented operating chain, and, in accordance with them, the newly invented human body capable of repeating the chains will emerge.[28] We see once again that Leroi-Gourhan's narrative of technical advancement includes a moment of profound interoceptive experience in which the subject, as he puts it, advances by *"palpating* the surface of the external milieu [*palpant la surface du milieu extérior*]."[29] In this way, gestures become evaluative, bringing back knowledge not only about the object but also about the worker's body, that is, about what gestures have to do, how muscles have to work, in order to produce better contact. Inchoate groping transforms the body into a receptor or, better yet, encourages a heightened attention to the sensory information that is always potentially available to a body that is skin and nerves and not plastic or metal. Haptic, visual, proprioceptive, kinesthetic, and conceivably auditory or even gustatory sensitivities join forces here to furnish the worker with the knowledge required to change the way she must move in order achieve an objective. By discovering in a groping, exploratory manner these new ways to move, elements of which might later be retained as new gestural programs, the worker contributes to culture and, eventually, to the constitution of her own body. Agency emerges as a result of embodiment, of possessing a body that moves and feels.

It is arguable that Leroi-Gourhan's most original contribution to cultural theory lies in his introduction of the word *"tâtonnement"* to explain how human beings propel the evolution of technical means. Etymologically, the verb *"tâtonner"* refers to the groping movements of the hand or other body part; it often implies the use of a prosthesis (a *"bâton,"* for instance), or the use of the hand *as* a prosthesis. *"Tâtonner"* is related to acts of situating, orienting, and, of course, palpating, touching an object or estimating the dimensions of a space. By analogy, *"tâtonner"* bears the figurative sense of intellectual searching, a hesitating movement of the mind as it tests out possible solutions, pursues various directions—so to speak—of thought. *"Tâtonner"* conveys the sense of exploration, whether

physical or cognitive: testing out a path not yet cleared or devising a sequence not yet inscribed. When used to refer to the order of thought, *"tâtonner"* in fact presents cogitation as a type of movement taking place in
space; to *"tâtonner"* is to parse or spatialize, even to create a space between
differentiations already made.

Leroi-Gourhan applies the term *"tâtonnement"* in a fairly narrow way
in *Évolution et techniques* and *Gesture and Speech* to mean the groping
movements that ultimately serve a "technical intentionality." However, he
makes room in his account to imagine that the palpating, exploratory movements of the worker or child are not always subordinated to a pre-conceived
goal, nor do they necessarily serve an intentionality that is primarily technical in nature. Theorists in several domains—Maxine Sheets-Johnstone
in evolutionary biology, Sally Ann Ness in anthropology, Michel Bernard
in dance studies, and José Gil in philosophy (to name just a few)—have
proposed that in many cases, the purpose of movement may be autotelic—
movement for the sake of experiencing more movement—or cognitive in
a broader sense. The moving subject may be seeking to understand something about the gesture itself (reflexive); the environment the gesture affects (exploratory but not locally instrumental); or the capacities and limits
of the body concerned.[30] Movement deviations to the learned pattern
(which Sheets-Johnstone believes are inevitable) produce differentiations
in performance, such that no two performances are ever exactly identical.
A more contemporary understanding of *"tâtonnement"* might associate it
with any intentional departure from the gestural chain, whether that intention be conceived as entirely conscious or part of what Merleau-Ponty
calls a "motor intentionality," and Sheets-Johnstone a "corporeal-kinetic
intentionality," occurring on the level of the neuromuscular body.

Leroi-Gourhan's texts only hint in the direction of what contemporary
research in cognitive science and movement theory increasingly confirms.
Yet he clearly anticipates findings that suggest the huge significance of movement experiment for the development of new techniques, technologies,
and associated operating routines. In addition, his theories concerning
the interdependence of motor experimentation and symbolic thought have
also turned out to be prescient.[31] *"Tâtonnement,"* even limited to Leroi-
Gourhan's more pragmatic understanding, evokes the fundamental and
indispensable inter-implication of cognitive development and motile activity. *Gesture and Speech* continuously posits the two as inextricably linked.
The emergence of a greater number of programs to choose from (and more
tools to use) is the result of a highly differentiated apparatus—the intricate
osteo-muscular structure of the human hand—as well as a larger surface of
neurons for registering and anticipating the movements the apparatus will
execute. According to Leroi-Gourhan, the hand and the brain engage in a

"dialogue in which the profit is mutual" (GP I, 59). Implied here, though, is that the "familiar knowledge" of "the hand and the face"—Derrida's short-hand for the teachings of *Gesture and Speech* (OG, 84)—presupposes more than an exchange between two partners. Leroi-Gourhan in fact argues that there are *three* factors at play: (1) a "bodily apparatus" (the "hand") facilitates a growth in the number of programs (operating chains or symbolic systems—the "face"). This growth in turn encourages (2) "the multiplication of possibilities for coordinating" movements (GP, 114). These "possibilites" of coordination are provided by none other than (3) the recursive structure of sensorimotor feedback. As he states clearly in volume 2, "from the beginning we have maintained a *triangle* of relations between the hand [body], language [program], and the sensorimotor cortex [interoceptive feedback]" (GP II, 76; added emphasis). This triangle of relations explains the existence of exploratory behavior and characterizes all animal motility and cogitation. However, it has unique implications, as we shall see, in the case of human beings.

"Putting-outside-the-self"

In *Évolution et techniques,* Leroi-Gourhan is satisfied to trace the emergence and development of innovations without wondering how their sheer quantity (and the quantity of new routines they engender) will affect other aspects of human behavior. However, in *Gesture and Speech,* the exponential increase in the number of programs available provokes another line of questioning. Here, he observes that rapid technological development made possible by exploratory "groping" radically changes the way gestural knowledges are registered and handed down. How, he asks, will humans record for future use such a rich legacy of gestural routines resulting from ever-renewed *"expériences du tâtonnement"*? Does the augmentation of the *habitus* demand a parallel increase in, or even a corollary transformation of, the skills capable of registering those accretions of experiment?

Although in the first chapters of *Gesture and Speech* Leroi-Gourhan insists on positing a profound continuity between humans and other animals, once he turns to the question of memory, of how to register longer and more complex operating chains, he is forced to acknowledge that the inventiveness of human beings entails the emergence of symbolic behaviors that distinguish them in incontrovertible ways. This acknowledgement introduces the most significant distinction he imposes in *Gesture and Speech*: the distinction between internal and external "modes of programmation," or forms of mnemonic registration. He begins by reiterating that all varieties of animal life share a type of internal, organic means of programmation in which traces of movement are left on a neural matter that is structured to receive them; at this level, the "inscription in the memory of numerous operating chains" takes place in the embedded, organic memory that surrounds the centers of voluntary motility (GP II, 20). But in the case of human evolution a salient difference emerges. Once the hand has been "liberated" by bipedalism, that is, once palpating, groping, and more intricate modes of contact and apprehension produce technological fruit, the invention of new means of mnemonic registration on other than organic supports becomes necessary. Accordingly, from approximately the Zinthropian on, as Leroi-Gourhan remarks, human animals begin to employ a second mode of programmation, one that makes use of "external" supports. The crucial difference between humans and animals is thus not the classical division between instinct and intelligence but that between the exercise of exclusively internal means of storing lived experience and the possession of *both* internal and external means.

It is important to note, however, that Leroi-Gourhan never states that humans rely exclusively on external modes de programmation. Nor do Derrida or Stiegler, for that matter; they, too, are aware that humans, like all other animals, possess "internal" modes of programmation, memory circuits connecting areas of the body to areas of the brain. But what is not sufficiently emphasized in their accounts is that the new external modes of programmation still rely on the first; that is, while human animals may employ external registering devices, from proverbs to videotapes, they cannot do so without developing the gestural skills, the operating chains, required to manipulate or manufacture these devices. An "internal" mode of programmation, neural-muscular memory, undergirds all tool use, whether the tool is a hand, a pen, a lever, or a mouse. External modes of programmation employ as supports the memory embedded in the very flesh of muscles and tendons, and this fact has consequences that have yet to be explored.

That gestures are themselves memory supports is a point that Stiegler's analysis of *Gesture and Speech* also raises. His comments are provocative, and therefore worth lingering over for a moment, but nonetheless sidestep Leroi-Gourhan's major point. Speaking of the difference between body and tool (and Leroi-Gourhan's productive undermining of their opposition), Stiegler notes that the first externalization of memory is *not* incarnated in either the tool or what that tool makes (the material product reflecting the procedures that brought it into being). Rather, the first externalization of memory is the hand itself *as* a tool. That is, insofar as working with objects gives muscular shape to the hand, the hand is not born but made, fabricated like a tool through its interactions with external matter. Interaction thus transforms an organic limb into a kind of prosthesis, rendering it external to itself. As Stiegler—rhetorically—asks:

"To articulate the living onto the nonliving"—to employ external tools and supports—"is that not already a gesture from after the rupture when you are already no longer in pure phusis?"[32] He seems to be suggesting that the hand is no longer "pure phusis" for the very reason that it has become a prosthetic form with its own program: "Prostheticity, here a consequence of the freedom of the hand, is a putting-outside-the-self that is also a putting-out-of-range-of-oneself."[33]

Stiegler's formulation is suggestive yet incomplete. His remarks open up a way of thinking about the body as external other (rather than pure self-identity) but do not allow us to think of the body as simultaneously *both*: prosthetically functional and intimately sensate (or, in Stiegler's terms, "out-of-range" and "within-range" at the same time). This is because Stiegler lacks a theory of gesture that could account for the internal-external technology that muscle memory *is*. It is impossible from within his paradigm to account for the type of agency—"technical intentionality" or innovative groping for contact—that Leroi-Gourhan explores in *Évolution et techniques*. In contrast, Merleau-Ponty develops a clear understanding of the gestural that accounts for its paradoxical nature as at once tool (sedimented *"acquis"*) and palpating openness to the world. Glossing Husserl's scene of hand touching hand, Merleau-Ponty notes how the hand can serve as a prosthesis extended in space while also providing sensory information to the nervous system that then seeks to "curve" the program, to establish better "contact." "In this bundle of bones and muscles which my right hand presents to my left," Merleau-Ponty observes, "I can anticipate for an instant the integument or incarnation of that other right hand, alive and mobile, *which I thrust toward things in order to explore them.*"[34] "To thrust" the hand toward something is already to mobilize a knowledge, an acquired way of moving that requires highly developed eye-hand coordination, a program with which the infant is not necessarily born. But to thrust the hand toward *that* object also calls for multiple adjustments of the program the adult has acquired, the constant proprioceptive, kinesthetic, and tactile evaluations that a hand—attached to a nervous system—is capable of achieving. It is because the hand is both an external tool (executing a learned routine) and an internal sensor (bringing feedback to the brain as it executes that routine) that it is able to *"tâtonner,"* that it can do the job of both *"bâton"* and mind-body composite. The remarkable aspect of gestures is that, as we see in Leroi-Gourhan's vision of the worker seeking "contact," they allow for living bodies to bring to bear a rich resource of acquired skills while simultaneously opening up these skills to revision in the course of being performed.

Returning to Leroi-Gourhan, we could say that the "touching," palpating, groping aspect of the human tool is precisely what remains *zoological* in the technical intention. The two bodies—the sensate and the prosthetic—are coimplicated and coextensive, capable together of what Merleau-Ponty calls a "double sensation" in which the hand as mnemonic device joins with the hand as sensory surface to suggest what should—no, what *could*—be done next. To imply, as Stiegler does, that the hand is definitively "outside the self" is to collapse the hand entirely into the tool and thus to ignore the sensate underbelly of corporeal gesturing, the existential substrate of programs, the ("internal") muscle memory responsible for the functioning of ("external") mnemonic devices. Ultimately, it matters little if the hand is replaced with a mechanical arm, or if a quantity of the body's force and even the bulk of its cognitive processes are assumed by a machine as long as sensory feedback produced through gestural manipulation of these advanced tools remains available to human bodies and minds. Otherwise, the programs the machine has encoded will no longer evolve to adapt to new, unpredictable situations.

Leroi-Gourhan is unequivocal on this point: he states in *Gesture and Speech* that the continuing evolution of skills and techniques relies not simply on the dialogue between a hand that can manipulate and a speech center that can articulate, symbolize, and store. Innovation also requires sensorimotor feedback from the moving body achieved *through performance*, that is, through the *"triangle* of relations between the hand, language, and the sensorimotor cortex" (GP II, 76; added emphasis). To neglect any one of these three contributions is to misunderstand the tool-making capacities of animate beings. The consequence of such a misunderstanding is clear in Stieglitz: the tool (or technology) emerges as the single agent in the history of humanity, defining the cognitive-symbolic capacities and the corporeal shape of the subject (the *"who"*). In contrast, Leroi-Gourhan advances a theory of distributed agency: tools (including symbolic tools, such as language and other mnemonic devices) help determine the movements the subject will make; but the subject's embodiment of these movements entails recursive interoceptive feedback that will also play an agentic role in the evolution of symbolic, technical, and corporeal instruments. Unfortunately Derrida, although attentive to the significance of sensorimotor feedback in other contexts, fails to weigh its full import when responding to Leroi-Gourhan in *Of Grammatology*. Derrida's omission, his reliance on what he calls the "familiar knowledge" of "the face and the hand," or "thought and tool," leads to a paradigm in which sensorimotor functions play no role at all. The logical consequences of this omission are serious; by neglecting the role of interoceptive feedback Derrida not only offers a skewed reading of Leroi-Gourhan, he also sends deconstruction down a path that leads to a disembodied theory of agency.[35] It turns out that the "familiar knowl-edge" of the hand and the face is not so familiar after all (OG, 84).

"The possibility of the trace"

So let us review this knowledge once again.

Leroi-Gourhan enters the argument of *Of Grammatology* at the point where Derrida is attempting to gather evidence with which to counter the ethnographically suspect distinction between societies "with writing" and societies "without writing." Leroi-Gourhan's theory of the gestural is pressed into the service of dismantling this opposition, one that buttresses the distinction between between *technè* and *physis* that is the very target of Derrida's critique. The paleoethnographer is a sympathetic (and use-ful) figure for Derrida because he defines writing as an external form of memory similar to all other external forms; "all societies without writing possess a range of means of preservation [*moyens de fixation*] in the form of proverbs, precepts, or recipes," Leroi-Gourhan states (GP II, 32; GS, 234). As opposed to Derrida's other interlocutor, the linguist Marcel Cohen (who upholds the distinction between societies with writing and those without), Leroi-Gourhan offers the first inkling that writing might in fact be coincident with the category "man" in the first place, and that there-fore a "science of man" has to seek man's *physis* in his *technè,* or tools. "To provide a uniform concept of man," Derrida states in his first explicit ref-erence to Leroi-Gourhan, "is undoubtedly to renounce the old notion of peoples said to be 'without writing' and 'without history.' André Leroi-Gourhan shows it well . . . the peoples said to be 'without writing' lack only a certain type of writing."[36]

Derrida thus appears to be in accord with Leroi-Gourhan, insofar as Derrida, too, contends that human societies, whether they possess writ-ing in the strict sense or not, all develop modes of programmation, or *"moyens de fixation,"* that rely on "external" (as opposed to organic) sup-ports (such as the nervous system). However, Leroi-Gourhan's notion of *"moyens de fixation"* is not as flexible as Derrida's notion of *"écriture."* For Leroi-Gourhan, the meaning of "writing" could *not* be extended to include the inscriptions performed entirely by an apparatus.[37] If the op-erational motions of the machine supply no *sensory* feedback, if a ma-chine has absorbed all motions into itself, then no lived experience of gesturing—and certainly no *"tâtonnements"*—can occur. (Therein lies the fundamental difference between a technique or tool requiring manipula-tion and a technology eliciting no sensory feedback whatsoever.) Writing proper (that is, writing involving, at the very least, the movements of digits and wrist) necessitates the participation of a body's centers of sensation and, to this extent, always offers a terrain in which something can be done that has never been done before.

Leroi-Gourhan exhibits a large—and arguably healthy—dose of technophobia in the concluding chapter of *Gesture and Speech*, which is devoted to a study of the ways contemporary societies compensate for the loss of manual activity in order to preserve the fragile equilibrium between programs and their performance. As we shall see, he is afraid that advanced technologies of inscription—from linear alphabetic writing to robotics—will eventually immobilize the human body. Derrida responds to Leroi-Gourhan's fear by insisting that although a greater range of technologies may indeed decrease bodily investment, the body's energies will nonetheless continue to surge forth in disruptive ways. But why is this so? To what does he attribute movement's disruptive force?

The reason why Derrida does not share Leroi-Gourhan's apprehension is that he does not locate the source of movement in the same place. For him, both the possibility of movement and the threat of its erasure, the "genetic" programs that prime the body to move and the modes of programmation that condemn it to move in prescribed ways, derive from a single structure: not the triangular structure of corporeal support (muscles that can be activated), learned programs (gestures or operating chains), and the sensorimotor feedback that alters them in a recursive loop, but instead the *possibility* of programmation itself. Derrida offers an almost dizzying variety of terms to suggest what he means by this fundamental, indispensable, and underlying pre-condition of all forms of life: "the possibility of the *grammè*," "spacing," "the unity of a double movement of protention and retention," "putting-in-reserve," and *différance*. However, he finally settles on "the structure of the trace" as most suggestive for his purposes. At whatever "level" of organic existence, he states, from "the amoeba and the annelid up to the passage beyond alphabetic writing or the orders of the logos and a certain homo sapiens," it is the underlying "structure of the trace" that exerts agentic force (OG, 84).

We could unpack further what Derrida means by "the structure of the trace" (its relation to the discourses of Lévinas, Nietzsche, and even contemporary biology [OG, 70]), but probably the best way to clarify Derrida's meaning is to link the trace structure to Leroi-Gourhan's notion of an apparatus—an "appareillage nerveux"—that generates actualized behaviors but has no stable or concrete existence in itself. For Leroi-Gourhan, the human nervous system (at a qualitative remove from that of the amoeba, it must be noted) is a "developmental system" of huge potential (Ingold, 292). This system is a *propensity* rather than a realized network, a potential to construct programs—not just a few but many and over the course of an entire lifetime. It is the history of *this* structure, an apparatus primed to construct programs (and not a history of the programs themselves), that Derrida believes should be written. That is, he calls for an account of a developmental system abstracted from the inventory of its actualizations.

But what would a historical study of such an abstraction show? It would show precisely what Leroi-Gourhan argues, which is that the innate propensity itself—to encode, to retain, to "put-in-reserve"—is nothing, it does not exist, without its imbrication in the concrete materialities of a singular body and a precise environment. That is, the only history that could be written is one that would not credit the developmental system with ultimate agency, even if the generativity of the structure is considered to be essential for the production of life. To be sure, the historian would have to acknowledge the structure of retention and protention; the movement of putting-in-reserve; the dynamic of a sedimented, approximated past as it projects a never fully predictable future—that is, the structure of the trace. But this historian would also have to attend to the innumerable performed movements, the actualized possibilities or *"tâtonnements,"* that provide the material to be placed in reserve in the first place. Finally, the historian would have to identify the environmental and social conditions providing occasions for agentic response.

Derrida enjoins us, however, to train our focus on the "structure of the trace," or "movement itself," as though they could indeed be treated in isolation. That is why he speaks not of precise movements, but of "the origin and possibility of movement" (OG, 84), not of specific instances of "writing," or "putting-in-reserve" but of "arche-writing" and the "history of the trace" (OG, 92). This emphasis produces a number of conceptual gains, but it also entails a significant loss. If Leroi-Gourhan understands agency to be exerted through an individual's "technical intentionality," registered as an *"incurvation,"* or departure, from a programmed operating chain, Derrida recasts this agency as nothing more than the inevitable consequence of a trace structure, a "developmental system" generating differentiations that appear to be accidental rather than directed, an expression of the system rather than part of a contingent, authored project to produce contact or obtain maximum grip within a specific environment. For Derrida, the structure of the trace—the condition of the possibility of movement and therefore of life itself—guarantees that no matter what kind of technologies are employed, and no matter what conditions for employing them obtain, differentiations will continue to proliferate, departures from programmed behavior will continue to occur. This is because the "possibility of the trace" (OG, 47) anticipates the possibility of both programs and their *"incurvation."* In short, the "possibility of the trace" underwrites the "possibility" of any movement (including "*tâtonnements*") whatsoever. The trace is, then, the pure force of an undefined, unlimited motility, a virtual motor power never fully present—never appearing "*as such*"—in any one movement type: mechanical, groping, or routine (OG, 84). Derrida's argument thus opposes the existential tendencies in Leroi-Gourhan's work by introducing a thinking of the mark of movement before the being that moves to mark, or "*la trace avant l'étant*" (DG, 69), the trace prior to being. Ultimately, what is at stake in the battle between Derrida and Leroi-Gourhan is the evolution of *philosophy*: Derrida attempts to move through but deviate from phenomenology in order to gesture toward an ontology of the pre-ontological trace.

"The reduction of the physical adventure"

At this point, one would expect Derrida to turn toward advanced technologies (robotics or virtual media) to prove that a trace structure underlies and maintains the equilibrium between "hand" and "face," and that, accordingly, differentiations will continue to proliferate no matter how immobilized the body might become. But instead, he returns to writing—in particular, linear writing—as the *technè* that illustrates in exemplary fashion how the stilling of the body results necessarily in a resurgence of motility and imagination. His decision to focus on writing is consistent with both the attacks on logocentrism he makes in other chapters and Leroi-Gourhan's own emphasis on "linearization," the standardizing of mythogrammatic multidimensionality, as a turning point in human history. Further, the example of writing allows Derrida to evoke a psychoanalytic understanding of the repression of the motile body, one in which the somatic is always (at least in his version) associated with a libidinal impulse. While productive in some ways, Derrida's focus on the discipline of linear writing (and on a psychoanalytic paradigm for interpreting its effects) leads him to ignore the knowledge-gathering and decision-making force of sensorimotor experience, the very aspect of movement that is highlighted in accounts by Leroi-Gourhan, Bergson, and Merleau-Ponty. What are the entailments of Derrida's choice to foreground writing? How does the example of writing obscure the agentic function of interoception as well as the crucial role of material conditions in soliciting its contribution? It is worth attending to the debate between Leroi-Gourhan and Derrida over the effects of linear writing if we wish to grasp more clearly what is at stake.

In the second volume of *Gesture and Speech,* Leroi-Gourhan turns his attention to writing. He maintains that long before cybernetic means of storage and transcription arrived on the scene, "linearization," or the process of reducing mythogrammatic multi-dimensionality to phonetic and alphabetic systems, had already initiated a trend toward less corporeal and imaginative engagement. To counter this argument, Derrida draws on Melanie Klein's experiments with school children in the process of learning how to write. Instead of confirming Leroi-Gourhan's teleological account of corporeal loss, Derrida argues, Klein's observations of children suggest that the body's energies cannot so easily be stilled. As Klein demonstrates in "The Role of the School in the Libidinal Development of the Child," the experimental flourishes supposedly tamed by linear writing surge forth as the child learns to compose letters on the page. She recounts episodes in which one of her patients, little Fritz, develops complex scenarios concerning a character named "i" while exaggerating (and relishing) the up and down movements through which letter "i"s are produced on the page.[38] With respect to these scenes, Derrida notes that "all the investments with which the operations of reading and writing . . . are charged" resurface during the period of apprenticeship as the subject indulges in gestural experiment, testing the range of movements that the disciplines of writing allow the body to produce (OG, 88). Thus, although "nonlinear writing" has to be "defeated" in the name of greater efficiency and "capitalization," the war against bodily investment is not, Derrida insists, won "one single time" (OG, 85).

The problem with Derrida's reply, and the reason why it fails to defeat Leroi-Gourhan's position, is that he points to only one type of movement behavior, what Klein refers to as the masturbatory, repetitive gestures that interrupt (but also in a way facilitate) the acquisition of writing. Derrida, following Klein, casts movement as the "return of the repressed," implying that the full range of unpredictable movements (recursively generated by sensorimotor feedback) could be collapsed into Fritz's repetitive, almost compulsive stroke. The imaginative and gestural labors of little Fritz might indeed be of value in the evolution of cultural routines, but they are more limited and reactive, less mindful and differentiated than the gestures Leroi-Gourhan identifies in *Évolution et techniques* as "*tâtonnements,*" swerves from routine to adjust to the specifics of the object and the situation. There is thus something not entirely convincing—at least to a movement practitioner—about a theory of disciplined movement that defines its unscripted "return" as primarily libidinal and reactive. The rewards of movement and of the sensations it affords are clearly—even in the case of handwriting—far more diverse.

Leroi-Gourhan's objective in the final chapter of *Gesture and Speech* is not to deny that programmed behavior calls forth the body's energetic response but to suggest that occasions for such response must be provided by material conditions, that is, by something other than "the structure of the trace." In this regard, it is worth recalling a passage quoted earlier in which he states that "acts accomplished for the first time by groping gestures inscribe themselves as programs in a sequence of different memories" (GP II, 18). Crucially, this "first time" may happen at any point, in infancy, adolescence, or adulthood—*but it cannot happen if the body is denied occasions to move.* His reservations about advanced technologies are based on his understanding that access to movement, threatened by machines, is vital to the continuation of what we might consider human ways of being. That is why he states that "it would be of little importance that this miraculous organ that is the hand were to lose its role if it were not the case that the hand's activity is closely related to the equilibrium of the cerebral zones it touches" (GP II, 61–62). Derrida in fact acknowledges the necessity of maintaining this "equilibrium," which he concedes is threatened by increasing reliance on external mnemonic or operational devices that obviate physical participation (OG, 85). This is the "familiar knowledge" of "gesture and speech, of body and language, of tool and thought" to which Derrida alludes (OG, 85). For Derrida, however, the equilibrium is *"toujours déjà"* menaced by that which initially brought it into being. Existence is ensured by the possibility of programming (or "putting-in-reserve"), that is, by the possibility of displacing the gestures of contact from human to technological hands. Thus the disappearance of writing in the strict sense does not worry Derrida, but it is a source of grave concern for Leroi-Gourhan. As he writes in *Gesture and Speech*:

> Reading will retain its importance for many more centuries . . . but writing is apparently about to disappear, rapidly replaced by dictaphone machines . . . In any case, science has nothing to lose with the disappearance of writing, and philosophy and literature will undoubtedly evolve in new ways. . . . Writing will pass into the infrastructure without fundamentally altering the functioning of human intelligence . . . *However, the loss of manual activity and the reduction of the physical adventure to a passive adventure are phenomena that pose greater problems.* (GP II, 262; added emphasis)

For Leroi-Gourhan, the "physical adventure" is endangered when the gestures responsible for moving the pen across the page, or dancing the fingers across a keyboard, are replaced by means of thought-capture that foreclose all activity on the part of the sensorimotor cortex.[39] Derrida responds by recalling that this danger does not appear with the invention of writing in the strict sense, nor will it increase once writing, as a "physical adventure," is gone. Externalization, for Derrida, is nothing less than the human body's "relation to death" without which life itself could not be conceived. From this perspective, the threat to motility, to the imagination, and to the very category of the "human" comes not from external modes of programming but from the *possibility* of putting-in-reserve (the *grammè*), the process of mark-making that defines life as a confrontation with the future through a rehearsal of the past. "From the elementary programs of so-called 'instinctive' behavior up to the constitution of electronic card-indexes and reading machines," Derrida contends, what has been enlarged is "the possibility of putting-in-reserve" *(mise-en-réserve)*. "If the expression ventured by Leroi-Gourhan is accepted, one could speak of a 'liberation of memory,' of an exteriorization always already begun" (OG, 84). Thus linearization, robots, and the electronic storage of experience may indeed decrease the number of movement opportunities, but to Derrida's mind, such reductions *realize* rather than pervert the authentic destiny of "Man."[40]

Yet an "exteriorization always already begun" is quite different from an exteriorization completed. And here lies the crux of the issue. Of course, the "externalization" of gestures and the concomitant loss of sensory experience has always begun, but it is frequently compensated for by tools that afford new interoceptive experiences and opportunities for *"tâtonnement."* As long as the act of putting-in-reserve remains a "technique of the body," it will involve a set of enchained gestures that stimulate nerve centers (producing new "inscriptions," or easily traveled pathways) while simultaneously lending the hand a muscular definition and producing movement experiences of a very particular sort. New modes of "putting-in-reserve" incorporate skills, or programs, *into the body,* leaving traces on muscles, ligaments, and tendons, retentive surfaces beyond the skin. Leroi-Gourhan is certainly aware that exteriorization has "always already begun"; *Gesture and Speech* is nothing if not a revelation of how deeply the impulse toward and possibility for the use of prostheses is implanted in the evolution of animate life (feline and primate as well as human).[41] As opposed to Derrida, however, Leroi-Gourhan fears that the process of exteriorization may eventually generate forms that *exclude* the constitution of animated bodies, thereby occluding the variety of agency he associates with the *"incurvation,"* or alteration, of the routine. *Gesture and Speech* is a phenomenological text (with a performative bias) insofar as it presupposes that human bodies come into being not because they are preprogrammed to be human by some cybernetic design (that is, are equipped with a set of genes that make them human or automatically give them a recognizable human shape) but rather because they realize kinetic dispositions, and thus osteo-muscular possibilities, through a culturally informed process of motor interaction with an environment—that is, through miming, imitation, and experiential *"tâtonnement."*

Logically, then, if humans are divorced from movement, if they are denied occasions to develop gestural programs through sensorimotor feedback, *they may fail to take shape at all.* The famous nightmare vision at the conclusion of *Gesture and Speech* presents precisely this scenario, one in which the arresting of movement permitted by technology limits interoceptive experience and places distributed agency, or animate cognition, in jeopardy. "Liberated from his tools," Leroi-Gourhan hypothesizes, "from his gestures, his muscles, the programmation of his acts, his memory, liberated from his imagination by the perfection of tele-diffused means, liberated from the animal and vegetal worlds, from the wind, from the cold, from bacteria, from the unknown of mountains and seas, the *homo sapiens* of zoology is probably at the end of his career" (GP II, 266). At stake are not simply human forms of kinesis but the very existence of cognitive activity itself. Leroi-Gourhan anticipates the findings of scientists in a diverse set of fields when he suggests that without opportunities for physical activity, without the ability to practice and develop a vast motor potential, humans may be unable to acquire and process the sensations afforded by gesturing. In the triangular (not binary) commerce of animation, these kinesthetic, tactile, and proprioceptive sensations are the very matter on which all differential symbolic orders and hermeneutic, perceptual operations depend.[42]

Coda: moving to read, moving to write

I now write these words as a significant temporal remove from Leroi-Gourhan's first meditations on the impact of advanced inscription techniques and Derrida's first defense of *écriture*. In the interim, new developments in word processing, computer animation, hypertext, electronic writing, and e-poetry have emerged, many of which Derrida lived long enough to witness.[43] As a coda to the preceding reflections, I would like to examine some exemplary works drawn from the domain of digital writing, both to test out the hypotheses already presented and to tease out of these works their own implied theory of agency as an entailment of embodiment. I will be interested especially in "digital" or "e-poetry," a genre that establishes an intimate association between the most embodied and the most disembodied practices of inscription. I choose this example precisely because it ushers technological modes of composition and dissemination into the generic domain traditionally identified with the expressive irregularities of the phenomenalized lyric voice. One of the paradoxical consequences of the permeation of our contemporary culture with computers has been the emergence of a cadre of computer-savvy poets, technicians of the word who have chosen to fabricate and disseminate their works through technological means Leroi-Gourhan could only have imagined. Predictably, in the early 1980s there were outcries from the poetry community that a lyric written on the computer (or, more to the point, *with* the computer) could only alienate further the living subject from her live audience. How could a computer-generated line, critics asked, capture the dialect or imitate the rhythms of moving bodies? How could cyber-authors who never put pen to paper, who never slapped a carriage back to begin a new line, gain an iota of the kinesthetic experience available to little Fritz? Wouldn't the demise of the body's motor investment in writing disturb that fragile equilibrium between program and performed movement crucial to Derrida and Leroi-Gourhan alike?

In recent years it has become clear that digital poetry, far from attenuating our relation to the human body, actually awakens this body and its kinetic energies in a variety of highly inventive ways.[44] The relation between fingers and font in digital writing might not be as immediate as the relation between hand and symbol that, according to Leroi-Gourhan, characterizes manual inscription; but this has not stopped poets—forever intrigued by lost immediacy—from sounding all the possibilities of that particular relation as it is manifested, distorted, and re-created in the digital realm. In fact, digital poetry has turned out to be the genre of computer-based registration that is most concerned with recalling to the user's consciousness a memory of the motions—both optical and kinetic—required to produce letters manually on a flat support. From this perspective, the gestures associated with computer use can be seen as perpetuating (rather than effacing) the operating chains responsible for our experience of handwriting as both a cultural discipline and a stage for expression. The motions associated with the use of paper and writing implement return in digital poetry both literally, as small motor movements requiring only the fingers and wrist (shifting the mouse, clicking, dragging, and so on), and figuratively, as replications of letter and word production acted out on the screen. Whether letters are constructed stroke by stroke by an anonymous program, as in Bill Marsh's "Aria"[45] or Jim Andrew's "Nio,"[46] or moved around the screen according to the hand motions of a real-time user, as in John Cayley's "riverIsland,"[47] Stephanie Strickland's "Vniverse,"[48] or "Text Rain" by Camille Utterback and Romy Achituv,[49] digital poems mime and displace the corporeal energy channeled by the gestures of handwriting. In fact, digital poetry makes it possible to retrieve—*and even amplify*—aspects of a subject's kinesthetic experience of manual inscription that simply cannot be captured by older print technologies such as the typewriter.

Arguably, the single most revolutionary contribution of the computer to poetic writing has been the accessibility of programs that "animate" words on the screen. To some extent, the constraints placed on poets by linear alphabetic writing were always available to subversion through typographic play. Concrete and visual poets have long tried to free letters from linear arrangement and an assigned place within a word. However, digital works distinguish themselves from these earlier efforts by the increased liberty of movement they accord to letters, words, and sentences—not to mention the hands that make them appear and the eyes that scan them. In the hands of today's e-poets, Flash, Director, and DHTML animation programs extend the visual, kinesthetic, and proprioceptive experience of the verbal construct in ways that earlier works could not. Through interactive technologies, programmers *and* users can move words and letters around the screen, make them flicker, pulse rhythmically, disappear, accumulate, or morph by moving their own hands in the same patterns that previously created the shapes of letters or, as in the case of Utterback and Archituv's "Text Rain," by moving any part of the body in unscripted ways. Software that sets the letter free of its positional constraints and allows it to dance on the screen offers digital poets entirely new ways of playing with the visual and semantic properties of words. In addition, these software programs encourage motility and in some cases greater movement experimentation, a *"tâtonnement"* that at times produces a-social, seemingly awkward movements outside of the gestural vocabularies normally employed (at least for reading and writing or interacting with a work of art). Whether generated by preprogrammed algorithms or initiated in real time by interactive users, the transformations and transpositions these letters undergo on the screen both recall visually and *demand physically* corporeal energies that drive the disciplines of handwriting and advance, gropingly, beyond them.

I will begin by looking at a short work by Philippe Castellin, a digital poet who explicitly conceives of the act of writing as a physical performance. His work extends Leroi-Gourhan's meditations in intriguing ways. Originally a sculptor and installation artist, Castellin produced "Le Poème est la somme" during the first wave of experimentation by poets with software animation programs. The work is based on an earlier sculpture-installation entitled "Man/Oeuvre"that was produced in collaboration with Jean Torregrosa in 1998.[50] "Man/Oeuvre," like the digital poem it inspired, transforms the space of viewing or reading into a stage on which masses and words—or, here, word-masses—are displaced through gestures executed over time. In the 1998 installation-performance, a set of large cinder blocks were stacked in four columns, each block bearing one word of the sentence "LE POÈME EST LA SOMME DE L'ENSEMBLE INFINI DES FORMES À L'INTÉRIEUR DESQUELLES IL SE SENT TOUJOURS ÉGALEMENT À L'ÉTROIT" (THE POEM IS THE SUM OF THE INFINITE TOTALITY OF FORMS INSIDE OF WHICH IT ALSO ALWAYS FEELS CONSTRAINED). The words of the sentence can be read either horizontally, from left to right, or vertically, column by column, in which case the sentence makes no grammatical sense. During the performance of the piece, the separate blocks were first placed all together in the form of a large cube; then Jean Torregrosa and Philippe Castellin employed a set of wheels to lift, transport, and rearrange the blocks, one by one, first into lines, then into columns. Sometimes these columns formed nonsense sentences, and sometimes the two artists managed to recompose a significant sentence, such as the one just quoted. In effect, the installation-performance poem transformed writing into a full-body practice. A repetitive gestural routine involving the torso, arms, and legs was essential for the production of inscriptions; blocks of letters became, literally, blocks of matter, transported—and thus given meaning—through the expenditure of a visibly large quantity of physical force.

In Castellin's digital remake of the same piece, "Le Poème est la somme" (1998), the energy required to displace words is transferred from the bodies of the producers both to the machine (a preprogrammed algorithm determines the position of each word on the screen) and to the hand of the interactive user (a click halts the movement of the letters or propels them into entirely different relationships). When the user pulls up the site she is confronted with a screen filled with traveling, flipping, flickering letters composing the original words found in "Man/Oeuvre" (plus the author's name and the date of the poem) in bright neon colors against a black back-

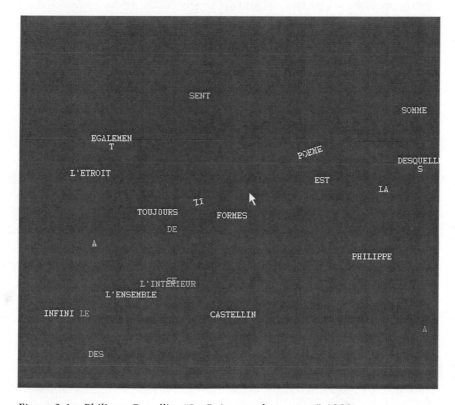

Figure 3.1   Philippe Castellin, "Le Poème est la somme," 1999. akenaton/DOC(K)S.

ground (Figure 3.1). These words float in seemingly haphazard directions for one to fifteen seconds before they suddenly halt in their tracks to form an ephemeral and disjointed page of legible signifiers. The circulating words never stop for more than a few seconds, just long enough to give the user time to obtain a visual impression, sometimes long enough to provide her with a readable text. The viewer responds to the kinetic quality of the animated words by following their movement—and their arrested patterns—with her eyes, thus tracing out a variety of optical paths that a linear text would not offer. The poem never seems to contain the same combinations of words twice; presumably, the permutations of syntax and content are limitless, *"à l'infini,"* even as the sum *("la somme")* of the poem remains constant, a given quantity of radiant signifiers framed by a screen.

Whereas the earliest manifestation of the poem, "Man/Oeuvre," operated its permutations only on the level of syntax (entire words could be rearranged, but not letters), the digitalized "Le Poème est la somme" begins to isolate letters as units of matter that can also be circulated, displaced, submitted to the gestures of the machine or the user who clicks on a word to stop or restart its rotation. This can be seen with the decomposition of the word "ÉGALEMENT," which appears on the screen as "ÉGALEMEN" with the "T" positioned beneath. Meaning "equally" or "also," "ÉGALEMENT" suggests that all permutations of the poem are equally valid and that there is no master text toward which the circulating letters are convening but only one that the user, by adjusting the mouse, provisionally makes. The scission of the word "ÉGALEMENT" into two parts further indicates that, on the level of their material existence, the letters are themselves nothing but building blocks, each equal to the other, just as the cinder blocks in "Man/Oeuvre" were exactly equal in weight, elements of matter that must be physically displaced by a moving body. As the sentence in "Man/Oeuvre" tells us, the poem always feels its infinity constrained by its static forms: "Le Poème . . . se sent toujours également à l'étroit." Poetry, it would seem, aspires not to fixity but to incessant movement: whether the result of physical gestures or programmed codes, the digital poem works in the service of both meaning construction (static, legible inscription) and meaning disruption (illegible but suggestive recombinations of the elements—kinetic and durable—of inscription). The more the poetic word is treated as a matter to be moved, the more the kinesis implicit in writing is evoked, threatening thereby to disturb the "equilibrium" between hand and face, motor memory and symbolic function—but in a direction opposite to the one Leroi-Gourhan had in mind. Instead of constraining movement (of the eyes, of the hands) to a greater degree, instead of trapping the body in ever more rigid disciplines, ever less flexible gestural routines, the interactive digital poem actually *challenges* our learned response to text. Skills acquired in literacy are temporarily undone as animation programs set written language—and the user—in motion.

The user who plugs into "Le Poème est la somme" not only observes but also takes part in a performance. She is brought into confrontation with—and is given the means to resist—the skills she has acquired to read and write. This reader is asked to *de*-skill, to liberate her optical movements from the strict regime of literacy, and to accept the explosive, unregimented shapes of words and letters as they dance erratically about the screen. Just as young children learning to write not only repeat obsessively the up-and-down gestures recorded by Klein but also enjoy drawing letters all over the page, truncating words, and placing their constitutive units in any arrangement whatsoever, so too the interactive user of "Le Poème est la somme" responds with pleasure to the inventive placement of the *T*, or to the upside-down "POÉSIE" which hurtles diagonally across the screen like a jet shot down in midflight. Here, inscription is resituated with respect to time (we feel time elapse), space (we become vividly aware of space as an active participant in communication), and movement (the gestures required for inscription are evoked through the trajectories of words on the screen as well as the gestures we can perform in re-making the poem). Finally, we recognize that the poem is composed not only of an infinite number of word sequences (as in Oulipian word games) but also of an infinite number of gestures new combinations of which we are invited to explore.

"Text Rain," by Camille Utterback and Romy Achituv, exponentially increases the performance elements mobilized in Castellin's "Le Poème est la somme." First created in 1999, "Text Rain" is a real-time interactive installation built with a program Utterback wrote herself ("C++"). Users, or more appropriately, interactive participants, begin by placing themselves before a screen; from the top of the screen, a "rain" of words "falls" vertically down at a leisurely pace. Both the vertical fall and the pace of the falling can be altered by the gestures a participant makes or by any object that is darker than a certain threshold determined in advance by the program. The projection of the participant's mirror image on the screen from the top of which the letters fall makes it look as though the participant were actually touching and supporting the letters with parts of her body (Figure 3.2). For instance, if a participant lifts her arm to a horizontal, the letters will rest themselves on this projected support. Participants may use their hands to scoop up the letters like trowels, wave their hands, swing their upper bodies back and forth, bat at the letters, or softly cup them in their palms (Figure 3.3). Each gesture on the part of a participant produces a different configuration at the level of the word and the sentence. But as soon as the participant steps out of the way, the letters, wherever they were halted, recommence their slow descent.

Figure 3.2   Camille Utterback and Romy Archituv, "Text Rain," 1999.
Courtesy of the artist.

Commenting on the installation, Utterback explains that the words falling in "Text Rain" were provided by an excerpt from a poem by Evan Zimroth entitled "Talk/You."[51] Each line of the excerpt falls three times, although "the rate of each line being 'dropped' depends on how much of a previous line has reached the bottom of the screen," in other words, on the quantity and nature of the participant's interventions.[52] For this reason, the program can be said to blur the distinction between writing and reading since the motions the participant makes with her body contribute to "writing" the work she reads. It is only by moving that she can capture—align and thus render legible—the words of the text; the participant must assume a posture, at least for a few seconds, to form a surface on which letters can alight. As Utterback notes, the letters of a single word are not programmed to fall at exactly the same pace. Unless the participant intervenes, lending a surface on which the letters may rest, the complete word will not appear legible to a stationary viewer. Alternatively, if the participant moves too quickly or too erratically, the letters will tumble around and never find their semantic partners or anticipated order on the screen.

Figure 3.3 Camille Utterback and Romy Archituv, "Text Rain," 1999.
Courtesy of the artist.

Participation—full-body participation—is necessary for the text to take both legible and illegible forms.

Zimroth's poem "Talk/You" provides a metacommentary on the installation; even its title suggests the dialogic nature of the project, the way meaning forms through an interaction requiring bodies as well as words:

> "I like talking with you,
> simply that: *conversing,*
> a turning—with or—around,
> as in your turning around
> to face me suddenly . . .
>
> At your turning, each part
> of my body turns to verb.
> We are the opposite
> of tongue-tied, if there
> were such an antonym

We are synonyms
for limbs' loosening
of syntax,
and yet turn to nothing:
It's just talk.

As the poem indicates, the participant in "Text Rain" is solicited to involve her body more thoroughly, more palpably, in a process somewhere between reading, writing, and dance. According to whether she turns away or toward the screen, the text recedes from or returns to legibility. The equilibrium between movement and meaning, sense and sign, is simultaneously disturbed and restored by the moving subject who responds to both verbal and kinesthetic cues. The body acts—is turned to "verb"—in the enlarged space of the reading performance. Bodily acts determine whether the text will indeed be text, a stream of legible words, or simply falling matter, rain. By treating letters as matter—here, a light matter, loosened from space, untied from the tongue—the participant can produce multiple meanings out of the textual given, procuring ever more "turns" of phrase. For instance, by gently moving the fingers back and forth, a participant transforms the word "turning" into "ruining," and then, letting the *r* drop, the variant "tuning around." Reading becomes a kind of physical play while writing becomes an interaction between a preexisting text and a moving body. The result is closer to "talk" than text—a unique, ephemeral "utterance" that, paradoxically, takes place in space.

"Le Poème est la somme" and "Text Rain" hint eloquently at the fact that gestures related to meaning-making can easily become gestures that challenge and obscure signification. They pursue further the experiments undertaken by Henri Michaux earlier in the century, which will be the subject of the following chapter. Working in the digital realm, Castellin and Utterback encourage users to pay attention to the movements involved in writing by requiring their magnification in performance. They demonstrate the link between advanced technologies of inscription and bodily investment, creating rather than eliminating opportunities for *"tâtonnement."* It is then not the case, as some media theorists have insisted in Leroi-Gourhan's wake, that computers now determine how we will move, for as many digital poems indicate, computers can in fact provide opportunities to move in unpredictable ways, to interact through the "limbs' loosening of syntax"—if only in an ephemeral performance space. Against the tradition of technological determinism crystallized in, if not inaugurated by, Heidegger (and the Heideggerian impulses of Leroi-Gourhan), it could be argued that advanced media technologies actually *increase* the opportunities for humans to exercise their haptic, proprioceptive, and kinesthetic sensitivities.[53] In digital practice, it turns out that the gestural routines associated with writing and reading persist and evolve: users of "Text Rain," for instance, follow lines of letters with the eyes; isolate the fingers so as to move each one separately; swirl the hands from the wrists or shoulder sockets in motions that can be reduced or—as in graffiti—enlarged. All these gestures may be assimilated, dissected, and recombined into other choreographies that evoke earlier manual tasks or extend beyond them. These writing and reading gestures themselves recall the gestures of drawing that came before them; indeed, they recall mark-making or imprinting gestures that have existed in human communities as far back as the Paleolithic, where Leroi-Gourhan found them fixed on cave walls.

It is tempting to come down on Derrida's side and conclude that kinesthetic, proprioceptive, and tactile feedback is indeed solicited by even the most advanced technologies of inscription. Yet this sanguine conclusion may ignore threats we have not yet weighed. Perhaps it is true that computers, developed in military and industrial contexts, can, under certain conditions, provide situations that encourage a literacy involving motile play. To employ Derrida's terms, perhaps the process of alphabetization, "linearization," "capitalization," and finally digitalization has not managed to achieve "the repression of pluri-dimensional symbolic thought" (OG, 86). Clearly, "Le Poème est la somme" and "Text Rain" both evoke visually the nonlinear mythogrammatic writing that Leroi-Gourhan mourned; they also render obligatory the supposedly lost practices of proprioceptive orientation and kinetic intervention in order to produce a pluridimensional performance of meaning. Ultimately, however, all I have shown is that the solicitation of the motile body and its interoceptive experience occurs in the cultural field of *artistic* production, not in the high tech industrial sphere. Derrida may be justified in arguing that linear writing (and, implicitly, all technological modes of programmation) cannot definitively suppress ("one single time") the unpredictable movements of the body or the subsequent creation of new programs. Yet is it entirely safe to state that Leroi-Gourhan was wrong, that humans in industrial environments who are "liberated" from the need to move will still retain opportunities for "*tâtonnement*"?[54]

To answer this question would require at least another chapter on conditions that scholars from Marx (in *Capital*) to Ingold (in *The Perception of the Environment*) have treated at much greater length. For now, it is sufficient to note that Leroi-Gourhan's groundbreaking study on gestures and their relation to the cognitive and technological development of human beings allows two conclusions to be reached. It is clear that to some extent, tools (including the hand) "liberate" parts of the human body so that speech and other high animal functions can develop. Transferring certain movements from the body to tools has permitted human bodies to discover new ways of moving and, through them, novel and perhaps more subtle experiences of fine motor articulation. However, as Ingold's genealogy of the machine demonstrates, it is equally clear that some technologies (such as advanced robotics) substantially alter the nature of the "physical adventure," limiting rather than liberating the human subject's ability to move. Leroi-Gourhan himself introduces this ambiguity when he fails to distinguish systematically between tools and technologies, or when he uses the same term to designate both the opening up and the foreclosing of opportunities for *"tâtonnement."* He speaks, for instance, of the "liberation" of the hand that occurs when bipedal locomotion "frees" the limbs and face for other tasks. Unfortunately, he also uses the term "liberation" to refer to the epiphenomenon of machinofacture and electronic processing in which the body becomes passive, "freed" *("libéré")* from the task of performing any movement whatsoever. But a reduction to a passive or stilled state is not a "liberation" in the same sense. Releasing the human body from the necessity to lift, turn, pry, hurl, stamp, and so on is not in itself a freeing of the body to move in new ways. What frightens Leroi-Gourhan in the case of machinofacture (and let us not forget, television) is the *passive attitude* of the user, the reduction of her motility to a standstill. Such a posture may very well save energy and time for symbolic and interpretive activity without motor investment, but in the long run it cannot be profitable to the brain. If innovation only emerges as a result of the *realization* of kinetic possibilities, then the "freedom" of an imagination without motor experience is illusive and the word "liberation" a misnomer. Leroi-Gourhan's strongest intervention in physical anthropology, the history of writing, and the theory of agency I have been attempting to develop in this book is his claim that neither perception nor cognition may take place without engaging a nervous system *in action*.

Leroi-Gourhan puts it this way: "How shall this outmoded mammal, with the archaic needs that have been the driving force of his entire ascension, continue to push his boulder up the slope if one day there remains only an image of his reality?" (GP II, 266). The vision of a man pushing a rock up a slope is well chosen, for it suggests that an experience of weight bearing is essential to the formulation of a new technical solution for the prosthetic bearing of weight. Similarly, the works of Castellin, Utterback, and Archituv offer an incipient theory of agency—the making of meaning and, by extention, the making of the world—as a recursive, unfolding dynamic between scripted performance and exploratory play.

If humans cannot interact with their images—both depicted and embedded in machines—then they might indeed be "liberated" from the exertion of the "push" but they will also relinquish the exhilaration of the climb. Leroi-Gourhan, for one, does not share Derrida's assurance that a fragile "equilibrium" between hand and face, movement and symbol, will always and inevitably be respected. It is entirely possible for him to imagine the stilling of the body as a *historical* development enforced by specific means and relations of production, and not, as Derrida would have it, as an ever-present threat to the life that requires programmation if it is to function at all. In Leroi-Gourhan's nightmare of technological determinism, the experiential handling of the tool that he identifies with developing a sensate, animal body is foreclosed not only because the gestural programs initially executed by humans have been absorbed into the machine's functioning but also—and more crucially—because the gestural programs for *interacting* with the machine have been rigidly prescribed as well.

In short, for Leroi-Gourhan, human beings as a zoological category will be "at the end of their career" when they are prevented from engaging in *"tâtonnement"* by more than a momentary disequilibrium between hand and face. The threat posed by the development of industrialization, its modes and relations of production, is that human beings may very well be brought to a point at which they are no longer "free" (in his first sense) to evaluate kinesthetically, proprioceptively, and through palpating touch the contingencies of a specific environment—to a point, that is, where their kinetic dispositions cease to be unfurled. Leroi-Gourhan reminds us of the historical factors at play, the conditions that can potentially limit our access to the interoceptive experience that may be our birthright not as "Man" but as *zoon*. On the one hand, Leroi-Gourhan anticipates the "waning of experience" diagnosed by Theodor Adorno and Max Horkheimer, the automation of our gestures dramatized by Bertolt Brecht and Walter Benjamin, and the surveillance of our sensorium analyzed by Michel Foucault, Jean Baudrillard, and David Howes. But Leroi-Gourhan also provides a theory of gesture that allows us to see the potential for the "capitalization" of humanity embedded in the very structure of motility itself. He teaches that we cannot move without a predisposition to "construct programs" (GP II, 13) and that technicity is lodged deeply within our animal being. *Technè* and *physis,* the routine and the sensate, are, as Derrida intuited, profoundly interdependent and mutually generative. Leroi-Gourhan's work is a salutory reminder, however, that their equilibrium might have to be politically maintained.

CHAPTER FOUR

Inscription as Performance:
Henri Michaux and the Writing Body

I N THIS CHAPTER, I will make a transition from theory to practice, from investigations in philosophy and the social sciences to aesthetic experimentation in the gestural realm. Henri Michaux, whose work I will introduce here, was not a movement practitioner in the strict sense. He did not define himself as a dancer but instead thought of himself as a writer who approaches writing as a gestural routine. Like the digital poets studied in the previous chapter, Michaux was interested in how writing and moving overlap, how one influences the form the other takes. However, he set out to explore the relation between writing and moving under entirely different circumstances, namely, within the frame of an artisanal writing practice. His goal was to produce a universally legible script; initially, he believed that he could unfold out of his own body a shared kinetic vocabulary that, when productive of marks, would reveal a fundamental sign-making capability available and transparent to all. To forge this movement vocabulary, he drew inspiration from the very same sources Leroi-Gourhan was unearthing during the postwar period: prehistoric cave markings thought to contain the kinetic bases of writing and drawing and thus defining for a generation of modernists both the human body (the shape it had to have to leave behind such marks) and the human mind (the ability to read these marks as signs).

A Belgian-born poet turned painter, Michaux belonged to the generation of mid-twentieth-century modernists intrigued by prehistoric inscriptions and their seemingly immediate relation to gestural routines. Similar in this regard to his contemporary Georges Bataille, Michaux was an avid reader of the prehistorians who had formed Leroi-Gourhan, such as Salomon

Reinach and Henri Breuil, scholars who understood Paleolithic and Neolithic cave paintings to involve both corporeal and graphic practices. During Michaux's period, discourses on prehistoric visual culture were diverse and heterogeneous, yet almost invariably they contained an implicit theory of gesture as fundamental to the production, appearance, and social function of marks. Artists and philosophers from Joan Miró to André Masson, Bataille to Merleau-Ponty, were exposed to accounts of prehistoric art not only through scholarly tomes but also through articles that appeared in modernist and avant-garde periodicals such as *Cahiers d'art, L'Esprit nouveau, Documents,* and *Ipek*. Given the period's primitivist fascination with the body as a resource for cultural renovation, it comes as no surprise that the vigorously corporeal quality of prehistoric markings inspired lively interest on the part of early twentieth-century artists.[1] The gestural energy of prehistoric markings suggested the possibility of spontaneity without convention, a form of expression with roots in the supposedly untamed and pure kinetic body.

The modernist interest in cave inscriptions reflected a broader romance with the primordial origins of sign making in general. Like other members of his generation, Michaux often expressed a desire to rediscover primordial signs, both plastic and scriptural, as an antidote to the alienation imposed by the visually impoverished and corporeally constraining signmaking practices of modernity. "Humans today are unhappy with their language," he stated in a 1984 interview. His turn toward painting was determined largely by a need to forge a less culturally specific, more universally intelligible medium. According to Michaux, the graphic could offer a solution to modernity's self-alienation, a way of inventing *"une langue universelle"* at once accessible to all yet viscerally connected to the communicative impulses of a single subject.[2] In *Par des traits* (By way of lines),[3] published that same year, he proposed his own primitivist version of Cratylism, the classical theory adumbrating a motivated relation between objects in the world and the signs designating them. The poem indicates that as Michaux turned to painting, he sought a set of signs, or simply "traits," continuous with and energized by the body's "gestes." Instead of seeking signs that could mime in iconic fashion the sounds and qualities of phenomenal entities, Michaux wanted to produce graphic signs indexing the tempo and quality of the body's movements. The conceit was that these signs, based on human gestures, would be legible to all. In this dream of a common language, inscription would be an emanation of the organic body; signs would be motivated, registering types and quantities of physical force. "Gestes plutôt que signes" ("Gestures rather than signs") he writes in *Par des traits:*

Départs
Éveil
Autres éveils
PAR DES TRAITS
Approcher, explorer par des traits
Atterrir par des traits
étaler
altérer par des traits [. . .]
Insignifier par des traits.[4]

Departures
awakenings
Other awakenings
THROUGH LINES
To approach, to explore with lines
To alight with lines
to display
to alter with lines [. . .]
To not signify [unsignify] with lines.

Michaux may very well have begun with the urge to "find a universal language" by means of "characters [*caractères*] clear to all without having to pass through words."[5] But what he actually performed was the *disarticulation* rather than the clarification of the written sign. In works such as *Narration* (1927), *Alphabets* (1943), *Mouvements* (1951), *Par la voie des rythmes* (1974), and *Par des traits* (1984), he distorted the characters of various writing systems by repeating patterns of movement modeled on but not coincident with the gestural routines of these systems. The progression from *"signes"* in the first line quoted above to *"Insignifier"* in the last is symptomatic of Michaux's development as a whole: the invention of the neologism *"insignifier"* indicates that his goal was not to create a universally intelligible written language but instead to bring the written sign to the very edge of its capacity to signify. Ultimately, he had no interest in communicating a specific meaning with his mimed signs; he expended his energy on examining meaning's contours, on discovering what meaning looks like and, more to the point, how meaning *feels in the body* while being made and unmade.

The vehicle for this miming of signification without achieving signification was, for Michaux, the gestural routines of several inscriptive technologies, not simply one in particular. His search for an alternative, more primordial and unmediated form of expression led him to combine distinct practices belonging to different writing systems—prehistoric, pictographic, calligraphic. Drawing attention away from what such signs mean, he approached writing as a performance, a "display" or presentation unfolding in linear time and in three-dimensional space and engaging a body alive with proprioceptive and kinesthetic sensations. Michaux transformed the act of writing into a practice that demanded a greater physical investment, or, more precisely, he emphasized that which is always present in the act of writing: the investment of corporeal energy in a set of movements combined in numerous ways. For this reason, he considered himself a *"primitif,"* destroying, through the force of his movements, the meaning that arbitrary, "civilized" signs possess, while forging a new, motivated meaning that "savage" signs were, in the modernist imagination, thought to embody. According to his own admission, however, Michaux never lit on the ideal embodiment of the perfectly transparent sign. Yet in the process of experimenting with the kinetic, kinesthetic, and graphemic elements of sign making, he managed to offer valuable insights into the performative nature of signing as well as the paradoxical implications of the primitivist project.

Kinetic desire

It was a common belief during the modernist period that gestural languages were more "primitive" than verbal languages in the double sense of "primitive": (1) "older," "first," "prior," and (2) "rudimentary," "undeveloped," "uncivilized." With respect to the history of human sign systems, languages composed of gestures were thought to have evolved earlier than languages composed of words; their chronological priority also suggested their greater fidelity to, their motivated one-on-one *correspondence* with, the objects and emotions they signified.[6] Because gestural languages are overtly kinetic, modernist painters and writers considered them to be more authentic, closer to the texture, rhythm, and intensity of the feeling or idea being communicated.[7] However, painters such as Michaux were working with inscriptive rather than performance media, and therefore could not show the movements themselves, only the imprints or traces of their performance. Foregrounding these traces *as* traces, as remainders of performed gestures, was thus one strategy available to artists invested in the primitivist fantasy of a direct, less arbitrary system of expression. If an artist could associate his own marks with the force of hypothetically "prehistoric" gestures, then those marks could share the aura of a language emanating from an earlier, purer source.

Michaux's earliest attempts to mime the gestures of inscriptive systems are contained in *Narration* and *Alphabets,* volumes in which the shapes of Western cursive writing and pictographic (perhaps Native American) systems serve as inspiration. By the early 1940s, however, he was gravitating toward prehistoric makings unearthed in the caves of southern France and Cantabrian Spain. According to Leslie Jones, Michaux gleaned much of his material for his earliest experimentation with mark-making not from the walls of prehistoric caves themselves but from the pages of scholarly monographs that, in his own words, he scattered liberally around the space

Figure 4.1   Henri Michaux, *Untitled (Alphabets)* (1943). Copyright 2008 Artists Rights Society, New York/ADAGP, Paris.

in which he was working.[8] The illustrations found in studies of Pale-olithic and Neolithic painting and notational systems were crucial to the development of Michaux's unique vocabulary of forms. By comparing pages from Michaux's *Alphabets,* composed between 1927 and 1943 (Figure 4.1) to Paleolithic representations of animals (Figure 4.2),[9] it is easy to see how Michaux's ink drawings imitate the graphic disposition of discrete figures as serialized in books on Paleolithic art.

It is likely that Michaux's greatest exposure to Paleolithic art occurred during World War II, when, resettled in the south of France, he acquired numerous back issues of magazines such as *Cahiers d'art* and *Minotaure.*[10] In images produced between 1943 and 1951 (e.g., Figure 4.3), it is possible to see the influence of the Aurignacian harpoon motifs (Figure 4.4) as well as the symbol-like markings found on cave walls (Figure 4.2). Reminiscent of these Aurignacian images is the severe horizontality, the insistence on vigorously repeated patterns of strokes, in Michaux's images. For images such as *Untitled (Alphabets)*, 1944 (Figure 4.5), he also derives inspiration from Castallón battle or spear-throwing scenes (Figure 4.6) documented in Georges Henri Luquet's *L'Art et la religion des hommes fossiles* (1926), which was popular reading among the surrealists and other artists of their generation.[11] Michaux's brief vertical strokes approximate the tangential, limb-like branchings of the Castallón figures dashing across the page and the lances captured midflight. *Untitled (Alphabets)*, 1944 (Figure 4.3), which preserves the serial presentation of archeological documentation, contains isolated sets of markings reminiscent of both symbolic pattern-ing and iconic rendering: on the lowest row, for instance, we see a series of pattern-type constructions that draw on the decorative aspect of the harpoon motifs (Figure 4.4), whereas elsewhere—in the fifth row, third column, for instance—we identify the schematic strokes of the anthropoid spear-throwers.

After the 1940s, Michaux would reproduce almost exclusively the less rigid, less pictographic, and more iconic figures associated with the Neo-lithic battle scenes. Although still fascinated with the sign-like or notational qualities of markings, such as those in the bottom row of Figure 4.3, he was nonetheless moving more toward the production of thicker, more ink-saturated lines disposed in less regular arrangements. However, instead of imitating the *visual* patterns of specific motifs, he was in fact attempting to mime, with his own body, the corporeal experience of a certain variety of "prehistoric" mark-making. He sought the experience of executing the strokes themselves, and it was to some extent of secondary concern whether the strokes resulted in sign-like configurations or in figures that appeared to be captured in movement.

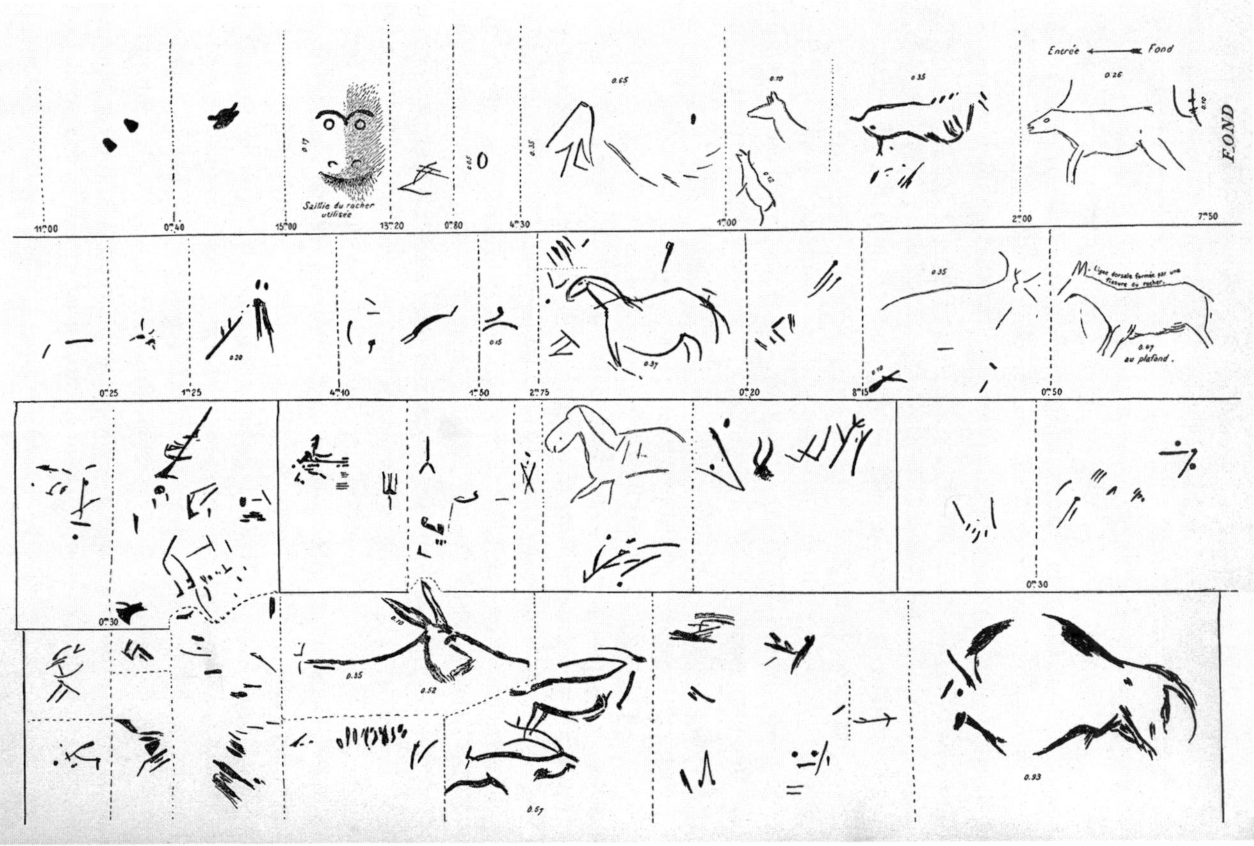

Figure 4.2
Henri Breuil, signs
and engravings,
Altamira. From
André Leroi-
Gourhan,
*Préhistoire de l'art
occidental* (Paris:
Editions Citadelles
et Mazenod, 1965).
Reprinted with
permission.

Yet even as Michaux experimented increasingly with strokes related to figuration and the production of composed scenes (suggesting nonserial relationships among discrete figures), he retained the grid-like, flat, non-scenic presentation he used in some of the images in *Alphabets*. By doing so, he was implicitly associating his clusters of marks not with the Neolithic depictions themselves—that is, with the way such renderings would appear to the eye of the spectator inspecting the original support—but with the artificial, taxonomic representation of cave art within the format of the scholarly tome. Within these explicit or implicit grids, Michaux traces bovine and equestrian figures in profile, preserving the archeologist's style of rendering the unclosed contours of figures without any visual reference to the irregularities of the actual support. Since cave painters were known to

Figure 4.3   Henri Michaux, *Untitled (Alphabets)* (1944). Copyright 2008 Artists Rights Society, New York/ADAGP, Paris.

have exploited the accidental irregularities of the support to suggest possible forms, it is clear that Michaux is alluding not to the artworks or objects as observed in the cave (or the museum vitrine) but to their reproduction in scholarly formats.[12] In *Alphabets,* the marking hand thus oscillates between two poles of attraction: the gestural and the archival. The artist's hand (and in some cases wrist, arm, and torso) is freed from the necessity to make

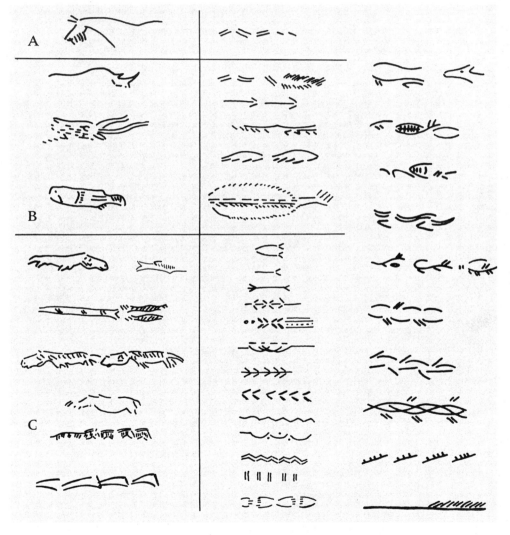

Figure 4.4 Henri Breuil, harpoon motifs, Altamira. From André Leroi-Gourhan, *Préhistoire de l'art occidental* (Paris: Editions Citadelles et Mazenod, 1965). Reprinted with permission.

recognizable signs and figures; yet at the same time, the scope of the artist's movements is tightly restrained by a gestural routine (also executed by the body), one that measures space into predetermined units and subsumes marks within a strict serial formation.

Michaux's critics have attended with enthusiasm to the gestural component of his inscriptive practice and have linked it, with good evidence, to the influence of prehistoric visual culture. What has largely been ignored, however, is the degree to which he maintains a spatial organization that dramatically limits the freedom of his gestures, an organization derived not from the phenomena we call "prehistoric" but from the techniques of archeological documentation forged to preserve those phenomena. The

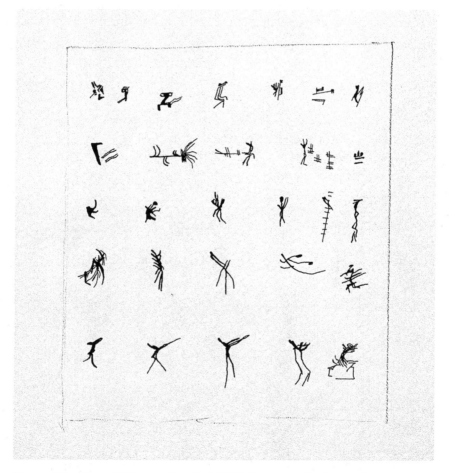

Figure 4.5   Henri Michaux, *Untitled (Alphabets)* (1944). Copyright 2008 Artists Rights Society, New York/ADAGP, Paris.

question that needs to be asked, then, is why, if Michaux was indeed striving to create a language composed entirely of personal signs, he constrained his gestural, supposedly more spontaneous practice of inscription within the highly charged disciplinary device of serial organization?

It is clear that Michaux was intrigued not only by prehistoric markings but also by inscriptive systems and supports of many varieties. As critics have noted, he not only took an interest in character sets, pictograms, hieroglyphs, and ideograms associated with specific written languages; he also explored, through an appropriation bordering on *détournement,* a wide variety of formats and technologies of display, such as the *abécédaire,* the chemical table, the geometric diagram, and the classificatory grids of archeological, geological, and botanical manuals.[13] Michaux experiments both with different inscriptive systems *and* with the protocols of spatialization associated with each of them. At the heart of his enterprise is a de-

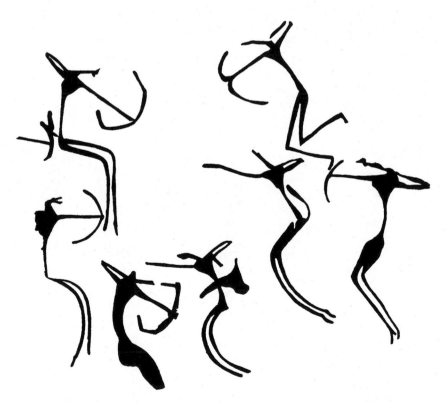

Figure 4.6   Prehistoric rock pictures. From Leo Frobenius and Douglas C. Fox, *Prehistoric Rock Pictures in Europe and Africa* (New York: Museum of Modern Art, 1937), 43.

sire to understand visually and kinesthetically the constitutive elements of inscription understood both as a set of signs and as a technology of distribution on the page.

Mouvements, the next major plastic work Michaux published after *Alphabets,* appeared in 1951 in the form of a polished, coherently conceived artist's book. Measuring 325 by 253 centimeters, *Mouvements* was originally an album containing reproductions of sixty-four ink drawings, a prefatory eponymous poem, and a "Postface." Here, the tentative experiment with writing systems and sign-producing gestures initiated in *Alphabets* and *Narration* is pursued further. The sixty-four reproductions are divided editorially into four discrete sections, two containing fifteen plates and two containing seventeen plates; each section is separated from the next by one blank page. The paper Michaux used for the original works reproduced in *Mouvements* was cheap, postwar regulation bond, apparently the only ink support he could afford at the time.[14] He was anything but economical in his use of this paper, however: by the time *Mouvements* was published, he had filled over twelve hundred pages with marks, only sixty-four of which were reproduced on vellum for the printed collection (the rest were distributed to friends, sold, or destroyed). In his "Postface," he recounts the story of the volume's genesis: "I had covered twelve hundred pages with these things, and all I saw there were flows *("flots"),* when René Bertelé [an editor of artist's books] took hold of them and, gropingly, reflectively, discovered in them sequences . . . the book you find here [is] more his work than my own."[15]

The four-part, sequential format imposed by Bertelé provides a particular narrative momentum to the volume. It establishes a sequence in which the reader, moving from one page to the next, is led to observe how an initially constrained—that is, horizontally oriented and consistently spaced—set of sign-like marks devolves increasingly toward random configurations. In each of the four sequences a set of marks similar to those found in Figure 4.7 (OC II, 563) lead, seemingly ineluctably, to a set of marks similar to those found in Figure 4.8 (OC II, 579). Marks that distantly recall Asian calligraphic characters (while simultaneously maintaining a connection to the Neolithic spear-throwers Michaux copied earlier) evolve slowly but surely toward larger, wilder doodles (Figures 4.9 [OC II, 568] and 4.10 [OC II, 569]). The series terminates when the scale is enlarged (Figure 4.11 [OC II, 576]) and the implicit grid explodes (Figure 4.8 [OC II, 579]), giving way to composition, an iconic reading, and the possibility of three-dimensional space. The sequential arrangement works to dramatize the tension between the rhythm of the gesture that marks and the rhythm of the gesture that spaces, or creates an interval. Eventually, the latter is overwhelmed by the former, as marking gestures transgress the disciplinary and disciplining grid within which the scriptural gesture is supposed to unfold.

I will supply a closer analysis of these mark clusters in a moment; for now it is crucial to note that the page sequences of *Mouvements* were constituted not by Michaux but by his editor and promoter, Bertelé. To his

Figure 4.7   Henri Michaux, *Mouvements* (1951). Copyright 2008 Artists Rights Society, New York/ADAGP, Paris.

credit, Bertelé does manage to create a narrative out of inscriptions; the reader-viewer of *Mouvements* observes if not the actual execution of the strokes, then at least, through the imposed order, evidence of their growing amplitude and intensity. Sequences of signs are arranged in such a manner as to imply that the increasing force and freedom of Michaux's gestures ends up loosening the bonds of the taxonomic imperative in a struggle that ends, time and time again, with the latter's defeat. However, it would be a mistake to ascribe to Michaux the intention to resolve the struggle between the supposedly freer force of gestural marking and the

Figure 4.8   Henri Michaux, *Mouvements* (1951). Copyright 2008 Artists Rights Society, New York/ADAGP, Paris.

disciplining force of the archival in quite that way.[16] Bertelé is clearly invested in presenting a particular version of *Mouvements* that might or might not be faithful to Michaux's experience, a version in which the author-painter seeks to break with the constraints of the written in order to cre-

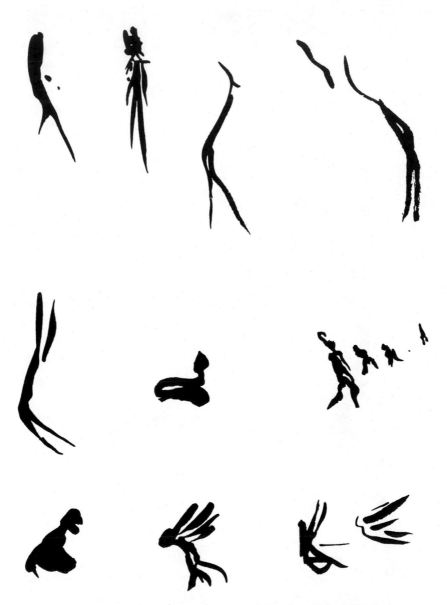

Figure 4.9   Henri Michaux, *Mouvements* (1951). Copyright 2008 Artists Rights Society, New York/ADAGP, Paris.

ate a more organic language, one that veers toward the figural as it reunites the subject with a "primitive" mythographic or pictographic imagination. In Bertelé's words, Michaux was seeking in *Mouvements* a "Writing from the beginning of the world, . . . a Writing taking us back to the primitive sources of communication [*les sources primitives de la communication*]."[17]

Bertelé is of course not alone in asserting that Michaux's project—not simply in *Mouvements* but throughout his career as a painter—was to

Figure 4.10   Henri Michaux, *Mouvements* (1951). Copyright 2008 Artists Rights Society, New York/ADAGP, Paris.

produce an inscriptive system capable of returning to "primitive" gestures and marks as a resource for the invention of a universal language. However, Michaux's own comments tend to stress the kinesthetic or sensual pleasures rather than the communicative aims of his procedures. In the eponymous poem accompanying the ink drawings, for instance, he

Figure 4.11   Henri Michaux, *Mouvements* (1951). Copyright 2008 Artists Rights Society, New York/ADAGP, Paris.

describes his motivation as an *"envie cinétique,"* a kinetic desire, or desire for kinesis. What he does not say, *pace* Bertelé, is that this desire for kinesis is coextensive with a desire to transmit a universally legible message. "Signs / not of rooftops, of tunics, or of palaces" ("Signes / non de toit, de tunique ou de palais"), Michaux's verse begins, signs "not of archives and dictionaries of knowledge / but of distortions, violence, perturbation / kinetic desire" (*"non d'archives et de dictionnaire du savoir / mais de torsion, de violence, de bousculement / mais d'envie cinétique"*).[18] In other words, the "signs" of *Mouvements* are not intended to decorate a support (one understanding of *"Signes . . . de toit"* as signs *belonging* to or *found on* a roof); nor do they represent, like a courtly hieroglyph, a scene (another understanding of *"Signes . . . de toit"*—signs *depicting* a roof). Because they are personal and idiosyncratic, generated by what Michaux calls the *"moi-je,"*[19] nor are they *"Signes . . . de toi[t]"* (*"your signs,"* a third way the phrase can be interpreted). These signs are decidedly not conventional or designed to be shared. Furthermore, Michaux explicitly remarks that they do not transmit the kind of knowledge that can be classified: *"Signes . . . non d'archives et de dictionnaire du savoir."* Instead, they merely evince a desire for kinesis, for motility. They are indexical rather than symbolic or iconic, but only insofar as they register that a movement (the movement that produced them) has indeed occurred. Michaux's *"mouvements,"* as he puts it, are a record only of the impulse to move.

"Form as a field of possibilities"

Whereas in his early years Michaux turned to paleographic documentation for examples of a kinetically charged pictographic system, in the 1950s Chinese calligraphy became his major source of inspiration. He owned a copy of Léon Wieger's *Caractères Chinois* (Chinese characters) in his personal library; as a child, but also later on as an adult, he spent many hours attempting to learn the rudiments of Chinese calligraphy (a point that will become important shortly).[20] The resemblance between Chinese calligraphic scripts and the marks contained in *Mouvements* has been established—perhaps too emphatically—by several of Michaux's critics. Frances Morris, for instance, finds that the collection is "a visual demonstration of [Michaux's] understanding of a Chinese approach. A few deft strokes, swift and spontaneous, identify a character as part of a group or alphabet disposed, like Chinese characters, neatly across the page."[21] As Leslie Jones has observed, however, many visual discrepancies complicate an easy analogy between Chinese characters and Michaux's marks. "The majority of Michaux's 'Mouvements,'" Jones notes, "have a torso-like center from which emanate 'limbs' of all sorts in contrast to the left-to-right, top-to-bottom, exterior-to-interior formation of Chinese characters that often center on an open core or void"; instead of laying down strokes "that circulate around the center" as in the calligraphic tradition, "Michaux worked from the center out and never followed a stroke order."[22] On closer inspection, not only do Michaux's *"mouvements"* fail to bear a resemblance to Chinese calligraphy characters but also their mode of production differs significantly from that of Chinese calligraphers. Working with the traditional materials of the Chinese form, Michaux "holds the brush as he would a pen—at an angle and resting on the second finger—while the Asian practice requires an artist to hold the brush perfectly upright with the handle resting on the third finger" (156).[23]

These differences in mode of execution must be contrasted with the continuities Michaux obviously wants to preserve. By switching from pen to brush and by working exclusively with *"encre de Chine,"* Michaux underscores his desire to evoke the tools of a practice that is at once writing and drawing, semantically significant and visually compelling. Further, by emphasizing the stroke to the detriment of legibility, Michaux displays his admiration for practitioners of Chinese cursive or running scripts, forms traditionally achieved only after complete mastery of the rigorously standardized clerical scripts.[24] He obviously wants to align his own efforts with those of innovators in the Chinese tradition who choose expression of individual motility over clarity of communication. By miming only certain aspects of the calligraphic sign-making tradition, he succeeds in maintaining a connection to it while simultaneously putting its methods to new use. For instance, he employs ink and brush, but he manipulates them in a Western way. He follows the Chinese calligrapher in combining individual, distinct strokes into character-like constructions, yet he reverses the orientation that Chinese characters demand. As in his 1975 collection *Idéogrammes en Chine,* he mixes up the elements of two inscriptive systems, imposing the grid-like distribution associated with East Asian signaries on characters that are not decidedly not East Asian, handling an Eastern brush as though it were a Western pen, and conducting the business of calligraphy not on a scroll but on a 9½ by 12⅝-inch Western paper support.

This last point is perhaps the most important, for it indicates something about his project that critics have failed to emphasize. Although in *Mouvements* Michaux may indeed be referencing the traditions of Eastern script, he is also deliberately observing the formatting principles of *Western* inscriptive systems. His support is the Western page; his reception apparatus the Western codex. Thus, as figurative as his marks might appear (suggesting at times the shapes of animals, plants, single-celled organisms, or the human body), they are in fact prevented from being received as fully iconic because they are contained within a 9½ by 12⅝-inch surface inserted into a volume of such surfaces. To this extent, *Mouvements* resembles *Alphabets,* for both reference noncodexical inscriptive supports—the cave wall or the calligrapher's scroll—while clinging nonetheless to a codexical *dispositif.* The grid-like presentation of Chinese characters echoes the grid-like presentation of paleographic artifacts that served as a compositional model for *Alphabets.* As was the case with *Alphabets,* again in *Mouvements* Michaux is limited by the scriptural economy of the page just as much as he is freed by the gestural possibilities of the body. His *"mouvements"* are only in part the recorded traces of spontaneous gestures. With the exception of the most extravagant cases, his marks tend to follow strict and redundant patterns of movement while staying respectfully within their designated squares. The gestural is certainly a crucial component of the exercise; gestural energy propels the direction of the strokes and determines the contours of the "signs." However, the space of the page is also strongly present both as a material reality that limits and organizes his gestures and as a cognitive frame that urges us to "read" these gestures as signs. The format of the page encourages the body to perform gestures that are consequently not those of cave painting or traditional calligraphy but rather those of Western writing. If, as critics such as Loreau have strenuously insisted, Michaux's purpose was to "root language and signs in the corporeal gesture [*le geste corporel*]," why, then, did he preserve and even emphasize the limited space of the page?[25] If he wanted to invent a language true to his own body, why did he discipline this body to perform within such a tight space?

For the space of the page is a tight one indeed. The original brush and ink drawings of *Mouvements* were executed on drawing paper somewhat larger than the surface familiar to French schoolchildren but clearly smaller than the surface generally employed by painters.[26] The pages of *Mouvements* retain the verticality of writing paper (they are longer than they are wide), and the "characters," or what I prefer to call "mark clusters," appear to have been applied from left to right and top to bottom. Michaux's choice of this reduced format places him in stark contrast with other artists of his generation who were also exploring the properties of the sign as a plastic element. At the time *Mouvements* appeared, the Italian painter Capogrossi and the French painter Georges Mathieu, two contemporaries to whom Michaux alludes in a short essay of 1954 entitled "Signes," were engaged in producing sign-like figures, but on large canvases, not codex pages.[27] Even when troping on traditional calligraphy, artists belonging to postwar movements such as *art informel, tachisme,* abstract expressionism, and *art brut* tended to move toward more impressive formats, producing their various marks (sign-like or not) by means of expansive, theatrical gestures.[28] Michaux's decision to explore the gestural while remaining wedded to the page was quite original; unique in his generation, he combined a surrealist preoccupation with everyday, nonspectacular materials with a clinical interest in his own motility that made him appear closer to artists such as Mathieu, Capogrossi, and Georges Noël than he actually was. His intervention in the field of painting drew from many sources and resembled that of many contemporaries, yet he diverged from them all in crucial ways.

Michaux turned toward painting at a precise moment in the Western history of the medium, the moment when writing—as inscription, but not necessarily *legible* inscription—emerged as a viable alternative to figuration. His decisive turn toward the visual during the 1940s was neither sudden nor capricious. He had already tried his hand at watercolors, gouaches, and inks long before 1951, the year he began executing the drawings that would become *Mouvements*. Even during the period when he was known solely as a poet, he took part in small gallery exhibitions, showing, as early as 1937, some of his watercolors and pastels.[29] Unfortunately, his career as an artist was interrupted by the war and did not really get under way until 1948, when the well-respected Galérie René Drouin displayed a striking collection of his gouaches. At least one significant encounter, however, marked the war years: at the end of 1944, Michaux met Jean Dubuffet for the first time and was "conquered" (his own word) by the energy of his paintings.[30] From that point on, Michaux was drawn into the circle around Dubuffet, exhibiting his works in shows with surrealists like Max Ernst and Masson and, at the same time, painters of the "new primitivism," such as Dubuffet and Wols.

"New primitivism" is a term coined by Sarah Wilson to characterize a handful of postwar movements that Michel Tapié has referred to, somewhat less convincingly, as *"un art autre."* The pivot between the "old" primitivism and the "new" was arguably provided by a specific event: Artaud's 1947 *"Conférence"* at the Théâtre du Vieux-Colombier, which was responsible for reigniting an interest in earlier aspects of surrealism (Artaud's work in particular) that wartime preoccupations had eclipsed. Wilson describes this "new primitivism" as "divorced from the spoils and the 'anthropology' of the Trocadero, the exotic fascinations of the returning Surrealists."[31] More to the point, the "new primitivism" also differed from the old insofar as it pinned its hopes not on the "talking cure" but on the revealed organic body of the artist. Exposing the supposedly raw impulses, rhythms, gestures, and marks of this body was now seen as a way out of the impasses of cubism, surrealism, and what Michel Leiris diagnosed as the "disillusionment of the Western man, ill at ease in his own skin" [la déception d'Occidental mal dans sa peau]."[32] In harmony with Brassaï, Luquet, and Bataille, Dubuffet brought attention to instances of inscription not previously considered aesthetically significant. Michaux admired Dubuffet's eccentric visual tastes; in fact, he credited him specifically with teaching an entire generation of artists and writers to "look differently at a wall, at graffiti" [regarder de façon différente un mur, un graffiti]."[33] Dubuffet extended in many directions the Surrealists' initial interest in marginalized art forms. He not only explored the expressive potential of wall inscriptions and uneven, grotto-like supports; he also brought greater recognition to the works of the insane and the incarcerated—"les fous, simples d'esprit, délinquents ou même assassins"—when he founded the Compagnie de l'Art Brut in 1948.[34]

Tapié, the famous promoter of art brut, was instrumental in ushering Dubuffet into the limelight. According to Tapié, Dubuffet placed a greater value on spontaneous compositional methods than his predecessors; he handled his materials in a way that foregrounds rather than disguises their properties, thereby making the rhythm of application visible, retraceable. In this sense, he theatricalized the painting process itself. Michaux's work was received by gallery owners and collectors as belonging to the emotionally raw aesthetic that Dubuffet and Tapié had championed. In 1948, two years after mounting an important Dubuffet show, René Drouin devoted his entire gallery to Michaux's watercolor washes, thereby underscoring the continuity between Dubuffet's art brut and Michaux's own version of working with wet paint. Exhibited in the same spaces as Dubuffet, Michaux was culturally positioned and discursively framed to be heralded as yet another member of the "new primitivism" of the postwar Wols-Jean Fautrier-Dubuffet generation.

It was in this atmosphere of exploratory theatricalizing of the painterly gesture that the drip canvases of Jackson Pollock and the notion of "action painting" were first introduced. Neither Pollock nor the principles of action painting would have been comprehensible to critics and gallery owners if Dubuffet, Hartung, Mathieu, Wols, and Michaux had not already prepared the French terrain. Michaux had not known of Pollock's paintings until Tapié took him to see them in Paris; in contrast to the prominent art critics of the period, Michaux displayed a marked receptivity to what one reviewer dubbed scornfully these "ink graffiti" ("graffiti d'encres").[35] Apparently Tapié, as well as many gallery owners, recognized a profound affinity between Michaux's ink marks and the drip paintings Pollock was producing in the late 1940s. From 1952 on, Michaux found his own works hanging in the same galleries as those of Pollock.[36] Given the immediately discernible differences between Michaux's delicate encres de

Chine and Pollock's explosive *"graffiti d'encre,"* it is surprising that so many critics and art historians—from Geneviève Bonnefoi to Jean Louis Schefer—have insisted on their resemblance. Pollock poured industrial paint while Michaux stroked on India ink; Pollock gushed in color, while Michaux dabbled in black and white. And yet, in the discourse of art history, Michaux has been most frequently and most consistently compared to Pollock. Why is this so?

According to the painter Claude Georges, Michaux and Pollock were equally innovative, and thus comparable, with respect to their "new attitude toward the work."[37] This attitude consisted in allowing the process of painting to assume agency, to dominate the intentionality of the artist; what Georges admired in both Pollock and Michaux was "this way of letting painting itself make the painting, this way of refusing to be obedient and docile with respect to the painter's *ideas*."[38] In the eyes of Jean Degottex as well, the two painters had embarked on a similar project at approximately the same moment, which was to eliminate the figurative from painting by exploring an *"écriture gestuelle."*[39] Finally, art critics indebted to Harold Rosenberg, such as Margit Rowell, have placed Pollock and Michaux side by side for the reason that each, in his own way, invests the gestural with the capacity to undo socialization, to return the body to its natural rhythms: "Gesture is a motivation, a tendency," Rowell writes in her chapter on Pollock; the gestural "corresponds to a fundamental human need, and because of this it is parasocial, paracultural. Gesture is the manifestation of a primal state of being."[40] Michaux shares with Pollock this primitivist notion of the gestural, Rowell continues, in her chapter on Michaux: with gesture, she says, we find ourselves "at the original source of all . . . creation, at the first, natural and spontaneous manifestation" of being; she concludes: "More than any other artist, with the exception of Pollock, Michaux sublimated his history in nature."[41]

But if both artists "sublimated" their personal history, drowning the contingencies of their cultural conditioning in a nature they rediscovered through gestural marking (and this is Rowell's contention), they nonetheless did so in utterly different ways. Setting aside for the moment the problematic nature of this primitivist account of Michaux's and Pollock's procedures (according to which both turned to the spontaneity of the gestural to unearth "a primitive state of being"), it is still necessary to account for the striking differences in their choices of format and modes of execution. It may very well be that, as Rowell has insisted, the model for Pollock's drip and splatter paintings was the child's *"expérience du griffonnage,"* the undisciplined enjoyment of materials and the kinesthetic pleasures of their application.[42] However, it is by no means incidental that the deepening of this experience in painterly terms was accompanied, in Pollock's case, by an expansion of the dimensions of the canvas support. Rowell acknowledges that Pollock's paintings of this period (1947–1950) "are of greater dimension than any he had produced before"; but for her, nothing was "modified" in the scribbling experience by this "change of scale" *("différence d'échelle")*.[43] That Pollock took the gestures of the "scribbler" *("griffonneur")* and expanded them until they could fill a space ten times bigger than that filled by Michaux's *"mouvements"* (e.g., Pollock's *Number 32* measures 269 by 457.5 centimeters) does not seem to trouble Rowell at all. Even as she underlines the exaggerated dimensions of his support, the magnified scope of his movements—"the pictorial matter follows the movements of his hand, arm, body"—she neglects to consider how the comparison with Michaux's project might need to be revised.[44]

Too often ignored in accounts of Michaux's work is the importance of scale. True, Pollock, similar to Michaux, tended to respect the borders of the support's rectangle; however, in Pollock's case, these borders encased and made available a surface (with a horizontal orientation) far larger than that circumscribed by Michaux. The gestures Pollock was referencing are those associated with mural painting or set design; they are larger than the gestures required for writing.[45] In contrast, Michaux not only preserves the scope of the gestural routines of character formation, he also chooses paper and ink over canvas and paint, thereby permitting his tool and his support to limit the variety of movements he can perform. Michaux's choices—to use ink and paper and to distribute the inked figures in rows—are part of a coherent strategy to respect the format of the codex even when venturing out onto the terrain of the painterly stroke. Bertelé's suggestion that the separate pages of *"mouvements"* be made into a book is thus in keeping with the general thrust of Michaux's procedures. When Bertelé anchored these pages with a spine and assured—by means of a prefatory poem and a "postface"—that, as in any codex, the pages of the volume would be turned from right to left, from front to back, he was merely extending the logic of the book that Michaux had established in the first place. Bertelé made sure that the pages of ink drawings would be framed on either end by traditionally laid-out text ("Mouvements" and "Postface"); this *dispositif* prepares the reader to approach the *"mouvements"* not as a spectator but as a *reader,* one who expects legibility, or at least intelligibility, to emerge from black lines on a white support.

What draws Michaux and Pollock together is perhaps less the formal qualities of their works than the art historical discourse that has been generated about these qualities. Both have been constructed—and at times have constructed themselves—as primitivists, disenchanted Westerners searching for the preenculturated, primordial self through paint. To the extent that Michaux was indeed seeking to reveal, as he wrote in the poem "Mouvements," a "man, displaying everything, flapping in the wind of his impulses" *("homme, tous pavillons dehors, claquant au vent bruissant de ses pulsiona")* (OC II, 436), he can be considered to have operated within the field of what Amelia Jones has called "the Pollockian performative,"[46] a field in which the self and its "impulses" are *engendered* phenomenologically in relation to a performance situation, rather than indexed belatedly by marks on the page.[47] It is clear from Michaux's own statements that he was striving to *produce* a new body through his gestures; it was not a matter of registering graphically the body he already was. A strategy had to be devised that would encourage the performance of spontaneous movements, or at least the performance of movements in a new *sequence* not previously determined by acquired skills. In other words, Michaux, like Pollock, needed to find a way to experience a body in the act of moving—and thus marking—in a new way.

The curious and perhaps singularly modern dilemma facing artists such as Michaux and Pollock was how to set up the conditions, often quite stringent, in which something resembling spontaneity could emerge.[48] As T. J. Clark points out with respect to Pollock's procedures (and in Pollock's terms), a high degree of "deskilling" was necessary, but, paradoxically, this deskilling demanded a "battery of techniques."[49] Whereas American artists tended to emphasize the ways they exploded previous techniques in order to return to "organic" movements and "authentic" subjectivities, the French of the same generation speak more frequently of the *"entraînement,"* or training in new protocols of execution, required in order to achieve similar goals. Sloughing off acquired habits of execution was something that could not be done simply by trusting "spontaneous" or "unconscious" impulses; if the French avant-garde had learned one thing from surrealism, it was this.[50] Rather, the artist had to become *more* conscious of habitual ways of doing things: he/she was called on to apprehend the discrete elements in a sequence of linked movements, in order to locate and exploit the fault lines between them. As Umberto Eco has written with respect to this period in French cultural history, the aesthetic of the *"informel"* and the "open work" involved a "rejection of classical forms," to be sure, "but *not* a rejection of that form which is the fundamental condition of communication," or the iterable line.[51]

No description could better fit Michaux's project in *Mouvements,* which could be construed as an effort to determine the formal—as well as the gestural—elements that make a mark susceptible to bearing signification.

Eco seems to be alluding to Michaux's work even more explicitly (although he was in fact referencing Pollock) when he observes that an *"informel"* art work "does not proclaim the death of form, rather, it proposes a new, more flexible version of it—*form as a field of possibilities.*"[52] In Michaux's case, the forms that served as "fields of possibilities" were not those of the image, but rather those of the written character and the spatial conventions of the page. That is, the forms to be "opened" and explored were those of a wide variety of different signaries and formatting systems, and therefore the techniques to be revisited were the gestural routines associated with writing in its many incarnations. Thus, when Michaux began to study Chinese training manuals, filling up the gridded pages of workbooks with calligraphic strokes, he was aiming less at perfecting a new skill than at getting rid of an old one. Accounts of Michaux's attempt to acquire the rudiments of Chinese calligraphy stress that he was a singularly unsuccessful student. The results, apparently, were always inadequate from a technical point of view. But his purpose was never to attain mastery, to become adept at an alternative—equally traditional and culturally specific—gestural routine. His goal was to understand, to become viscerally aware of the physical demands of *many* inscriptive systems—Neolithic, calligraphic, pictographic—in order to liberate movement possibilities residing within the anatomical body as it moved to create—or more precisely, to mime— a plethora of forms. In short, the challenge for Michaux was to perform a new gestural routine in order to render less familiar, less necessary, and less *natural* another acquired one. In *Mouvements,* Michaux was interested in documenting, encyclopedically, the greatest number of mark-making movements he could execute without exceeding the bounds of an implicit, sign-defining grid. Such an encyclopedic approach might suggest new combinatory possibilities, new choreographies, and these choreographies in turn materialized impulses located less in some unconscious depth of the self or the precultural body than in the body that performs signs.

"Je peins pour me déconditionner"

Mouvements documents Michaux's effort to unlearn how to write; as Michaux himself wrote in 1972, "je peins *pour me déconditionner* [I write to decondition myself]."[53] To underline that such deconditioning requires an apprenticeship in expressive operations of another variety (rather than the elimination of training altogether), Michaux chooses for *Mouvements* the format of a child's primer. On his mark clusters he imposes a serial formation drawn not from authentic examples of achieved Chinese calligraphy (scrolls and wall hangings in which characters are rarely justified on both margins) but from the gridded exercise sheets used by Chinese schoolchildren during the apprenticeship phase when they are just *learning* calligraphy. This invisible grid of the primer thematizes visually the fact that Michaux is involved in a process of *"entraînement."* At the same time, however, this grid also evokes the child's ambivalent experience of learning good penmanship. The child is forced to master the discipline of writing according to linear or other culturally specific spatial conventions, thereby submitting to a limited set of expressive instruments and possibilities. Yet in the very act of being disciplined, the child is also acquiring the skills necessary to deform the shapes, dislocate the syntax or order, and play with the arrangement of characters on the page, thereby discovering expressive possibilities in the system that cannot be entirely predetermined or controlled. As any parent, schoolteacher, or psychologist can confirm, for many children, learning to write is an experience that incites a good deal of inquisitive experimentation and creative resistance. In *Mouvements* Michaux is as interested in the resistance as he is in the discipline.

A closer examination of the mark clusters on a single page of *Mouvements* reveals that the artist's impulse to perfect through repetition is challenged by an equally strong impulse to vary and innovate. The single page is a better clue to the nature of Michaux's project than the sequence of fifteen or seventeen pages, since he alone (as opposed to Bertelé) determined the order of mark clusters on any given page. Therefore, I shall return to a single page from the third sequence briefly discussed earlier, isolating it from the context in which Bertelé placed it. Figure 4.12 (page 2 of the third sequence) is a good place to begin, for it is fairly representative of a large quantity of pages in *Mouvements*. The neat four-by-four ordering of character-like marks within the implied grid is typical of many pages, as are the thickness, density, and length of the constitutive strokes. In addition, this page has the advantage of being neither the first nor the last in a sequence and thus remains unburdened by having to hold a significant place in the dramatic arc created by Bertelé. We can attend, then, more closely to the drama taking place within the limits of the individual page.

What is immediately apparent to the eye is the downward, vertical thrust of the primary strokes composing the clusters. Although there are exceptions to the rule (see, in particular, the mark clusters located in the third row, first and fourth columns), most of the mark clusters possess a strong, defining vertical line that thickens as it descends, an attribute that tells us that Michaux repeatedly began his stroke from on high and lowered his hand as he proceeded. Alternating with this downward stroke is often a horizontal squiggle or line set (as in the mark clusters in the top row, first and third columns). Judging by this group, one is tempted to conclude that in executing the mark clusters on this page, Michaux's hand, wrist, and arm followed a consistent gestural routine, one composed largely of vertical slashes and horizontal swings, with very few meditated circular motions. Visible as well are the types of brush mark made by altering the degree of pressure exerted by the hand as it advances the brush toward contact with the support. In the mark clusters in the second row, first and third column;

Figure 4.12   Henri Michaux, *Mouvements* (1951). Copyright 2008 Artists Rights Society, New York/ADAGP, Paris.

the third row, second column; and the fourth row, third column, it is possible to discern the work of a brush that has been pressed to the paper and then swiftly lifted, leaving behind a rapidly narrowing trail. Such dramatic marks index the body's movements within a three-dimensional space, as opposed to lateral or longitudinal movements in a two-dimensional space. Indexes of pressure applied in the three-dimensional space of the artist are typical (and integral to the legibility) of calligraphic characters, but are largely foreign to conventional writing systems of the West.

This page of *Mouvements* is representative with respect to the sequence in which Bertelé has embedded it. It is likely that the second page, (Figure 4.12), the one preceding it (Figure 4.7), and the one following it (Figure 4.13) were completed if not one after the other, then at least closely together in time; the stroke used in Figure 4.12 is the type of stroke used to produce many of the other figures in the sequence. Yet this page retains a certain integrity and uniqueness. Just two pages later (Figure 4.14), Michaux has introduced an entirely new stroke, a new theme, one is tempted to say: the diagonal swing stroke (the entire third row, for instance), which hardly appears in later pages of the same sequence, such as Figures 4.15 and 4.16. On the one hand, it would be possible to argue that Figure 4.12 contains the germ—the stroke vocabulary or lexicon—of the entire sequence. The diagonal swing can be discerned in the mark clusters in the third row, fourth column, and the fourth row, second and third columns. But then it would be necessary to explain the appearance of a figure such as the one in the lower right-hand corner in Figure 4.16. This cluster of marks is probably not a prolongation or augmentation of any stroke type found in Figure 4.12. Its production has required an entirely different movement, a longer, slower, continuous application of ink involving rotation at the level of the elbow. It was probably generated not by any combinatory potential present on the first two pages of the sequence but by a sustained stroke made by exerting uniform pressure as the hand moved across the page. Strokes like these are responsible for the pronounced verticality of all the figures on the page, except the horizontal strokes found at its bottom. Those horizontals are a reaction to the verticals above; they maintain the same sort of rhythm, pulse, scale, and scope but simply move in a different direction. Michaux follows the momentum and directionality of the gesture—the same gesture—until the body swerves, a new impulse is manifested, and a new directionality appears.

My reading is intended to emphasize both the integrity of the single page of markings and the systematicity of the entire approach. Typically, Michaux establishes a gestural routine composed of three to five strokes; he then adds a new element not initially constitutive of the original set, which initiates a substantially different gestural routine. To the extent that each set involves a limited set of strokes executed with slight variations, Michaux is remarkably consistent. However, frequently the new element added (degree of pressure, privileged direction of the thrust) changes the

Figure 4.13   Henri Michaux, *Mouvements* (1951). Copyright 2008 Artists Rights Society, New York/ADAGP, Paris.

visually evocative power of the strokes entirely. That is, they can change quite rapidly from resembling Chinese characters to resembling Neolithic markings as a result of only one addition to the gestural routine. That addition is extrapolated from one of the possibilities offered by previous strokes. Michaux appears to be practicing an abstraction of the principles—and

Figure 4.14   Henri Michaux, *Mouvements* (1951). Copyright 2008 Artists Rights Society, New York/ADAGP, Paris.

movements—that make script script-like, characters character-like. This gestural process of abstraction or schematization (through rapidity and repetition) allows him to access not some authentic, primordial body but simply a set of movements (and movement experiences) normally unavailable to the writing body that his particular culture has taught him to be.

Figure 4.15   Henri Michaux, *Mouvements* (1951). Copyright 2008 Artists Rights Society, New York/ADAGP, Paris.

One could argue that in *Mouvements* Michaux is trying to invent a new signary by exploring every possible stroke combination, a point buttressed by the evidence of his enormous production of "sign"-filled pages. But to make this argument, one would have to identify a trend toward consistency, a search for regularity. In this respect, however, the mark clusters of *Mouvements* are in contradiction with one of writing's most basic fea-

Figure 4.16   Henri Michaux, *Mouvements* (1951). Copyright 2008 Artists Rights Society, New York/ADAGP, Paris.

tures: limited differentiation, the reduction of the quantity of marks that can bear meaning within any one system to a precise number. No writing system of a single culture (or language) could be as heterogeneous as those found in *Mouvements*. Since the character set (and associated gestural routine) changes slightly—or dramatically—on every page, *Mouvements* resembles more closely a compilation of scripts, an encyclopedia of signaries, than a single, achieved system. Ultimately, what the pages of the volume indicate is that Michaux was less interested in forging a personal character set, "a language all his own," in Bertelé's words, than in using character formation, and the generative gestures of inscription, to explore untapped gestural and graphic possibilities within the practice of inscription itself.[54]

Thus, despite the critical insistence on writing as tool, evidence suggests that Michaux was invested in writing as *practice:* he was seeking to discover the essential elements of sign making as a "technique of the body," or a *"chaîne opératoire."* With respect to the visual phenomenality of the sign, he wished to explore all the potential graphic instantiations of that social unit called "the sign," as well as the types of spatial relationships allowed between signs. He knew that he could not transgress the socially determined graphemic and spatial limitations on sign making without losing the formal sign-quality of his marks. What he could do, however, was suggest sign-*ness* (without actually signing) by exploiting the combinatory possibilities provided by signs of all varieties. He therefore mimes the literalness or iconicity of the pictogram, the evocative power of the ideogram, the simplicity and easy iterability of the letter, the discreteness of the cuneiform imprint, and the decorative quality of the hieroglyph. Further, the implicit grid structure he employs not only evokes the child's primer but also establishes an "unnatural" and nonfigurative relation among the various mark groupings on the page.[55] They almost invariably stand in relationships dictated by symbolic rather than iconic representational conventions. The threshold with narrative painting is rarely crossed, and the reader's urge toward a figurative (iconic) reading of the marks is thwarted by the reimposition, either on the page at hand or the next, of a seriality that is inscription's most defining feature.

Michaux thus mimes signing on two levels: he approximates the graphic features of the sign on the level of the visual, and he reproduces the kinetic properties of sign *making* on the level of the gestural. By respecting the rhythms of sequencing or seriality as well as the types and qualities of stroke permitted to character formation within a tight space, he manages to inhabit (in the sense of *habitus*), the gestural routines of not just one but several writing systems. It seems logical that he would turn toward calligraphic and pictographic systems in order to increase his field of exploration; such systems generally require more kinetic investment on the part of the writer than linear alphabetic systems. In *Mouvements*, especially, the calligraphic allows him to experience his body, as a writing body, in a new way. He seems to have appreciated this augmentation of the choreographic possibilities offered to him by alternative writing practices. Flirting with the constraints of these more gestural systems, he often appears to reach the limit point of each routine he initiates; on some pages his strokes are longer and his characters larger, more figurative, or more schematic than permitted by even calligraphic conventions. But it is perhaps only by experiencing those transgressions physically as well as visually that Michaux's body comes to know what it is to have a signing body, a disciplined body capable of inscribing marks that resemble, or could operate as, signs.

"Their movement became my movement"

Significantly, in later remarks on *Mouvements*, Michaux tends to stress not the visual qualities of his marks but the kinetic experience of making them. The sheer number of pages he filled with these marks testifies to the aim of the project: to *move* in a sign-making way. Since it is exclusively scholars of literature and art historians (and not dance ethnographers or theorists of movement) who have approached Michaux's ink drawings, it makes sense that an entire aspect—perhaps the most important—of his practice has until now been ignored.[56] Yet a mere glance at his manifold writings on the subject of writing reveals clearly that even if the initial impetus for creating *"mouvements"* was a desire to invent an ideal signary, in the end it was the opportunity to perform a wide variety of inscriptive gestures that proved the most compelling aspect of the experiment. In "Signes," for instance, he emphasizes the gestural rather than the visual motivation while speculating on the genesis of *Mouvements*. "I have to speak now about my signs," he concedes: "But where am I with these signs? Surely not where everyone else is [Sûrement pas dans la voie principale]."

> I made thousands of them two years ago. But were these really signs? They were gestures, rather, interior gestures [*gestes intérieurs*] for which we have no limbs, but only a desire for limbs, ways of tensing, ways of reaching [élans], and all of them executed by lively ligaments, never thick, never weighted down with flesh or closed in by skin [*et tout cela en cordes vivantes, jamais épaisses, jamais grosses de chair ou fermées de peau*].[57]

When Michaux wrote "Signes," *"la voie principale"* of painterly experimentation with sign-like figures was that cleared by Mathieu and Capogrossi. The latter, Michaux claims, discovered a *"signe de base,"* a schematic cell from which all other signs would issue (OC II, 430). Mathieu, too, according to Michaux, located something "irreducible": "the final point, the Alpha, the metaphysics of authority" (OC II, 431). In "Signes," Michaux acknowledges that his experience in *Mouvements* produced something quite different: neither an essential sign (Capogrossi) nor a definitive signature (Mathieu) but instead "movements . . . pieces of movements [*des émiettements de mouvements*]," too numerous and too heterogeneous even to merit the appellation "signs." By leaving *"la voie principale,"* however, Michaux manages to wander into a whole new arena of investigation, one in which gestures and movements become more significant than the marks they leave behind on the canvas or page. His singular accomplishment is to have relinquished (or at least deferred) the dream of an absolute, essential sign (a dream pursued more rigorously by Capogrossi and Mathieu) in the interest of reanimating the body's seemingly limitless sign-making capacity.

But this limitless sign-making capacity is a dream of another sort. The marks Michaux leaves on the pages of the *Mouvements* series are not truly produced by *"gestes intérieurs."* How could they be? If an external body did not execute the gestures, then no marks would remain, and there would be no *Mouvements*. *"Gestes intérieurs"* are imaginative and virtual rather than performed and materialized; as such, they are infinite, or if not infinite, then at least unhampered by corporeal constraints ("never thick, never weighted down with flesh or closed in by skin"). The "gestures for which we have no limbs but only a desire for limbs" belong to the virtual body, the body before it has been shaped by one—or *any*—culture. Of course, Michaux cannot gain access to this virtual body except in his imagination; the orthography of every character set, in whatever civilization or language, obeys the gestural conventions and regimes of that civilization. Furthermore, the shapes any character set can assume are determined by the physiological limits of human digits, the degree of acceleration wrist movements can attain, the scope of circular flexibility in the joints, and so on. Nonetheless, the virtual body serves as a blueprint for movements beyond those allocated by an individual culture; in the act of trying to execute these imaginary *"gestes intérieurs,"* the real body reaches beyond its cultural conditioning, beyond the disciplines of inscription to which it has been subjected since childhood, and gains the knowledge of what it can and cannot do in its struggle to overcome the routines of a specific practice.

Allusions to this ideal, precultural (virtual) body appear throughout Michaux's works. One of the central themes of his earliest publications is in fact nostalgia for the body before its physical training in pedagogical situations. He taxes his early childhood physical *"entraînement"* with having severely limited and deformed his potential to move freely in space. In "Observations," a short text published in *Passages* (1950), he attributes his restricted way of moving, and thus his self-alienation, to an elementary school training in *"Gymnastique suédoise,"* "this Western gymnastics with its mechanical gestures which divide the body from itself [*qui écartent de soi*]."[58] The Swedish "occidental" training is contrasted with that offered to the Hindu dancer or the African drummer.[59] Michaux's conventional primitivism resurfaces here as he indulges in the fantasy of an alternative physical training that would correspond to, rather than distort, the body's natural rhythms. In an untitled poem immediately preceding "Observations," he explains his recent predilection for playing the tom-tom as an attempt to relocate his own natural rhythm, or pulse ("I play the tom-tom . . . to feel my pulse [*je joue du tam-tam . . . Pour me tâter le pouls*]") (OC II, 342–443). Not that he actually dances to the tom-tom, Michaux assures his reader. Beating, moving to the beat, does not allow him to recover a full, originary freedom of movement he believes forever lost. However, what does return in the process of drumming is an amorphous, unchoreographed wealth of *"mouvements"*: "In the end, I was intrigued . . . by movements, by the influence that movements could have over me." And this wealth of movements, we learn in the note he provides, is precisely what had been repressed by an elementary school training in "this damned occidental stupidity, Swedish gymnastics" (OC II, 344).

The drum thus gives him a sense of what his body, shorn of its Western training, might be able to do. A brief glimpse of this virtual body appears as well in "Arriver à se réveiller" ("Managing to Wake Up"), a kind of Proustian recollection of awakening as spatial and temporal but also corporeal disorientation. "Without knowing exactly what kind of being I am . . . and moving in contradictory ways . . . I try with my numerous feet to pull myself out of sleep."[60] Michaux's preconscious body appears to him first as an insect body, then an animal or machine body, before losing these potential of ways of being and emerging as a human ambulatory mechanism. The text presents in its own terms an intuition that is far more developed in Eastern religions and spiritually oriented physical practices: that the body is a set of articulations that, with devoted practice, can be sublated into a Divine Body capable of moving in all ways. This Divine Body is associated in Michaux's works either with the preconscious body (caught between sleep and waking) or with that of the child. In "Dessiner l'écoulement du temps" ("Drawing the Passage of Time," 1957), however, he admits that even the child can only experience this "extraordinary," virtually limitless range of movements in fantasy: "In my childhood reveries . . .

I never was a prince or a conquerer," he notes, "but I was extraordinary in my movements [*mais j'étais extraordinaire en mouvements*]. A real prodigy in movements. A Proteus of movements."[61] Once again, as in "Signes," pure freedom of movement is relegated to the virtual; anything visible, performed on the stage of the social, is immediately a reduction of the kinetic possibilities entertained by the mind. The more the child moves internally, virtually (by means of *"gestes intérieurs"*), the less his real body is displaced ("there was no trace of these internal movements in my attitude/posture"). Indeed, his physical apathy grows in direct proportion to his internal agitation. The same ratio holds true for *Mouvements* during the making of which (as the author tells us in his "Postface") a total indolence germinated an *"inouïe mobilité,"* an unsuspected potential for kinesis, that achieved external form not as dance or athletic movement but as the movement series that was required to inscribe: "For most of my life, spread out on my bed, for interminable hours during which I never got bored, I brought to life two or three forms [at a time] . . . I filled one with an unheard-of mobility [*une inouïe mobilité*] of which I was at once the double and the motor, although I remained immobile and sluggish" (OC II, 598).

Michaux's description here in the "Postface" is telling: he describes himself as both the "double" and the "motor" of the *"inouïe mobilité"* the form (the sign-like mark) achieves. In other words, even while lying in bed (and thus eliminating as many habitual movements as possible), he provides the source of the kinetic energy that allows the inscriptive gesture to be performed and the sign-like mark to be inscribed. To that extent, he is the "motor," the source of the kinetic energy that is capable of "infusing" the inscriptive form with motility. Yet he is also simultaneously the "double" of this form's motility; he moves according to the way the form moves. As Michaux puts it, "their movement became my movement." As the "motor," then, he is the form's cause; but as the double, *he is the form's effect.* That is, the movements required to make the forms actually produce a new moving self and, as a result, a new "technique of the body." The self produced by this technique, this new gestural routine, is not some absolute, essential self but just that form of being that appears when he is inscribing the marks, a *performative* self phenomenalized by a set of inscriptive gestures and the particular quality of movement they require in order to be performed.

Moving as a body that inscribes

But can a movement-form really be called a "sign"? Michaux asks himself this very question in the conclusion of his "Postface." "Voilà," he attempts a reply, pointing rhetorically at the volume; Bertelé "urged me to take up once again the composition of my ideograms, resumed time and time again over a period of twenty years and abandoned for lack of success. I tried again," he tells us, "but gradually the forms 'in movement' eliminated the thought forms, the characters of composition. Why? I liked making them more. *Their movement became my movement.* The more I made, the more I existed. The more I wanted. Making them, I became utterly other (OC II, 598; added emphasis). If there exists a being called "Michaux" at this moment of kinetic possession, one who could be said to exist in ontological terms, it is not a "Michaux" as Cartesian mind but a "Michaux" as gesturing body. The self revealed is nothing *but* movement, or to put it differently, the self *is* the way the self moves. This does not mean, however, that the self's movements are untainted by cultural inflection (or freed from anatomical determination). Michaux, in movement, has not rediscovered some originary, essential way of moving but only a way of moving *as a body that inscribes.* The movements that define him are still those associated specifically with the gestural routines of inscription, and further, the dimensions of the page continue to circumscribe the space within which this self can be performed. Even though Michaux rejects the precise routines of the writing systems to which he has been exposed, it is the possibilities offered by miming symbol or character formation that dictate the scope and type of movements he can execute and thus the being he can become.

Ultimately, Michaux's comments reveal that his lifelong attempt at alphabet invention was less a quest for a universal language of intelligible signs than an exploration of the kinesthetic experience of making them, the experience, that is, of being a *writer* in the most literal sense, a practitioner of the physical technique called writing. Michaux was not a dancer or an athlete; he could not explore the sensations of his moving body through practices that were not his own. What he could do was seek to experience the sensation of the moving body by enlarging a practice with which he was all too familiar. His idea was to experiment not with any gestures whatsoever but specifically with the gestures of sign making, or the gestures of making sign-like things. In this respect, he is like a choreographer in quest of a new movement vocabulary entirely his own; by working through a previous training consciously, conscientiously, he discovers unexploited movement possibilities in the gestures he has already learned or is in the process of learning. Feeling the body move returns him to an experience of motility as a continuum underlying culturally imposed divisions of movement into communicative or instrumental units. The choreographer does not suddenly enter that continuum, as if miraculously freed from the need to shift weight, retain balance, pause for breath. Instead, the

choreographer extends, parses, and combines learned and borrowed gestures in new ways.

Michaux never achieves an ideal Archimedean point beyond culture,
beyond history; instead, through operations of skilling and simultaneous
deskilling, he reaches a point where the possibilities within the larger
practice we call inscription become more numerous and the movements a
sign-making body can make are exponentially increased. Michaux re-
launches the energy vectors of a corporeal practice we call writing in order to sound a broader range of the body as an instrument for making
marks. To the extent that he practices inscription as disarticulating and
recombinatory, a transgressive remixing of the given rather than an ex ni-
hilo creation of the purely other, he belongs to a radically antiprimitivist
tradition of theorizing resistance as parodic citation, or the performative
repetition of cultural codes. Michaux's accentuation of the gestural component in inscription has important implications for contemporary theories
of subjectivation, such as Judith Butler's theory of the performative construction of the gendered subject or Pierre Bourdieu's theory of subjectivity as constituted through acquisition of the *habitus*. Writing is just one
form of practical knowledge, one element of a much larger body of iterable corporeal practices; but what Michaux's experiment suggests is that
by exploring writing as a movement practice, we learn that our subjectivity is kinetically as well as discursively conditioned, and that we can resist our conditioning through citational practices involving movements as
well as words.

CHAPTER FIVE

The Gestural Performative:
Locating Agency in the Work of
Judith Butler and Frantz Fanon

T HE PHILOSOPHER who has presented the strongest case for approaching resistance as recombinatory and parodic is without doubt Judith Butler. In the realm of speculation, she has devised a theory that accounts in large measure for Michaux's attempts to alter acquired gestural routines through reiteration. Michaux's practice, however, constitutes both an actualization of Butler's theory of the performative and an implicit critical commentary on it. The continuities between the two are clear: both are interested in the conditioning of human subjects, and both discover within this very conditioning the means to subvert it. But there are also significant differences between Butler and Michaux that this chapter will reveal. By approaching Butler through Michaux, we can discern precisely which elements of her theory of subject construction need to be rethought. Her works are an excellent resource for analyzing the cultural function of performatives in general, but they are less convincing with respect to the role of the *gestural* performative in particular. At times, she seems to argue that subjects are constructed entirely by linguistic acts or enunciative positions afforded by discourse. At other moments, she allows for the possibility that "acts" other than speech acts—what she refers to as "acts, gestures and behaviors"—play a role in the construction of the subject. Speech acts and gestural acts, though, are not the same thing, a fact she does not consistently take into account. She tends to juxtapose theories of subject construction derived from linguistics and poststructuralism with those emerging from anthropology (the ritual theory of Victor Turner, in particular), treating verbal performatives and gestural performances as identical ontological forms. Her frequent recourse to anthropological approaches complicates the models she inherits from J. L. Austin, Derrida, Foucault, Lacan, and Althusser in ways she herself does not explore. Yet this confusion of paradigms (and acts) proves productive in the end. Her arguments in works such as *Gender Trouble: Feminism and the Subversion of Identity; Bodies That Matter: On the Discursive Limits of "Sex"*; and the frequently anthologized "Performative Acts and Gender Constitution"[1] are sufficiently wide-ranging (and her references sufficiently broad) to suggest a robust theory of the gestural performative that I would like to present in this chapter. I will attempt to bridge the gulf that remains between a theory of inscription as a performance of subjectivity, proposed in the last chapter, and Butler's theory of subjectivity as an inscription performed. As opposed to Michaux, Butler has a meager account of both embodiment and interoception. While insisting that inscriptions are "incorporated," "parodied," or "recombined," she neglects to theorize the performing body's proprioceptive, kinesthetic, even affective experience of moving in prescribed ways. This is a significant lacuna, for as I will show, it is ultimately kinesthetic experience, the somatic attention accorded to the lived sensation of movement, that allows the subject to become an agent in the making of herself. In the last section I turn to the example of racialization as opposed to gender construction, suggesting that as Butler anticipates, they both pose formidable obstacles to somatic experience (our ability to "drop away," as Merleau-Ponty would have it). However, through a reading of Frantz Fanon's "The Lived Experience of the Black Man," I suggest that a tenacious belief in and demand for such experience may be one of the greatest challenges to social construction the subject can pose.

Citing like a girl

The first shift that must be made when moving from Michaux to Butler is that the body in the equation has to be theorized from the start as a gendered body. Gender is not a privileged category of embodiment in Michaux, although of course it is implicitly evoked in his representation of the autobiographical self as a male subject. In contrast, Butler insists repeatedly that the identification of the body with a particular gender is coincident with social visibility and subjecthood as such. Sometimes it is difficult to determine precisely at what point Butler believes the en-gendering of the body occurs; this is in part because she works with a number of different theories of childhood development (Freud, Lacan, Torok, and Abraham) and subjectivation (Foucault, Althusser) that often enter into conflict with one another. In one of her strongest formulations—the one that returns most consistently in her works—she states that recognition of the body *as* a body is coincident with that body's gendering. "Bodies," she writes, "cannot be said to have a signifiable existence prior to the mark of their gender; the question then emerges: To what extent does the body *come into being* in and through the mark(s) of gender?"[2]

What remains opaque in this passage (as in many others) is whether the subject experiences any body-sense whatsoever prior to being discursively "marked" or "gendered." If coming-into-being means for Michaux to have bodily sensations, for Butler that is clearly not the case. In Butler's formulation, "coming into being" and possessing a "signifiable existence" appear to be one and the same thing; existence is only existence if it is "signifiable," a meaning transmittable as a sign to other bodies that are also legible as signs. In another unequivocal formulation, she puts it this way: "there is no recourse to a body that has not always already been interpreted by cultural meanings" (GT, 8). But it is one thing to say that human subjects have "no recourse" to a body without a cultural filter. It is quite another to say that the body has no "emergent" sense of a sensorimotor body in pregendered terms (to evoke Daniel Stern). As many theorists have remarked, Butler is equivocal when treating the problem of interoceptive experience.[3] Do sensations exist and exert pressure in their own right? Do they play any role whatsoever in the establishment and mutation of "cultural meanings"?

A further ambiguity troubles Butler's account. It is not clear in *Gender Trouble* that the gendering of the body—as a process of becoming-a-sign-for-others-to-interpret—occurs to the same extent or in the same way irrespective of the sign system engaged. Let us say, for the sake of argument, that the "mark" of gender ushering the subject into being (into "social legibility") is an anatomical "sign," the vagina. In most cultural scenarios of childbirth, the vagina is a sign—some would call it an "index"—of the female sex that the doctor or midwife knows how to read.[4] As soon as it is perceived, the vagina immediately becomes a sign circulating within a network of signs; it cannot remain a culturally neutral element of anatomy. Whether or not we believe that a vagina is linked of necessity to a female member of the species, it is clear that the objective ("material") element of anatomy, as soon as it is framed socially, will be charged with associations that are culturally imposed, not simply biologically determined. In any given setting, a certain number of attributes will be ascribed to the subject possessing a vagina, and a set of cultural assumptions about these attributes will be transmitted to the subject both through discursive acts and through patterns of behavior. From the perspective of a Butlerian analysis, the vagina-as-sign (like the penis-as-sign) is a constructed not a natural entity, and its discursive existence will be determined by the rules of discourse, not by anything intrinsic to its function or its neuronal connections to centers of sensation.

Following Althusser, Butler argues that the "mark" of gender is purely discursive (rather than anatomical), produced not by the child but by the discourse that precedes her and therefore conditions her "coming into being." That is, upon birth, anatomy is transformed into (interpreted as) a discursive category; the infant possessing a vagina is interpellated as a female child, given a female name, referred to as "she," and from that point on other socialized beings surrounding the infant will insert her into a prefabricated system of signs by which she is situated, culturally interpreted, constructed, overdetermined, marked. In Butler's scenario, the interpellation of the infant as a female child in effect creates her very "femaleness," exposing her to a battery of expectations for which neither her anatomy nor her physiology (i.e., hormonal composition) can be held responsible. The body is a "surface inscribed with meanings," in Butler's terminology, a form whose distinct parts have been assigned incontrovertible valences within a limited and limiting male/female dichotomy of signification.

But let us imagine a slightly different scenario, one in which the gender "female" is ascribed to a human figure not because of what that figure possesses anatomically but because of the way this figure moves. Such a scenario is analyzed by Iris Marion Young in "Throwing Like a Girl: A Phenomenology of Feminine Body Comportment, Motility, and Spatiality," a work Butler herself cites.[5] In the case Young describes, the identifying feature is not an element of anatomy but an acquired behavior, throwing a ball, a behavior that both reinforces and derives from a former en-gendering of the subject through discursive but also other, for example, punitive, means. Young cites a study authored by Erwin Straus that classifies one set of movements as typically female and another as typically male, arguing that a gestural routine, seemingly acquired, results of necessity from precise physiological differences between the sexes. Young responds by insisting that it is not biology that makes a girl "throw like a girl" but rather cultural conditioning. The reason girls do not mobilize the same quantity of force as boys, she states, is that the former have been taught to experience space—and their bodies in space—in a different way. Instead of mobilizing the entire body to propel an object, as boys do, girls concentrate the motion in one limb, misjudge the space they can encompass, and thus fail to "reach, extend, lean, stretch, and follow through in the direction" of their intention.[6] This is because, according to Young, "feminine existence lives space as enclosed or confining"; the female subject feels herself "positioned in space" rather than actively positioning something or someone else in space.[7] As a result of years of being observed and inhibited, the female body tends to underestimate its ability to fill and traverse space: "Typically, the feminine body underuses [sic] its real capacity, both as the potentiality of its physical size and strength and as the real skills and coordination that are available to it"; the space "that is *physically* available to the feminine body is frequently of greater radius than the space that she uses and inhabits."[8] Denied to the female body, it would seem, is proprioception as well as kinesthetic attention; in other words, not being able to feel oneself move in space is a peculiarly gendered experience. Further, this gendered privation of sensitivity to the moving self appears to be predicated on and produced by discursive commands and warnings: the young girl is "told that she must be careful not to get hurt, not to get dirty, not to tear her clothes, that the things she desires to do are dangerous for her. Thus she develops a bodily timidity that increases with age."[9] Young's analysis implies that not just throwing, but many other gestural routines as well are shaped, their elements and qualities determined, by cultural rather than physiological imperatives.

To a certain extent, the Butlerian approach can be applied to the scenario Young offers. Clearly, it is a pure construction to say that throwing a ball weakly and without good aim is a sign, or "mark," of being a "girl"; the association is not motivated by a biological difference between the throwing capacities of men and women. Nothing intrinsic to the female body requires that she throw in a weak and aimless manner. That she does so is merely a result of discursive conventions that produce physical inhibitions; and, tautologically, these physical inhibitions then legitimate further discursive reinforcement, as in phrases such as "she throws like a girl." Cultural rules, embedded in discourse, produce the behavior they claim to describe. Or, as Butler might put it, discursive acts performatively bring the gendered body into being.

What Butler's paradigm does not quite succeed in communicating, though, is that such acquired gender traits (gestural routines like throwing) bear a much less solid relation to a gendered anatomy than do the genital organs themselves. Statistically speaking, an overwhelming majority of subjects possessing vaginas show evidence of other attributes gendered female; but this is a claim that need not detain us here. What should give us pause is that most subjects who "throw like a girl," while still retaining other attributes gendered female (both anatomical and behavioral), can indeed learn to "throw like a boy." A female subject can learn to imitate, and thus "cite," in Butler's sense, the arm-shoulder-torso movements engaged by the normative boy in the act of throwing. As a result of repetition and training, bodily experience of the behavior (here, the gesture of throwing) can produce a situation in which the performance of the act does not correspond to the discursive existence it is given. Through retraining, dissonance can be created on the level of the gestural, and thus discursive norms can be brought into confrontation with movement practices in such a way as to subvert cultural expectations and challenge dichotomous structures.

It is clear, then, that the vagina as a mark of gender and the gesture ("throwing like a girl") as a mark of gender do *not* function at the same ontological or phenomenological levels. If we are to understand how performatives work to create the bodies they name, and if we are to gain any understanding of how resistance to the name occurs, then certain crucial distinctions between types of marks have to be maintained. Both the gesture and the anatomical feature are discursively mediated, received as "marks" of gender only because they are associated, in and by discourse, with one gender or the other. The crucial difference I want to underline here is that gestural routines are particularly vulnerable to processes of de-skilling and re-skilling; these processes undermine the culturally regulated body-discourse relation and produce intense kinesthetic and affective experiences of dissonance. To a surprising degree, an acquired action, an operating chain such as throwing a certain way, can be unlearned, and in certain cases resignified. In short, the moving, trained, and trainable body is always a potential source of resistance to the meanings it is required to bear.

Gestural routines arguably provide a broader field of experience rich with possibilities for experimentation, refinement, and—in a cultural frame—subversion. Practices involving the limbs and head are clearly visible and, because they involve several linked movements, can often be manipulated, remixed, thereby causing overt dissonance with respect to the gendered identities they are supposed to support. Is it possible, then, that "marks" of gender obtain differing degrees of hold on us, and that they offer different opportunities for resistance, depending on whether they are practices ("marks" as gestures or behaviors), parts of anatomy ("marks" as penises, vaginas, breasts, facial hair, etc.), or, a third category I will investigate at greater length, statements, or positions of enunciation? Are the three types of marks exactly the same? Do they all maintain the same relationship to the body they designate or produce the same effects?

The significance of these questions lies in their potential at once to complicate and enrich Butler's theory of the performative production of the gendered subject. Although throughout *Gender Trouble* and *Bodies That Matter* she shifts constantly between an analysis of discursive acts and an analysis of physical acts (what she calls "acts, gestures, and behaviors") she never pauses to consider the differences between them. This is at once the weakness of her theory and its most suggestive element. A closer look at what happens when a model of the performative derived from *speech* act theory is applied to gestures and behaviors reveals an essential feature of the body's gestural existence: Gestures, like discursive acts, need to be *repeated* in order to produce a socially legible body. In a sense, the most important point Butler makes is not that different varieties of gender (and en-gendering) "marks" are "read" by other cultural subjects but that these marks must be *repeatedly* presented and *repeatedly* read. The subject "performs" its gender and acquires a material body precisely insofar as it does so again and again. In this sense, then, the manifestation of the "marks"— if we consider these marks to be gestures—involves the acquisition of a kind of skill; not only being gendered but also being sexed, Butler will add, is something one acquires through mime (Leroi-Gourhan's "imitation by *dressage*"), adopts through verbal coaxing ("verbal communication"), or reaches through experiment ("the experience of groping [*tâtonnement*]").[10] As Butler states in a provocative passage in *Bodies That Matter*: "Construction [of the gendered body] not only takes place *in* time, but is itself a temporal process which operates through the reiteration of norms; sex is both produced and destabilized in the course of this reiteration. [The sexed body is] a sedimented effect of a reiterative or ritual practice."[11]

This formulation would seem to suggest that simply possessing the anatomical sign for female-ness is not enough to ensure the stable gendering of the subject or, what amounts to the same thing for Butler, material embodiment, since it would be impossible to reiterate "having a vagina" once one indeed has one. Rather, the anatomical feature must be interpreted as meaningful, and it is in this shift from being to being-for-the-other that construction occurs. So, too, must the gestures the gendered subject executes be perpetually reinserted into a dichotomous linguistic account: for example, "throwing like a girl" or "throwing like a boy." What it *feels* like to perform the act of throwing is never at issue for Butler since, in her stringently antiphenomenological axiomatics, feelings are always mediated by words that make those feelings available while alienating us from them. But if we follow Butler's argument to its logical conclusion, the repetition of gestures should produce as much dissonance as the repetition of discursive acts. If, as I argue in earlier chapters, the period of apprenticeship is an especially delicate one, replete with opportunities for gestural experiment and kinesthetic sensation, then the process of learning to bear the gendered gestural "mark" should also provide sufficient somatic knowledge with which to destabilize the mark and the hegemonic signifying system to which it belongs. But Butler does not pursue the implications of the comparisons between gestures as marks and words as marks that her argument puts into play.

Butler's expression "mark(s) of gender" is a notoriously vague way of referring to the signifiers—both embodied and verbal—that situate the body in the cultural sphere or, in a more radical formulation, that allow for its "coming into being." The term "marks" suggests that visual signs alone (marks can be seen, not heard) allow the body to achieve the status of significance, or interpretability. And indeed, there is a strong impetus at work in *Gender Trouble* to present "marks" as exclusively visual phenomena, available only to the eye. Visible properties of the body, such as dress, haircut, cosmetics, but also genitalia and secondary sex characteristics (facial hair, dimension of hips, and so on) constitute the "marks" that enter a hegemonic discursive economy productive of the body's "meaning." The word "marks" emphasizes that the gendered body is all a matter of exteriorization; what it feels like to have thicker facial hair, or wider hips, is qualitatively identical (from the outside) to the experience of what it feels like to wear lipstick or sport a buzz cut. It does not matter what it feels like to the subject because recourse to feeling has been lost (if it ever existed); the experience of having wider hips is always already culturally mediated by what it signifies in a given cultural situation. Even if having these hips produces a different way of walking, of bearing weight, and eventually of experiencing aging, the primary experience of hips is that they signify, culturally, just as wearing lipstick does. Frequently, Butler asserts that these marks are like inscriptions printed onto the body, inscriptions that become a legible text for culture to read. The specificity of the mark as a form of writing is a crucial element of her approach, one that relies on Derrida's (and Freud's) understanding of somatic and perceptual experience as a matter of laying down tracks, forging routes in the density of cerebral material. The term "marks" should not be taken lightly, then, since it evokes a tradition of analysis that employs a vocabulary drawn from the act of inscription that we now need to examine at closer range.

The dispersal of the subject

We should begin by noting that the *visible mark* of gender, such as wearing lipstick, and the *gestural mark* of gender, such as throwing without aim, are utterly different entities. This is not to say that there are not a lot of gestural "marks" involved in the visible ones; putting on "lipstick" involves a good deal of learning and also requires a specific set of movements, even an "operating chain." My point is simply that these distinctions between various types of "marks"—trundled together in Butler's text—are extremely important. Without attending to them, it is impossible to provide a more nuanced account of the en-gendering of the body, of its modes of social legibility, and, as I will suggest in my conclusion, of the multiple ways in which resistance to culturally dominant modes of subjectivation occurs. If, as Butler assures her reader repeatedly, the body is not merely a surface covered with marks, a passive support of inscription, then it is still necessary to determine just what kind of a support or surface the body is. The body also exerts pressure on discourse, Butler insists; however, she provides no account of how, when, and why this pressure makes itself felt.

Having drawn attention to the ambiguities introduced by the term "mark," I now want to examine in greater detail the sites in her argument where those ambiguities can become productive of a more nuanced theory of gender as embodied by gestures as well as words. To be sure, we must wait quite a while before encountering in Butler's works even an incipient theory of gesture; but if we are patient, such a theory does emerge. In *Gender Trouble* she is concerned primarily with establishing her first major insight, namely, that the subject (including its gender) is "conditioned" by discourse, and thus anything beyond the discursive must wait for another moment to be treated in full. In the early chapters she argues forcefully that there is no such thing as a "prediscursive" or "extradiscursive" moment of being, because all being is *being-for-another*—appearance, representation, social legibility, citation. For *this* Butler, all forms of being are filtered through speech acts, caught in the net of discourse, or, alternatively, denied discursive existence and thus relegated to the margins of social legibility. Butler mirrors this structure in her own text, where anything sensed or sensual is banished to the zone of the "inchoate," the untheorizable.

However clear this position might at first seem, it is rendered less secure by a multiplication of reiterations in which both the diction and the paradigms employed change. In fact, Butler brings to bear so many distinct (if overlapping) discourses in the course of her exposition that the status of the linguistic in the constitution of the subject becomes more difficult to define. There are at least five separate models of linguistic conditioning at play in *Gender Trouble,* and it is worth listing them and measuring their relative weights on her argument in order to determine precisely at what level she imagines language's intervention in subject formation to be located. I ask for my reader's patience as I clarify Butler's linguistic model of the verbal performative before demonstrating how it both facilitates and betrays an understanding of how the gestural performative works.

First and foremost, Butler is engaging Foucault's analysis of "discursive formations" as it is theorized in *The Archeology of Knowledge and the Discourse on Language* and *The History of Sexuality.* She will spend most of her energy applying a Foucauldian model of subjectivation to a study of gender and the body, and therefore my emphasis will also lie here. Second, Butler is invested in Althusser's theory of interpellation as adumbrated in "Ideology and Ideological State Apparatuses" in which the subject comes to exist "by virtue of [a] fundamental dependency on the address of the

Other."[12] Third, Lacan's Symbolic also makes regular cameo appearances throughout *Gender Trouble* and becomes the authorial voice in *Bodies That Matter,* especially. The Symbolic (as opposed to the discursive formation) provides "names" with which bodies can achieve social legibility and significance. Fourth, there appears in Butler's work a less rigorous but nonetheless facilitating use of the word "language," a general term that seems to mean something larger than "discourse," assimilable perhaps to the French *langue* meaning all words in general, or all elements of verbal and written linguistic signs in their diachronic multiplicity. Finally, Butler relies heavily on Derrida's reformulation of Austin's notion of the "performative speech act," especially in *Bodies That Matter* and *Excitable Speech: A Politics of the Performative.* Speech act theory is central to Butler's entire project, for it allows her to posit the necessity of reiteration, the ritualized repetition of speech acts that constitute the subject over time, and this necessity, in turn, allows her to develop a notion of subversive re-citation that we must situate at the very heart of her theory of parody as a form of politics.

Both Foucault and Derrida offer an important caveat that Althusser and Lacan do not. For the latter, the subject's constitution in language is definitive, unequivocal, and apparently not subject to revision. As Butler puts it, "in Althusser's notion of interpellation, it is the police who initiate the call or address by which a subject becomes socially constituted. . . . The call is formative, if not *per*formative, precisely because it initiates the individual into the subjected status of the subject" (BTM, 121). Further, for Butler's Althusser, the constitutive act is a matter of pronouns, "you," "he," "she," or, in Emile Benveniste's slightly modified schema, "I." Identifying the subject *as* a subject in effect conditions that subject, but it does so with pronouns, not with "predicates" and "adjectives," those parts of speech that will become increasingly important to Butler as she elaborates a theory of the repeated and diachronically unfolding construction of the subject through discursive acts, or statements. Similarly, the weakness of Lacan's notion of the Symbolic, for Butler's purposes, is that it situates the subjectivation of the subject at a precise moment of development and does not provide for the reiterative restagings responsible for securing the subject's social (phantasmatic) identity.[13] This is not to say that Althusser and Lacan lose their purchase for Butler. Much to the contrary: she retools their paradigms and makes them work well in the service of her own theoretical goals. But the advantage of the Foucauldian and Derridian models is that they establish the constitutive instance as necessarily multiple. For Derrida and Foucault, discursive acts do not remain consistent throughout time: discursive formations themselves change (Foucault), and the occasions for the reiteration of the speech act are never self-identical (Derrida). In other words, content (the verbal substance) and context (the existential situation of utterance or inscription) both play a role in altering the discursive act through which the subject is performed and received.

"Discourse" is a particularly fruitful term for Butler because in the philosophical texts she cites it is poised between two fields: the field of "acts" and the field of "words." Like "speech act," "discourse" can be allied with *praxis,* as in the syntagma Butler deploys (somewhat ambiguously), "discursive practice." Alternatively, "discourse" can be interpreted more narrowly as utterance, linguistic emission, unrelated to a corporeal operation. Although Butler would never want to dissociate discourse from practice, saying from doing, both possibilities are, as I will try to show, at play in her work. On the one hand, she clearly wants to draw the body into close proximity with the speech it utters (see especially *Excitable Speech*); on the other, however, she creates a theoretically unbridgeable gulf between discourse and how the body feels as it executes the movements that discourse interprets and renders socially legible. Presumably, any experience of movement the body might have is filtered—in Butler's stronger terms, "constituted"—by discursive performatives. That is, the discrete discourses belonging to the discursive formation provide only a limited set of interpretative tools for understanding the body, which can therefore be neither a source of awareness and knowledge nor a generator of language. It is in this sense that the body is cut off from discourse, that the two are dissociated in Butler's paradigm. At least on a first reading, the regulative function of the discursive formation appears to overwhelm, to keep in line, any friction the body's materiality might create.

Butler's own definition of "discursive formations"—"historically specific organizations of language"—is rather thin, but it rests on a large body of ruminations we will find elsewhere in Foucault. In *The Archeology of Knowledge and the Discourse on Language,* Foucault develops a theory of discursive formations with respect to two categories, individual self-expression (authorship) and disciplinary "fields," such as "psychopathology, medicine, or political economy," both of which will be pertinent to Butler's own model of subject construction.[14] In the first instance, Foucault introduces the term "discourse" in order to battle the firmly held belief that a corpus of written works can be "defined by a certain expressive function." A corpus does not incarnate a voice, he insists; it is not "the expression of the thought, the experience, the imagination, or the unconscious of the author" (AK, 24). Further, a corpus is not a "unity" of articulations but rather a heterogeneous aggregate of "irruptions," or discursive events, the rules of which must be studied in *historical* rather than linguistic or stylistic terms (AK, 25). For Butler, this will mean that a subject's supposedly "expressive" discursive acts (and, as a corollary, gestural acts) are in fact not the phenomenalization of a unique individual essence called "the self" but rather a set of citations drawn from the discursive (and gestural) possibilities for the subject's self-representation available at a given moment. In the second instance ("psychopathology, medicine"), Foucault is interested in showing that "fields" of discourse are not formed around a preexisting object (such as the madman) but instead constitute the object by means of a set of statements. Discourses are not languages with grammatical rules but sets of statements internally related and correlated according to a logic peculiar to the conditions in which the discourse emerges. A "language [*langue*]," he writes,

> is still a system for possible statements, a finite body of rules that authorizes an infinite number of performances. . . . The question posed by language analysis of some discursive fact or other is always: according to what rules has a particular statement been made, and consequently according to what rules could other similar statements be made? The description of the events of discourse poses a quite different question: how is it that one particular statement appeared rather than another? (AK, 27)

It is easy to see how the second question animates Butler's own inquiry. She, too, is concerned with circumscribing the social horizon within which gender possibilities (combinations of statements or gestures) may be, at any given moment in history, produced. She seeks therefore to determine the discursive formulas ("linguistic sequences") that are used not to describe constatively but to bring into being performatively a certain type of heterosexual subject. She wants to understand the power structures allowing "one particular statement [to] appear rather than another," one particular subject to appear rather than another, even when the objective, ahistorical rules of a language would permit other representations to be produced. Foucault's notion of "discursive formations" is indispensable to her argument, for it allows her to shift the focus from style as an expression of substance to the "discursive act," the performative utterance or gesture, as a product of a set of historically determined possibilities. "Irruptions" in the field of discourse (variations in the field of subjects) are conditioned rather than prevented by the discursive rules governing the generation of "linguistic sequences." A discursive analysis will therefore have two parts: it will attempt to account for how these "linguistic sequences" reflect specific social forces (here, the heterosexual imperative) and it will explore how possibilities for subversion are both "enabled" and "restrained" by discursive rules organizing the "linguistic sequences" concerned.[15]

Foucault's theory is without doubt the principal conceptual structure undergirding, even while producing discrepancies in, Butler's eclectic mode of argumentation. If we hope to understand better just what a "discursive formation" is and how it might generate "resistance"—in both verbal and gestural registers—we have to return to the texts in which Foucault defines the working tools of his analysis before applying them in *The History of Sexuality,* a text Butler frequently cites. *The Archaeology of Knowledge,* a combined translation of the two original French works *Archéologie du savoir* (1969) and *L'Ordre du discours* (1971), presents the most sustained and painstaking exploration of the discursive formation as a word-based but not exclusively linguistic phenomenon (not exclusively linguistic because productive of power relations within institutional and political structures). Here, Foucault provides as clear a definition of "discourse" and "discursive formation" as one can hope for. A "discourse" is "defined as the group of statements that belong to a single system or formation," for example, "clinical discourse, economic discourse, the discourse of natural history, psychiatric discourse" (AK, 108). Meanwhile, a "discursive formation" is "the law of such a series . . . , the principle of dispersion and redistribution, not of formulations, not of sentences, not of propositions, but of statements" (AK, 107).

But what is a statement *("énoncé")?* What are its "particular modalities of existence"? The "statement," Foucault responds, is neither a sentence nor a proposition. Unlike the latter, a statement serves specifically to make a *position for subjectivity available in discourse.* Statements create an "enunciative situation," they performatively bring into being a discursively valid subject—and that is why they are interesting to Butler. A statement requires that the subject assume precisely the same enunciative position each time the statement is pronounced. In contrast, a proposition is considered to have been repeated with exactitude if the *meaning* is the same, even if the situation of utterance and the subjectivity it instantiates have changed.[16]

The statement, then, is an enunciative operation that requires language and yet is productive of something beyond language, namely, a position a subject may hold, a power to inhabit language (and thus, for Foucault, culture) in a certain legitimated, coherent way. The position or site of enunciation the statement carves out for the subject is generated neither by an individual nor by a collectivity; it is, quite simply, a position allowed by the discursive formation to which the statement belongs. In this formulation, the concepts "authorship," "intentionality, and "agency" are rendered obsolete. The subject who performs the utterance (similar to the subject who performs the gesture) "is not the cause, origin, or starting-point of the phenomenon of the written or spoken articulation"; thus, the enunciative position provided by the verbal performance is nothing more than a "particular, vacant place that may in fact be filled by different individuals" (AK, 95).

The system would be purely tautological (a formation produces a subject that can be a subject in that formation) and largely uninteresting—at least for a theory of gestural resistance—if the formation itself did not generate and depend on linking multiple enunciative positions, not always in coherent or seamless ways. At any one point in time, Foucault contends, there are several statements available for the subject to make, multiple positions for him to fill. For instance, Foucault registers a "disparity" in the types of enunciative positions that can be assumed by the physician, his primary example in *The Archaeology* (AK, 54): playing many roles at once, the physician is offered statements that allow him to assume the position of a "perceiving, observing, describing, [or] teaching" subject (AK, 53). Interestingly, Foucault registers this multiplicity of subject positions *not* in order to unify them under the canopy of some existential subject named "the physician" but instead to demonstrate how the "various enunciative modalities" "manifest his [the unified subject's] dispersion" (AK, 54). In other words, the discursive formation brings into performative being not an integrated but rather a *dispersed* subject, one able to inhabit a variety of discursively constituted enunciative positions, the relations of which can only be marginally regulated by the laws of the discursive formation. Ironically, the discursive formation as it is pictured here is more enabling and generative (disseminating) than limiting and consolidating; by seeking to establish a purely discursive level for the analysis of the subject, Foucault replaces a cultural myth of the unified, intentional subject with the figure of a discursively constituted but dispersed one whose fulsome, phenomenal identity can be seized in no one group of statements, in no one "performance."[17]

Let us imagine, for a moment, what this might mean translated into the gestural register. First, this multiplicity of positions of enunciation might be compared to the multiplicity of skills or operating chains with which, in Leroi-Gourhan's analysis, a subject is equipped. The moving subject, in this scenario, would have at her disposal a rich background of chains to be recombined, just as the physician, in Foucault's example, might end up integrating in new ways the enunciative positions he can inhabit. Statements, affording enunciative positions, are "performative" in the sense that they lend an identity to a subject that does not exist prior to the statement. If we shift Foucault's thinking to the order of the gestural, we see that the gesture, similar to a "statement" (or performative speech act), defines a subject for culture, makes her legible to others; but by mastering a plethora of gestural sequences, and therefore a plethora of identities, the subject might recombine these identities in potentially subversive ways. Such a situation is dramatized by Michaux: When he juxtaposes the gestures necessary to produce various sign sets—calligraphic, Arabic, pictographic, and so on—he is attempting to access a motility flowing between them, a body defined by no single one. In this version of resistance and agency—which is, for now, incomplete—the emergence of the unpredictable and the new is exclusively a function of recombinatory audacity. In Foucault's paradigm, there is no reference to the kinesthetic experience that emerges from such juxtapositions, for the reason that he is speaking of statements (which produce far less kinesthetic feedback) and not gestures. But as we saw in the case of Michaux, the experience of recombination can itself produce kinesthetic knowledge ; the subject not only recombines existing elements of programs (enunciative positions) but also experiences the elements of these programs on the order of movement. And performing subjectivity, here, becomes a body-moving rather than meaning-making phenomenon. Interestingly, the experiential aspect of dispersal and recombination is noted not by Foucault but by Butler—and only when she buttresses Foucault's paradigm with another one that allows her to meditate on the processual (temporal) nature of subject constitution.

From iteration to alteration

In order to clarify how subversion might occur, and thus to forge a set of political practices that could replicate such conditions, Butler turns to yet another theory of the power of language in subject construction: Derrida's theory of the performative speech act as adumbrated in "Signature, Event, Context." As many commentators have noted, Butler's debt to Derrida's theory of performative iteration is extensive indeed. The influence of this theory can be felt throughout *Gender Trouble* (especially in the last chapter, where it is applied to "behaviors") but nowhere as forcefully as in the introduction to *Bodies That Matter*. Here, Butler makes her first full-fledged attempt to fold Derrida's theory of performative iteration into the rich batter that Foucault, Lacan, and Althusser have already provided. First, in high Foucauldian style, she states that for the purposes of her argument the "matter" of bodies (as well as gender and sexuality) will be understood not as prediscursive but instead as discursively constituted, "the effect of a dynamic of power" embodied in "discursive practices" (BTM, 2). But then Butler informs us that a second condition for the discursive construction of the subject also obtains: this time following Derrida, she argues that the performative speech act constituting the subject—the statement that lends him an enunciative position and thus identity—must be reiterated many times. "Performativity," she writes, must be understood "not as the act by which a subject brings into being what she/he names, but, rather, as that reiterative power of discourse to produce the phenomena that it regulates and constrains" (BTM, 2). Of course, "that reiterative power of discourse" is not something Foucault alone has established; rather, it is the central tenet of Derrida's position in "Signature, Event, Context." A few pages later, Derrida's influence emerges yet more clearly: "Performativity" is citational; it is "not a singular 'act,'" Butler asserts, "for it is always a reiteration of a norm or set of norms, and to the extent that it acquires an act-like status in the present, it conceals or dissimulates the conventions of which it is a repetition" (BTM, 12). The necessity to repeat speech acts or statements is thus built into the temporal structure of human existence and not into any one, given discursive formation. As a signifying being, the human subject must continue to instantiate herself in discourse (she must *repeatedly* assume positions of enunciation) if she is to go on "mattering," at all.

Here, resistance appears to arise from two interlocking phenomena: first, the subject's dispersal into numerous enunciative positions, that is, numerous performatives (and thus the possibility of recombining verbal or gestural chains), and second, the necessity to repeat performative acts (and thus the possibility in the course of performance of inflecting them in unpredictable ways). Butler concurs with Foucault insofar as she insists that verbal performances (and their combinations) are to a large extent governed by laws, or "norms" specific to the discursive formation; however, Butler's emphasis is different. If Foucault identifies as the source of "dispersion" (and therefore incoherence) the number of different enunciative positions offered to the subject within one discursive formation, Butler, following Derrida, locates the source of potential incoherence (and therefore subversion) in the fact that a single performance must be reiterated, an enunciative position repeatedly assumed, if it is to acquire and retain its effect. For Derrida and Butler, it is the nature of temporality, and not the discursive formation, that ensures that the subject will construct dissonant identities in language; it is language itself that produces a subject who is inconsistent, innovative, and dispersed. This is the gist of Derrida's critique of traditional speech-act theory in "Signature, Event, Context," a work that has been as central to the development of performance studies as it was to the acceleration of the linguistic turn.

Beginning with the act of writing, but soon broadening the context to speaking and communication in general, Derrida argues that the primary condition of language is that its units and sequences must be iterable. Otherwise, he remarks, they would not be recognized as part of a conventionalized, shared system of signs and could not operate within a signifying system. Transferred to the register of movement, this means that gestures must also be recognized as part of a conventional signifying system, that they are semiotically charged skilled behaviors and not untrained vehicles of pure expression. (If they were not conventional, they could not be recognized as gestures, as units of signifying movement, at all.) Paradoxically, though, the fact that signs are iterable means that their field of action cannot be circumscribed, their potential meanings cannot be controlled. Repetition can always become *alteration,* and it is this resource within sign languages, the condition of iterability, that both requires the establishment of strict conventions of performance and presages their transgression. The etymological root of the word *"itérabilité,"* Derrida claims, is the Sanskrit *itara,* meaning "other" *("autre").* The logic embedded in the word's historical evolution from otherness to sameness thus "links repetition to alterity."[18] Derrida proceeds to extend this logic from the individual sign to the performative speech act, which is conventional, ritualized, and iterable, thus vulnerable to alteration. Derrida's strategic move is crucial to the development of Butler's argument; if, as she contends, subjects are discursively brought into being by performative speech acts (or in Foucault's vocabulary, "statements" and compelled "rituals of confession"), then enunciations of subjectivity are not only repeatable but also potentially alterable in the course of being performed.

Under normative conditions, conventions of articulation and reception (the laws and rituals governing what the subject can say and do) ensure to some degree that repetition will successfully constitute the speaking subject in a consistent way. Similarly, in the gestural register, social codes impress on the mobile subject the necessity of gesturing in a coherent, legible fashion. But these conventions are notoriously susceptible to a wide variety of subversions, both intentional and unintentional. Derrida's forceful critique of Austin is lodged precisely here: to Derrida's mind, the vulnerability of all signifying acts—including the performative—is not sufficiently taken into account in Austin's framework. Austin does underline that performative utterances, in order to take effect (and produce the state they signify) necessitate "that the *circumstances* in which the words are pronounced be . . . appropriate."[19] But the contextual demands of the performative speech act in fact invite irregularities, inconsistencies, even perversions. In order for the performative to be "successful"—in Butler's terms, to constitute a coherent subject—it must offer precisely the same enunciative position to the subject each time it is pronounced. In other words, performative speech acts labor under the strain of having to produce a subject of enunciation that always speaks from the same place, with the same intention, and with the same predetermined, accompanying gestures in order to do its linguistic and cultural work.

As Derrida points out, this is the fragile but also promising state not simply of performatives ("I promise"; "I pray") but of *all* signs, the underlying principle of which is that they may be reiterated, or cited, in enunciative contexts both "appropriate" and not. Derrida thereby dilates the performative; suddenly its vulnerability to alteration characterizes all acts of communication—from written promises to spoken descriptions (and, I would add, Butler's "gestures, acts, and behaviors"). The danger that rules might be broken, that a statement might be cited out of its proper order (or that a gesture might be performed at an inappropriate time) is always present. "Citationality," iteration within or without the conventional context, is Derrida's term for this danger, this condition of potential *détournement* affecting acts of "communication."

Thus, in contrast with Foucault, Derrida implies that the production of alteration, or variation in performance, is not a result of dispersion, the multiplicity of discourses (and enunciative positions) available at any one point in time, but a characteristic of signs themselves. He states unequivocally that it is signs that "bear a force of rupture [*comporte une force de rupture*]," thereby attributing to language—not to discursive units and the power relations embedded in their formations—a type of energy (even agency) that discursive formations cannot hope to contain. In short, the power to alter belongs to language alone, not to some body or heroic agent of history or formation of a new discipline. If the subject is compelled to perform her identity repeatedly in language, this is not because her true identity lies *beyond* language but because language generates identities endlessly due to its own law of "supplementarity" (GT, 140). Butler echoes this conclusion in her own words: "The theories of feminist identity that elaborate predicates of color, sexuality, ethnicity, class, and able-bodiedness invariably close with an embarrassed 'etc.'" "Etc." is Butler's way of indicating the linguistic placeholder for that which it supposedly is not. "Through this horizontal trajectory of adjectives," she proceeds, "these positions"—"white," "middle-class," "female"—strive to encompass a situated subject but invariably fail to be complete. This failure, however, is instructive, she reassures us. "What political impetus is to be derived from the exasperated 'etc.' that so often occurs at the end of such lines? This is a sign of exhaustion"—presumably, the inability of the subject to discover herself in the enunciative positions she can assume—"as well as of *the illimitable process of signification itself*." And here, Butler reveals her cards: "It is the *supplément*, the excess that necessarily accompanies any effort to posit identity once and for all" (GT, 140; added emphasis).

In this tour-de-force summation, Butler deftly shifts the impetus for reiteration, the continuing effort to perform one's identity in discourse, from a subject's sense of a nondiscursive phenomenality onto "the illimitable process of signification itself" (GT, 140). That is, for Butler, the "etc." represents an excess in language, *not in being.* If we glance at her source, Derrida's *Of Grammatology,* the reasoning behind this shift is exposed. For Derrida, supplementarity guarantees not the retrieval or completion of the subject in language—the addition of more positions of enunciation, more opportunities to perform the self—but rather the "speculary dispossession" of subjectivity.[20] The need to keep talking, to keep performing, *to be a subject for others at all,* is a "law of language," not of embodiment or history. Alteration in reiteration is not an adventure of self-realization or resistance; it is not the result of a change in discursive formation. It is simply the product of the "law of the supplement . . . which at the same time institutes and deconstitutes me," appearing as aleatory as it is inevitable (OG, 141). The "law of language" emerges as the ultimate law, the ultimate source of agency and power.

Gesturing as citational

Butler's move from Foucault to Derrida may be enabling in some respects, but it does not help her to resolve the problem with which we began, the problem of agency in both gestural and verbal realms. She is forced to credit iterability itself, the prime characteristic of language, with what she calls "a certain agency": "the force of repetition in language may be the paradoxical condition by which a certain agency—not linked to a fiction of the ego as master of circumstance—is derived from the *impossibility* of choice" (BTM, 124; original emphasis). In *Gender Trouble,* Butler magnifies the law of language (supplementary reiteration) to encompass all systems of signs: "all signification takes place within the orbit of the compulsion to repeat; 'agency,' then, is to be located within the possibility of a variation on that repetition" (GT, 145).[21] But as soon as Butler denies "the fiction of the ego" and places agency squarely in the "orbit of the compulsion to repeat," resistance becomes a very slippery project indeed. Within the theoretical model she has borrowed from Derrida, there is no way to produce variations voluntarily. The linguistic sequence or performative act may be "lifted" "from the chain [*l'enchaînement*] in which it is given,"[22] and, as a result, "radical resignification" may indeed occur (BTM, 22). However, there is no subject who does the heavy "lifting," and signification thus emerges as the result of a purely linguistic law.

At the end of *Gender Trouble* Butler turns her attention from verbal performatives to reiterated "behaviors, acts, and practices" that she insists are governed by the same imperative, a *linguistic* compulsion to repeat. The tension between the performative speech act as an iterable linguistic unit and the performance of subjectivity as an embodied and contingent *act* nonetheless begins to obtrude. In the concluding chapters, "Subversive Bodily Acts" and "From Parody to Politics," Butler attempts to knead together the most purely text-based paradigm she has introduced thus far (Derrida's model of the *supplément*) with a paradigm of embodied behavior derived from anthropological ritual theory and performance studies. In an almost perverse refusal to theorize the differences between them, Butler employs simultaneously and without reservation two distinct vocabularies, one concerning "behaviors," "acts," "practices," and "gestures" drawn from Victor Turner's *Dramas, Fields, and Metaphors* and Clifford Geertz's *Local Knowledge,* the other characterized by terms such as "supplement" and "systems of signification" harking back to strictly linguistic modes of analysis.[23]

It would be disingenuous to fault a theorist for juxtaposing vocabularies and paradigms from discrete realms of analysis, since this is what theory so often does. And in some cases, Butler's remixing of "linguistic sequences" drawn from different discursive domains is both suggestive and exhilarating. However, in the case at hand, the juxtaposition reveals the serious fractures rather than the productive continuities between the discrete discourses. Butler seems to want to be able to refer in one breath to "bodily gestures" and "discursive acts" (GT, 140) without having to account for the difference between a "corporeal sign," a sign that *is* a moving body, and a verbal sign that is pronounced by that body. She claims that behaviors, gestures, and speech acts are all "*performative* in the sense that the essence or identity that they otherwise purport to express are *fabrications* manufactured and sustained through corporeal signs and other discursive means" (GT, 136; original emphasis). The phrasing of this last sentence operates a conflation of the discursive and the corporeal; stating that identities are fabricated "through corporeal signs and *other* discursive means" (added emphasis) makes it seem as though corporeal signs *were* just another variety of discursive means. But for the performing subject, the "corporeal sign" is more than discursive. The viewer of the "repeated acts" constituting gender identity may indeed produce a discursive transcription and interpretation of those acts, a legend for the gesture or "corporeal sign"; the subject who is moving may accept this interpretation as well. But the fact still remains that the gesture and the word inhabit different registers of experience as well as signification; corporeal and verbal signs possess different supports and therefore bear a different relation to the body they purportedly bring into being.

Paradoxically, the richness of Butler's work lies precisely here, at the point where the fracture between the corporeal and linguistic sign, the performed gesture and the performative speech act, opens wider. At first, she seems determined to underscore the proximity of performed gestures to speech acts. As in other ritual social dramas, the action of gender "requires a performance that is *repeated*" (GT, 140; original emphasis.) "Actions" of gender are, like performative speech acts, governed by ritualized conditions of iteration. The "repetition" of the gesture, Butler continues, "is at once a reenactment and reexperiencing of a set of meanings already socially established" (GT, 140). Consistently repeated, the "various acts" composing the gestural regime produce the gender they are believed to express: "Gender ought not to be construed as a stable identity or locus of agency from which various acts follow; rather, gender is an identity tenuously constituted in time, instituted in an exterior space through a *stylized repetition of acts* . . . in which bodily gestures, movements, and styles of various kinds constitute the illusion of an abiding gendered self" (GT, 140; original emphasis).

We can easily see how Butler has mapped a linguistic theory of subject construction through the regulated repetition of speech acts onto a scene in which gestures—not words—provide "the illusion of an abiding gendered self." Butler has created in this passage the outlines of what I call the *gestural performative,* coded and carefully policed movements that constitute an embodiment, a kinetic, corporeal support, for cultural (discursive) meanings. Presumably, the same rules obtain for the gestural performative as for the verbal performative. Just as the repeated citation of speech acts can either consolidate or subvert a normative identity, the reiteration ("citation" in a metaphorical sense) of gestures can either "reconsolidate naturalized identities" or produce "a dissonant and denaturalized performance that reveals the performative status of the natural self" (GT, 146). But a new problem appears: if the alteration of linguistic chains is a result of a *linguistic* law of signifying excess, why would the alteration and subversion of "acts" of gender, or kinetic chains, ever come to be? Unfortunately, the reasons why a "dissonant and denaturalized [corporeal] performance" should ever occur remain a mystery. In the linguistic example, an "excess" attributable to the functioning of the *linguistic system itself* is what encourages the proliferation of ever more sequences, ever more "cultural predicates" and "etc.'s." But what constitutes a similar "excess" on the order of the gestural? It is clear why gestures must be reiterated (social coercion), but what law propels their *alteration?* Why would gestures change over time and why would their cultural meanings evolve?

The body speaks back

The key to the solution, I believe, lies in a foreign term (at least "foreign" with respect to Butler's stringent antiphenomenalism) that manages to insinuate itself into her prose, namely, "reexperiencing"—found in the sentence quoted above: "This repetition is at once a reenactment and *reexperiencing* of a set of meanings already socially established" (GT, 140; added emphasis). Where, one cannot help asking, does this word "reexperiencing" come from and how does it differ from "reenact"? Is there actually a moment for Butler when subjects "reexperience"—and not simply act out again—a set of preestablished meanings? What would "reexperiencing" a "meaning" mean?

"Reexperiencing" a meaning is obviously not the same thing as reenacting it for others. An "act" and an "experience" are certainly co-implicated but they address different registers, only the second of which has epistemological connotations. "Reexperiencing" a "set of meanings already socially established" entails recognizing, once again, the meanings that a particular action is conveying to others. Butler may simply be referring to the way in which, through the repetition of an action, we regain a sense of what a gesture signifies within an intersubjective space. However, in recognizing the meaning the act is conveying to others, we inevitably become aware of movement as a conventional meaning-making practice. Such an awareness affords in turn the possibility of a critical distance from that practice. The subject, in "reexperiencing" social meanings, becomes alert to the distinction between meaning-making for others and being a material support for that meaning, or, more precisely, being a material *and animate* support for that meaning. In other words, the term "reexperience" offers the possibility that through repetition, through reen*act*ment, the subject may reexperience her own moving body *as an embodied sign*—that is, as a sign *and* as a form of embodied animation. Achieving awareness of the moving body as an embodied sign can, in certain cases, draw attention to moving as well as signing, or to moving as a sign-supporting endeavor in which movements are not necessarily identical to the meanings they support.

Following Butler, it is the act of repetition itself—an *act,* though, *not merely a repetition*—that allows for the "reexperiencing of a set of meanings already socially established." Butler's rich term—to "reexperience"—allows us to explore the possibility that perhaps it is only through repetition, and not acquisition, that we gain the experience we need to separate momentarily from our social roles. If this is the case, not only does conditioning "enable" the variations in performance it is supposedly designed to curtail, but it is absolutely essential (as I have claimed in earlier chapters) for developing the capacity to acknowledge the social construction of our movements. The reenactment of conditioned gestures is what affords the opportunity to sense a discrepancy between "a set of social meanings" and the complex kinetic-kinesthetic operations upon which they depend. Unfortunately, however, Butler does not explore the analytical promise of her term, nor does she pursue the implications of her notion that repeated *acts* render some form of experience in the process of iteration. The argument merely falls back on "repetition" (as opposed to the "reexperience") to explain the generation of discontinuities and dissonances. Such discontinuities and dissonances can only be attributed to accident, since the subject's own awareness of embodiment is never seriously considered as a possible source of agentic change.

Tweaking Butler's formulations just slightly—and stretching the analogy she herself puts into circulation—one could say that gestural "formations" (like discursive "formations") compel subjects to perform gestural routines (like discursive acts). These routines are similar to statements that provide positions of enunciation, for they too render the subject socially legible, they too produce a body coherently marked. The body's gestures would in this case be like marks that can be "read," discursively interpreted and given meanings according to discursive laws. However, if we are to follow Butler further, the body pressed into the service of inhabiting and promoting "socially established" meanings could not be seen simply as a silent material support, a surface that can be forced to signify in any way (according, for instance, to linguistic play). In Butler's own words, the capacity still exists to "reexperience" social meanings in the course of reenacting the gestural routines to which they apply. That is, conventional meanings associated with gestural "marks" could be reexperienced as such, that is, as conventional gestures bearing conventional meanings. Then dissonance could arise from a *gap* between the meaning discursively attributed to the movement and movement itself as an animate (as opposed to disembodied) support. Such, at least, is the promise of Butler's phenomenological claim at the end of "Subversive Bodily Acts."

Yet Butler's thesis depends on our willingness to accept three premises that contradict the logic of this claim: 1) that embodied signs (gestures) are identical to disembodied signs (words); 2) that a *linguistic* law demands iteration and affords alteration in both cases; and 3) that therefore all alteration (and subversion) of the gestural routine is a result of a repetition governed purely by the linguistic law of iteration as opposed to a reenactment mobilizing an animate, sensorimotor system governed by laws of its own. None of these premises can be maintained if we give any currency to the notion of "reexperience" generated through the repetition of gestural routines. Thus, when Butler introduces the term, and more broadly, when she addresses *performance* as opposed to the performative, she contradicts her own constructivist stance, hinting at the epistemological force of a properly kinesthetic-somatic experience of performance that could be *meaning-making* as well as subservient to meanings already made.

Responding in *Bodies That Matter* to accusations of "somatophobia"[24] received after the publication of *Gender Trouble,* Butler offers the following compromise: It is not in fact the case that "on the one hand, the body is simply linguistic stuff or, on the other, that it has no bearing on language. It bears on language all the time" (BTM, 68). But precisely how does that "bearing on" make itself evident? How is the body registered on the surface of language? "Bear on" implies the exertion of a kind of pressure, like that of an imprint on a vulnerable surface. If the body "bears on language all the time," then, given Butler's formulation, the inscriptive pressure of language on the body must be matched by *the inscriptive pressure of the body on language.* But at what point, and in what way, does the body inscribe itself on language? If the body is not simply a passive surface, then it must leave its own types of imprint, it must produce its own variety of knowledge to which language will attend in its own, albeit limited way.

By the end of *Gender Trouble* Butler finds herself at a strange pass with respect to the body and its "reexperience" of the cultural meanings embedded in—but detachable from—gestural practice. In earlier chapters, she has eliminated the possibility held out by Foucault in *The History of Sexuality* that the body's "pleasures" and "sensations" (experienced in the act of executing certain movements) might provide a source of friction within the meaning-making machine. Butler time and again rejects recourse to a prediscursive or extradiscursive order of bodily "pleasures" and "sensations" as she attempts to root out the last traces of emancipatory rhetoric she finds in texts by Foucault (as well as by Monique Wittig and Julia Kristeva). To be true to her argument, Butler has to reduce "reexperiencing" to a cognitive act in which it is *meaning* that is reexperienced, not the body's own sensations of reenacting. But what does it mean to "reexperience" a meaning if not to live it with one's body, to struggle to achieve (or fail to achieve) harmony between a movement practice and its symbolic import.

To "reexperience" the socially established meaning of a curtsy, for instance, would be to know that one is conveying "grace" and "femininity" (the "set of meanings already socially established") as one rotates the femurs outward in the hip sockets and drops weight into the knees. But what if in performing the curtsy the subject felt not only "feminine" but also sore? What if the socially established meaning of the act were over-whelmed, at least momentarily, by the somatic experiences of pressure, friction, and pain? What if, in other words, the body spoke back?

These are questions that Butler, at least in these works, chooses not to pursue.[25] In the course of "Subversive Bodily Acts," she treats "reexperiencing" as a purely cognitive operation of seizing (or re-seizing) the "already socially established" meanings of one's kinetic acts. She thus fails to theorize "reexperiencing" as a movement process involving kinesthetic-somatic awareness of the body as it tries to inhabit these meanings. She loses a valuable opportunity to consider the dual nature of "reexperiencing" movement. At least for the practitioner, what is reexperienced is both the cultural meaning of the movement ("My curtsy is feminine and grace-ful") and the sensation of performing it ("It strains my knees to hold this position for a long time"). The gendered body that comes into being in the process of moving is not simply a signifying-body, a corporeal *sign*. What is also brought into being as a result of moving in a certain way, as a result of reiterating a gestural performance, is another type of "etc.," a kinesthetic, proprioceptive, and somatic experience that exerts a force on language all its own.

It is for this reason that gestural performatives and verbal performatives are not identical. Both "bring into being" a gendered body that may not have existed in that form prior to the performance. However, the gesture is both a sign, a parsed unit of a continuum, and a potential movement experience, an exertion of energy that belongs to a continuum of energy exertion. It is entirely possible to consider gestures from the perspective of words (many linguists still do).[26] Similar to verbal phrases (performative speech acts), gestures can also be analytically decomposed. Just as words are conventionally meaningful "packages of speech production" that can be divided into "tone units" (to cite Adam Kendon), gestures are conventionally meaningful "packages" of movement production that can be divided into "gesture units."[27] An effort to reduce gestures to words, however, always comes up against the demonstrable reality that a gesture contains a far fuller range of movement than simply the meaningful component, what Kendon calls the semiotically loaded "stroke." As Sha Xin Wei has eloquently argued, no matter how relentlessly linguists attempt to "divide the stream of gesture into equivalence classes," no matter how hard they try to "subsume gesture into the category of spoken language," there remains the "parsing problem": "Where and when does one gesture end and another begin?"[28] This problem plagues the analysis not simply of semiotic gestures, such as pointing or waving, but all gestures, including those that "mark" a certain gender as well as those that belong to skilled gestural routines.[29]

Thus there are limits to the assimilation of gestures to a variety of performative act. Assuming a position of enunciation, representing oneself in discourse, provides different opportunities from those afforded by the enactment and reenactment of a gendered self. A problem Butler never overtly acknowledges is that speaking in and of itself, although it does indeed involve the lips, tongue, nose, and vocal cords, demands a far smaller commitment from the kinetic body than executing gestures or gestural routines, from "doing the '*onioi*'" (or, in another tradition, curtsying) to donning such gendered accessories as stockings, high heels, or a tie. If "gender," "sex," "body," and "materiality" were simply a matter of consistently reiterating the same performative *speech* acts, then indeed, little pressure from that "excess," that unnameable extradiscursive body that supposedly "bears on language," would be registered. The fact that we so rarely register the pressure of unpleasant sensations is proof that even the larger en-gendering techniques of the body (such as modest smiling or curtsying) have a remarkably firm grip on the body. The socially preestablished meanings of these acts are difficult (and sometimes impossible) to dislodge. This is due, according to Mauss, to the social efficacy of the gendered gesture, the validation it confers, the position of "enunciation" it accords. However, when enacting a gendered gesture produces unpleasant sensations that can no longer be tolerated, when "efficacy" is eclipsed by tension or pain, then pressure from *something other than language* has made itself felt. This "something other than language" is, I submit, agentic. It instantiates a nonlinguistic law that culture, in its turn, must at times observe.

Finally, it is the doing-body, not the speaking body, that senses most urgently the dissonance, the lack of adequation, between a cultural meaning and the embodiment of that meaning, between what the subject is supposed to be signifying and how she feels. And this sensation of dissonance is a product not of repetition in language but of *repetition in practice*. Further, the embodied, sensate subject, the one who executes the gestures that constitute gendered identities (or their parody), is not an "excess" in some abstract sense but a singular body, brought into being again and again by adapting to particular (not universal) and enculturated (not "human") ways of moving. Embodying performative gestures is always a contingent performance, one that generates an experience of the body *as it moves,* not a body as it looks in the mirror, or as it is instantiated in words. Experience of the body may indeed be "discursively conditioned" (GT, 17), but through repeated opportunities to perform, discourses—and with them the subjects they constitute—are in turn *kinesthetically* conditioned. How we feel in the process of enacting our discursively constructed gender behaviors—how we feel when citing gestures and conveying their preestablished meanings—

has an impact on the ways we perform gestures and the new meanings they acquire. The repeated experience of performing discursively mediated gestures can produce sensations that compel us to alter the variety, quality, and sequence of the movements that realize our words.

The dissonance of race

There is no doubt that Butler's theory of performativity, however problematic, succeeds in presenting a major challenge to phenomenological celebrations of interoceptive experience. Even if we maintain, as Butler appears to, that some variety of extralinguistic experience is available (if only in the form of a dissonant "reexperience" of the meanings one's body is supposed to convey), we must admit that, *pace* Merleau-Ponty, social forces can seriously constrain our ability to "drop away" from cultural meanings at will. At the very least, Butler forces us to acknowledge the huge impediments to interoception erected by the gendering of the subject through the enforcement (and rewarding) of particular positions of enunciation and ways of behaving. It seems reasonable to inquire, then, whether equally formidable constraints are placed on the *racialized* subject as he or she attempts to experience the body as a source of resistance against the violent oppression of racial stereotyping. If gender is imprinted on the moving body at birth, at what point and in what ways does race become a mark that bodies bear? Do racially identified verbal and gestural performatives construct the racialized subject, frustrating all attempts to live the body beyond their reach?

I want to close this chapter by considering the barriers to interoceptive (or "somatic") experience encountered during the process of racialization, barriers I have associated with the stilling of the body caused by advanced technologies (in Chapter 3) and with the gendering of the body (in this chapter). In this case, I will allow Frantz Fanon's *Black Skin, White Masks* to frame my approach, thus shifting vocabularies slightly but always keeping in mind Butler's arguments and the pertinence of her terms. I cannot hope to take on the issue of racial subjectivation in any thorough manner, but intend simply to explore Fanon's understanding of its consequences on embodiment and agency as he depicts them in a short anecdote from *Black Skin, White Masks*. My questions will be as follows: Is the raced subject, similar in this regard to Butler's gendered one, depicted by Fanon as forever alienated from the sensations and related meanings that constitute a unique embodiment? Do marks of race, like those of gender, short-circuit any agency that might inhere in a heightened sensitivity to the gesturing self?

One of the first French philosophers to examine the consequences of racial socialization and its effects on bodily awareness was Jean-Paul Sartre, a major influence on Lacan (and thus Butler) as well as Fanon. In *Being and Nothingness*, Sartre only mentions in passing that race plays a role in the dialectic of identity, the constitution of the self through a relation with *"autrui"* (others). However, his comments provide a basis for the more profound meditation on bodily awareness and its relation to gestures that Fanon pursues in *Black Skin, White Masks* of 1952. *Being and Nothingness* is also the source of many of Butler's own theoretical presuppositions (filtered through Lacan), so Fanon's nuanced critique of Sartre serves, albeit indirectly, as a critique of Butler's work as well. Through a reading of Sartre's understanding of the body, Fanon ends up confirming that what he calls "first person experience," or interoceptive awareness, *must* be accessible to consciousness if any freedom from stereotyping constructions is ever to be won.

If bodily awareness assumes a positive value in *Black Skin, White Masks,* in Sartre's monumental tome this is not the case. The body is introduced in *Being and Nothingness* as an inescapable materiality, what Sartre calls the "facticity" of the self that determines the limits of what the subject can be. "Facticity," Sartre acknowledges, is what ensures that the subject will have a point of view *at all;* without the facticity of the body we simply would not exist in human form. But the body is nonetheless something we "suffer," a condition that no permutations of language will let us escape or forget . Although the nature of a subject's facticity apparently includes both social and biological determinants, Sartre chooses to begin by associating facticity with the specific situation into which a subject is born: "my *birth,*" he writes, "as it conditions the way in which objects are revealed to me (. . . there are barriers in my hodological space)."[30] This very general and inevitable condition—simply the fact of being born at a specific place, at a specific time—is seconded by more precise, socially constituted situations, including *"my race* as it is indicated by the Other's attitude with regard to me (these attitudes are revealed as scornful or admiring, as trusting or distrusting)" and *"my class* as it is disclosed by the revelation of the social community to which I belong inasmuch as the places which I frequent refer to it."[31] Although Sartre does not explicitly mention gender as a salient category, it makes sense to imagine gender as yet another "situation," like race, into which the subject is born.

Fanon adopts in large measure Sartre's model of how the subject is fixed ("revealed") in racial or class terms, for it allows him to posit race as a social rather than biological factor in the body's facticity. But for Fanon, race is not merely one element of contingency among others; instead, race is the historically specific form of contingency that governs the rest, making it virtually impossible for the raced subject to experience existence in other ways—as "the revelation of a community" (class) or as "the way in which objects are revealed" ("hodological space"). Racialization works insidiously to undermine not only accidents of birth and nuances of class but even the subject's experience of other, less socially determined aspects of his facticity, such as orientation in space, a kinesthetic background, a sensitivity to touch. Fanon agrees that, as Sartre puts it, one's corporeal facticity is always to some extent mediated, primarily by others' perceptions and the words they use. But Fanon notes that in the case of the black man, the perceptions of others—*white* others—reduce him to an epidermal existence and thereby produce an alienation from bodily awareness more devastating and far-reaching in its effects. "If," Fanon muses in "The Lived Experience of the Black Man," "Sartre's speculations on the existence of 'the Other' remain correct (insofar as, we may recall, *Being and Nothingness* describes an alienated consciousness), their application to a black consciousness proves fallacious"; this is because "the white man," Fanon pursues, "is not only 'the Other,' but also the master, whether real or imaginary."[32] Whereas Sartre's dialectic of (white) identity includes a moment when the subject *recognizes* himself in the other and is recognized by the other in turn, in Fanon's dialectic of identity this moment of mutual recognition cannot occur.[33]

For Fanon, the colonial situation presents a particularly virulent challenge to black subjectivation, for it imposes a form of linguistic interpellation and visible marking that—*pace* Butler—subjugates *without enabling*. "As long as the black man remains on his home territory, except for petty internal quarrels, he will not have to experience his being for others," Fanon begins (F, 89). During his childhood, a black man might manage to avoid confronting the withering regard of the white other by which he is transfixed. But inevitably, "in the weltanschauung of a colonized people, there is an impurity or a flaw . . . For not only must the black man be black; he must be black in relation to the white man" (F, 89–90). This state of enslavement, the state of being little more than a "being for another" *("être pour l'autre")* cannot be overcome *("dépassé")* by a black subject within a white environment. *"L'autre"* is not a similar being, one who depends for his identity on recognition from the other in turn, but rather "the master, real or imaginary." Under the eye and through the voice of this "master," the colonized subject is incapable of living his "blackness" *("être noir")* in any other way than that defined by the colonizer—as an appearance, a visible spectacle, a mask. The black subject has no access to the type of experience Sartre posits as necessary for the acquisition of subjectivity: a self-reflexive grasp of the body's own invisible processes and the way they inform the subject's "projects" and way of being in the world. Fanon puts it as follows: "In the white world, the man of color encounters difficulties in elaborating his *body schema*. Knowledge of one's body is a purely negative activity. It is a knowledge in the third person" (F, 90; added emphasis).[34]

The colonized subject, Fanon tell us, has been deprived of his "body schema" by the infiltration of an insidious "historical-racial schema" that appears not at birth but once exposure to the white world has begun. Citing Jean Lhermitte's *L'Image de notre corps* (The image of our body), Fanon explains: "The data I used [to construct a self] were provided not by 'remnants [*résidus*] of feelings and notions of a tactile, vestibular, kinesthetic, or visual nature'"; instead, the elements of what he calls a "historico-racial body schema" have been furnished "by the Other, the white man, who had woven me out of a thousand details, anecdotes, and stories" (F, 91). Rehearsing the normative psychophysiological scenario, Fanon observes: "I thought I was being asked to construct a physiological self, to balance space and localize sensations"; he, too, should have been able to continue constructing a body schema from the *"résidus"* of interoceptive sensations. But, according to his allegory of racial subjectivation, he is prevented from doing so by the forceful intervention of both the white gaze and the white word:

> "Look! A Negro!" It was an external stimulus that pricked me in passing.
> "Look! A Negro!" I attempted a smile.
> "Look! A Negro!"
> (F, 91; translation modified)

In this drama of interpellation, "the body schema, attacked in several places by an "external stimulus" ("stories," and "anecdotes") collapses, giving way to an epidermal "historical-racial schema" that will prove difficult to displace (F, 92). The body schema, which Fanon tells us is built from an interwoven fabric of sensations, is replaced with a label, an affect-laden sign ("A Negro!"), a mark in Butler's sense. As in Sartre's scenario, "it is language which teaches me my body's structures for the other";[35] but here, in Fanon's example, the structures of the body have been reduced to nothing more than a skin color and a set of stereotypes that no somatic sensitivities can mediate in turn.

At stake in Fanon's narrative is precisely what we saw earlier in the account of subjectivation offered by Butler: the subject's ability to know her body as a positive presence and thus to differ from the role she has been called on (by and for others) to perform. Ostensibly, neither the gendered nor the raced subject has access to interoceptive sensations—or a "body schema"—that would mediate and inform the self. However, Fanon differs from Butler insofar as he posits a normative social conditioning—situated in the protected sphere of the African home—in which a sense of the body is encouraged and even celebrated rather than eclipsed by a racial socialization that is occurring on both the verbal and behavioral registers. What appears in Butler's account as a generalized distortion—every subject in culture is gendered and thus every subject undergoes alienation from sensation—is treated by Fanon as a pathology peculiar to the colonial condition. In order to measure the distance that separates Butler from Fanon, and thus a poststructuralist gender critique from an existentialist theory of racialization, we must recall that it is to the classic theory of the body schema that Fanon is alluding in *Black Skin, White Masks*. Fanon's references are to the "postural model" of the body, an avatar of the body schema developed by Henry Head that informs the work of Merleau-Ponty. Fanon adopts a psychoanalytic model that situates body awareness somewhere between the primarily kinesthetic-proprioceptive *body schema*, or "postural model," introduced by Henry Head in the 1920s and the scopic *body image* presented by Paul Schilder in 1950. As opposed to Butler, who is writing after the shift in psychiatric terminology introduced by Schilder, Fanon is writing *as this shift is occurring*. He thus preserves Head's notion that interoceptive sensations inform comportment while acknowledging the role that visual images can play in the construction of an embodied sense of self.[36]

Head's ground-breaking work in the areas of neurology, aphasia, cutaneous sensation, and proprioception laid the groundwork for the psychological approaches to which Fanon was exposed during his training and which he mobilizes to serve his anticolonial critique in *Black Skin, White Masks*.[37] At the same time, Fanon would have been familiar with Henri Wallon's studies on the significance of visual experience to identity formation, studies that were popularized by Lacan. Wallon's clinical research on the tension between optical perception and interoceptive sensation furthered the notion that a subject's sense of her own body depends heavily on visual images, especially those coming from without. Lacan's adoption of Wallon's studies and his melodramatic exaggeration of the significance of the "scopic drive" set psychoanalysis on a new path and resulted in an almost complete eclipse of Head's research (if not for its retrieval in the work of Merleau-Ponty). Paradoxically, Schilder, often credited with developing the notion of the "body image" and thus contributing to the neglect of Head's theories, actually strikes a balance between Head's emphasis on somatic sensations and Lacan's emphasis on an alienating visual gestalt.[38] It is Schilder who insists that the body schema contains and integrates *but is not subsumed by* visualizations of the body, and that this body schema, which he then renames the "body image," is at times available to consciousness, influencing the way a subject behaves through a recursive self-correction that allows the image to evolve in time.[39] In sum, Schilder's elastic model of an evolving body image is far closer to Fanon's understanding than is the Lacanian model favored by Butler. Whereas in the Lacanian-Butlerian scenario every form of kinesthetic, tactile, and proprioceptive sensation appears to be foreclosed by the gaze (dramatized as the mirror image but also inhering in the images of others one introjects), in contrast, Fanon seems to believe that at least a semiconscious, operative body awareness is available to—and constitutive of—the subject beyond or before the grip of a colonial world.

Fanon's use of the term "body schema" clearly situates him in a particular tradition, one that accords to the body a capacity that poststructuralists later deny. To his mind, the body schema—as an empirical reality but also an idea—is a tool with which to resist racial stereotyping and the domination of the colonial eye. In evoking the body schema in this context, Fanon not only enriches the work of the clinicians he studies but also anticipates the return in numerous scientific disciplines to a conception of interoception as a fundamental and abiding resource of individual agency.[40] As Fanon illustrates in "The Lived Experience of the Black Man," it is precisely an ability to feel the body poised or moving through space (a body *schema*) that the black subject lacks. To exist solely as a legible surface without depth, as a black skin without cutaneous sensation, is the *"malédiction corporelle"*—the embodied curse—of the *racialized* body" (F, 90). Fanon associates the eclipse of a body schema to which the subject may consciously attend with a very particular historical predicament. And Fanon *must* posit the existence of a more-than-visual sense of the self, obfuscated by colonialism, if he is to ground his critique of colonialism. He thus indirectly argues for the possibility of a somatic existence that Butler asserts is unavailable to all subjects of social conditioning and interpellation. Since, in Fanon's understanding, a first person experience of the body can supplement—and in the case of racial stereotyping, contradict—the body image that others have forged and imposed on the subject, it is absolutely critical that such a first person experience be reclaimed.

But how does Fanon propose to reclaim this lost sensitivity to the sensations of one's own body? How can the effects of a colonial socialization be reversed? More to the point, how can a subversive *re*experiencing of colonial "meanings" be achieved through the reenactment of the gestures a colonized subject is required to perform?

Suffering the body

The pages of "The Lived Experience of the Black Man" trace a trajectory familiar to readers since Aimé Césaire's *Notebook of a Return to the Native Land* in which a colonial subject, in search of lost identity, assumes a series of borrowed voices and masks before reclaiming an authentic self. What is fascinating about Fanon's version is that although he desires solidarity with others, his primary commitment is to a sensory reclamation of himself. The two alternatives Negritude offers him are thus rejected in turn: Neither an affirmation of an African community at one with the cosmos (derived from Leo Frobenius) nor the recuperation of a courtly, civilized ancestry (Victor Schoelcher's contribution) can rescue the subject from the pervasive sense of self-alienation he feels. Even the dialectical assumption of race as a situation that can be overcome (Sartre's solution in *Black Orpheus*) fails to convince Fanon.[41] For ultimately Fanon seeks to satisfy his need for a body schema that will reflect the specificities of his own embodiment, an embodiment that includes a racialized body image he shares with other black subjects but that could integrate other sensations as well.

Fanon's first step, then, is *not* to seek a collective solution to the dilemma of self-alienation, even though he recognizes such alienation in others (and is certainly not blind to the need for political resistance). Privileging introspection in "The Lived Experience of the Black Man," he sets out to recuperate the most intimate and inarticulate variety of knowledge about himself, attempting thereby to reverse the process of subjectivation that a colonial situation has imposed. This intimate knowledge would, if achieved, demonstrate the equality of his race by confirming what Sartre terms his *"pour soi,"* the possibility for a black subject to be *for himself,* rather than simply for others. By recovering a kinesthetic-proprioceptive-tactile self-awareness, Fanon hopes to regain for his race what colonization took away: a body schema, the ability to feel oneself stationed or moving in space. For ultimately, in the words of Fanon, the result of colonial subjectivation has been nothing other than a loss of *Erlebnis* understood as lived experience, bodily awareness, and the riches of sensation. As he describes the situation allegorically, when confronted by the withering, reifying white gaze, the subject finds himself deprived even of the power to localize his own being-in-the-world: "in truth I say, my shoulders slipped away from the structure of the world, *my feet no longer felt the caress of the earth*" (F, 116–117; modified translation; added emphasis).

This experience of slipping through the air, of failing to feel the earth beneath one's feet, evokes a state of confusion, even suffering, but this suffering, Fanon reminds us, is the very opposite of the suffering Sartre associates with bearing the facticity of a situated, material core. "Jean-Paul Sartre," Fanon states emphatically, "forgets that the black man suffers in his body quite differently from the white man" (F, 117). Fanon's assertion is a direct response to Sartre's argument in *Being and Nothingness* that the body is *"suffered,"* that the facticity of embodiment is a type of imprisonment in an earthly form.[42] To Sartre's mind, awareness of this facticity is also an awareness of one's limits, a knowledge that one's projects and possibilities for becoming are constrained by what the body can and cannot do. Sartre describes the body "suffered" as a *"fond"* (background), evoking the same term found in Heidegger and Merleau-Ponty. But for Sartre, this *"fond,"* or somatic background to consciousness, is not to be unambiguously celebrated, for it is always tinged with a sickly glow. He famously associates this vague background of bodily awareness with "nausea": it reminds us that we are bodies that have autonomous functions, decay, and grow old.[43] Yet ultimately, "suffering the body" is still a highly significant state because, for Sartre, it frees us ever so slightly from the hegemony of those understandings we derive from without (from *autrui*). In Fanon's interpretation, though, what is suffered by the black subject is precisely the *inability* to "suffer" the body, to access consciousness's lived material core. The *"corps souffert"* is denied to the racialized subject, who can only know his body "in the third person," as a body observed. Suffering the body, for Fanon is salutory and liberational insofar as it offers a counter to the "historico-racial body schema" that steals the subject's interiority away.

Finally, if Fanon cannot feel the caress of the earth beneath his feet, not only does he lack a register of apprehensions that should inform his understanding of his position, his orientation in space, but more, *he is deprived of the empowerment derived from that understanding;* he cannot recursively self-correct, seek greater contact, *"tâtonner,"* and thus *act* in a less automatic way. One of the most curious aspects of the existential philosophy Fanon adopts is that whereas on the explicit level it grants to consciousness alone the potential for self-creation (consciousness "transcends" the texture of facticity), and while the facticity of the body thus appears to "imprison" the subject and limit his possibilities, it is also true that such facticity can be mobilized to counter the "suffocating reification" that is the colonial subject's fate. Implicitly in Sartre's discussion, kinesis and the sensations it engenders are also a source of possibilities offering freedom from situational constraints. For instance, when experienced as potential, as the "*possibility which I am* of walking, running, or of playing," Sartre says, the leg becomes not an observed attribute but a guarantee of multiple mobilities as well as, potentially, an experience of muscular strain.[44] To apprehend the leg as part of the body we *suffer* is to apprehend the self as a set of "I can's" (the "*possibility which I am*") and thus as much more than an incarnation of the other's words or gaze. It might very well be, then, that in "The Lived Experience of the Black Man" Fanon is lamenting not only the lack of access to sensorimotor awareness but also the loss of the particular agency that inheres in that awareness, the potentially subversive understanding that comes from *reiterating* performatives, *reexperiencing* their cultural meanings, while simultaneously living the body as a plethora of other possible meanings one could be.

In the final pages of "The Lived Experience of the Black Man," Fanon, deprived of the interiority he seeks, fights nonetheless to restore a sense of facticity, a rootedness and a fulsome embodiment that would of course bind him while setting him free:

> Yet, with all my being, I refuse to accept this amputation [the amputation contingent upon abjuring one's "blackness"]. I feel my soul as vast as the world, truly a soul as deep as the deepest of rivers; my chest has the power of infinite expansion. I was made to contribute and instead they prescribe for me the humility of the cripple. When I opened my eyes yesterday I saw the sky in total revulsion. I tried to get up but the eviscerated silence flowed back on me with paralyzed wings. Irresponsible, at the crossroads between Nothingness and Infinity, I began to weep. (F, 119; translation modified)

Lacking a foothold ("my feet no longer felt the caress of the ground"), the subject must choose either to adopt the Universal (but empty) subjectivity envisioned by the authors of Negritude ("Infinity"), or he must resign himself to being absolutely nothing, no-body, at all ("Nothingness"). The two postures the colonial situation allows him are in fact interdependent, two faces of the same coin; for to be "Infinite," to have a soul as "vast as the world" and "as deep as the deepest of rivers" may be rhetorically powerful but it is existentially void if at the same time the living body—the chest—can be located in no particular place (it possesses the "power of infinite expansion" and is thus nowhere to be found).[45] Of course, faced with these two impossible alternatives, Fanon's subject can do no more than fall silent, and then fail even to recognize this silence as his own. Instead, he attributes the silence—and even the paralysis of his own legs—to some disembodied, "eviscerated" force. Utterly alienated from the state of his own body, he falls back on the bed, stilled, unable to move.

Fanon finally admits his confusion, his lack of orientation, in the concluding lines: "Irresponsible, at the crossroads between Nothingness and Infinity, I began to weep." However, instead of rolling over to plunge into the dreamworld, as does the protagonist of Césaire's *Notebook*, Fanon's subject merely breaks down and cries. If we have been waiting for a dramatic retrieval of agency at the end of the chapter, some militant statement of determination or assertion of identity to serve as a conclusion, then we are disappointed by this seemingly "irresponsible" move. But if we understand crying itself to be the most radical solution available—at least at this juncture—then we may be comforted that Fanon's subject will indeed find his way. Crying is a movement behavior involving violent convulsions rather than words. It is a gesture that puts us in contact with a prepersonal motor system that is invisible to the colonizer's gaze. Attending to this convulsive motility with interest and respect, privileging it in a narrative search for the lost self, can afford a knowledge if not of some immutable essence of selfhood then at least of an innate capacity to reflect. The knowledge that we can have a reflexive awareness *is valuable in itself.* Fanon's recourse to weeping can be seen, then, as the first step toward reclaiming a body schema, a *"pour soi."* The lived body, in all its limiting *and enabling* facticity *("possibility which I am"),* returns to consciousness in the form of a sob. Fanon's chapter must end here, with crying rather than speaking, because it is only this sort of gesture (along with Nietzsche's laughter) that can restore to the subject a body of sensation previously denied. The gesture of crying is performative insofar as it is iterable and gains its meaning within a system of gestural signifiers the meanings of which are culturally prescribed. However, the gesture of crying is closer to the involuntary, autonomous body than most of the words we speak or the gestures we perform. For this reason, crying accords access to an interiority that culture cannot entirely control. If the racialized subject must take part in the meaning-making systems of an alienating culture, at least this subject can struggle to reexperience what those systems physically require. Crying contracts and releases us violently, insisting that we witness, for ourselves, how it feels to reexperience despair.

Conclusion: Illegible Graffiti

THE STUDIES I have assembled here suggest that our gestures are neither natural nor inevitable but rather contingent expressions of the kinetic energy they organize. The kinetic continuum has already been segmented, sliced into operational or significant units, by the time we recognize movements *as* gestures, yet gestures nonetheless remain part of that continuum, pulled by the body's tow. Gesturing is a motor phenomenon and therefore part of the natural world; at the same time, a gesture is a unit of significant, visible shape, a quantity of employable force, and therefore part of the cultural world. It is by gesturing that bodies become inscribed with meanings in cultural environments, but it is also by gesturing that these inscribed meanings achieve embodiment and inflection.

Throughout this book, the act of writing has appeared as a kind of leitmotif, returning in each chapter either as a privileged example of a gestural routine that provides potentially disruptive kinesthetic experiences or as a figure for inscription (mark-making) in general, the process by which culture leaves its imprint on both the body and the mind. I would like to close by studying this figure more attentively in order to gather together the various arguments I have presented while situating them within the genealogy of critical theory as it has developed in France and the United States.

Writing is a very specific kind of gesturing, one that rarely invites scrutiny as an instance of motility. Yet "to write" is to deposit potentially significant marks on a support and simultaneously to perform the precise movements that allow one to do so. Insofar as writing involves the moving body in "real time," it affords an experience of animate form that can be addressed as intransitive, that is, as kinesthetic experience. My fingers, hand, wrist, arm, shoulder, trapezius, and neck (at the very least) are actively engaged in the gestural routines of writing, whether these routines involve paper or wall, keyboard or skin. In the course of performing the gestural routines of writing, specific parts of my body are given an opportunity to feel themselves in motion. At present, I choose to thematize my awareness of writing as an occasion for kinesthetic experience; but I am not obliged to do so. Alternatively, I might be more concerned with what I am writing (the meaning of the signs I "commit to space")[1] or with the clarity and elegance of my chosen font. But these expressive or aesthetic concerns can at any moment be eclipsed by a sudden shift in attention, a return to the experience of gesturing itself. Arguably, such an experience is always available, and an awareness of its availability is implicit, even when the act of writing appears to be directed toward quite different ends. Thus, what the writer discovers while writing is both inscriptions *and* movements, or as Sartre once put it, *"jambages"*: the vertical lines of letters (the technical sense of *"jambages"*) and the rhythmic, measured stride of the digits as limbs *("jamb*ages*")*.[2]

This *implicitness* of the corporeal substrate of writing is thematized more often than one might suspect. In fact, theorizing the gestural component of inscription has been a secret preoccupation of philosophy and aesthetics for a long time. A glance at the major texts of continental philosophy reveals the startling frequency with which the act of inscription is evoked as an exemplary instance *not* of communication or expression but of an opportunity for an experience of the body in the here and now. Writing (philosophy) is an opportunity to experience the body as a kind of resistant materiality that threatens to render momentarily illegible the marks on the page. When Hegel wants to illustrate the contradictions of self-consciousness in *The Phenomenology of Mind,* he describes himself holding his pen, writing the words *hic* and *nunc* even as those words, by being written, lose their power of deixis.[3] When Husserl wants to practice the *epochè* and confront the incontrovertible *"voici,"* he touches the blank page in front of him, sensing his orientation, the posture and intentionality of his body vis-à-vis the writing space.[4] Similarly, in the powerful overture to the "Cogito" chapter of *Phenomenology of Perception,* Merleau-Ponty describes himself putting pen to page as though it were a central kinetic (and kinesthetic) element of the exercise, part of a *situated* thinking about thinking according to Descartes. Sitting before the window of the café, shifting his eyes from street scene to ink meander, Merleau-Ponty senses his hand as it marks out the time in which thinking occurs. He then comes to figure thought itself as a kind of gesturing, a temporally unfolding cerebral (neuronal) *"tâtonnement"*: "my thought *strains toward* it [the idea of the cogito], *finds its orientation* and *makes its way* among objects without my needing to have them expressly in mind."[5] Finally, when Derrida, in *Memoirs of the Blind,* seeks to probe the relation between sensation and reflexive consciousness, presence and deferral, he too chooses the act of inscription as exemplary illustration. Driving home at night, the philosopher scribbles an illegible graffiti *("graffiti illisible")* on the dashboard, noting how "a hand of the blind man ventures forth alone . . . it feels its way, it gropes, it caresses as much as it inscribes [*Une main d'aveugle s'aventure solitaire . . . elle tâte, elle palpe, elle caresse autant qu'elle inscrit*]."[6]

For these philosophers, writing is indeed an act in league with the past and the future, but it also requires that a body move through the space of the now. The gestures of writing can make the body present as well as absent; they do more than "commit" the word to space; they actually submit space to, as Derrida puts it, the caress. But what does it mean to say that writing is a form of caress ("A hand . . . caresses as much as it inscribes")? On a first reading, Derrida seems to be suggesting that the gestures of writing, an acquired set of enchained small motor movements, are caress-*like;* they resemble a type of touching that we, as members of a particular semiotic community, recognize as gentle and noninvasive. Derrida's figure of the caressing hand has the rhetorical effect of transforming a gestural routine into a gestural language. By stating that to write is to caress, Derrida implies that strokes of the pen possess a semiotic value, that they themselves convey the same meaning (tender concern?) as conveyed by the strokes of a hand on a surface of flesh. Still, a gestural routine is not the same thing as a gestural sign system, which nonetheless requires a gestural routine for its transmission. The two orders (the semiotic and the instrumental) should, at least for the moment, be kept distinct. To be precise, a gestural sign system is a conventional set of bodily movements that can be culturally specific and vaguely evocative (such as a nod or a wave) or, alternatively, codified into a universal "sign language" in which each gesture corresponds, like a symbol or icon, to a letter, word, or idea. In contrast, the gestures of writing are "techniques of the body"; like other such techniques (swimming, sculpting a spearhead, applying lipstick), they are constructed, operational, syntactic sequences executed with the intention to fabricate an object, leave a mark, or accomplish a task.

However, as I have frequently argued in this book, it is not always easy to keep these two orders apart. And this, in fact, is the point about gestures: *they move.* They are not inherently fixed in either an instrumental or signifying register. Because gestures depend on the involvement of a sensorimotor apparatus in order to be performed, they are peculiarly susceptible to dehiscence; they can separate from their assigned meanings or tasks to become conduits of somatic absorption or, alternatively, spectacles, examples of themselves in scenes of instruction or self-conscious stagings that change their semantic inflection. This mutability or plurifunctionality of gestures is evoked in my citation from Derrida's *Memoirs of the Blind*: as he stresses, the writing hand "caresses *as much as* it inscribes." In other words, the gestures of the writing hand, recast as a variety of "caressing," can also express attitudes and emotions. A sharp analyst of Artaud, Derrida knows full well that the gestures of writing are expressive: one can stab a piece of paper, traverse its space in order to slash or rip it apart.[7] As Melanie Klein has also argued, the gestures of inscription, learned initially in an instrumental context as an obligatory discipline, can be pressed into the service of transmitting a libidinal impulse, an inappropriate emotion that graphologists are quick to note. But the protean nature of gestures does not end here. The locution "[a hand] feels its way, it gropes, it caresses as much as it inscribes" suggests further that the body performing inscriptive gestures is more than instrumental or expressive, spectacular or sentient; the body engaged in the gestures of writing is exploratory as well. "Caressing" the space of inscription is one way for the body to orient itself in, parse, and divide up space by means of self-displacing *"tâtonnements."*

Derrida is neither the first nor the last to discover in acts of inscription the fecund ambiguity of the gestural. The three valences of gesture he alludes to briefly in his anecdote—expressive/communicative, operational/technical, and rhythmic/exploratory—overlap in other important accounts of inscription as well. In "The Hands of Gargas," for instance, Leroi-Gourhan demonstrates how Paleolithic digital imprints function simultaneously as a sign system of conventional hand signals (expressive/communicative); as indexes of the gestural routines that produced the signals (operational/technical); and as a means of dividing up and exploring in a tactile, proprioceptive manner the natural space of the cave (rhythmic/exploratory). For Merleau-Ponty as well, gestures, as embodied signs or performances, are remarkably ambivalent and can be approached in a number of ways. However, as he observes in *Phenomenology of Perception*, there is one occasion that forces on us an approach we cannot evade, and that is the occasion of pain. The incontrovertible *"voici"* of pain constrains us to attend to our bodily gestures in a more pointed way. What is said about pain, though, can be extended to any stress applied to the agents that accomplish our tasks. Sensations are not a hermeneutic, a grid applied to interpreting movements, but a quality of the movements themselves. Even as I write for a future in which I may be absent, I can find myself clenching my fingers, hardening my wrist, pinching my shoulder blades, furrowing my brow. Sensations of discomfort (or pleasure) interrupt our more practical or expressive routines, but they reward us by providing the experience of movement in all its multiplicity.

By some accounts, we can choose freely to shift our awareness from our intended goal to the limbs that are accomplishing it. We can "drop awareness" into the body, as Deidre Sklar has put it, or "drop away," in the words of Merleau-Ponty (PP, 469), consciously turning our awareness "inward," toward that vanishing point where we might "feel" our "body as a continuum of kinetic sensations."[8] When we are engaging interoceptive awareness, Sklar writes, we momentarily break the hold of the *habitus,* we "unbraid" movement practices from ideological ends and open up the possibility of no longer perpetuating "social structures at the level of the body."[9]

Such a critical sensitivity to our acts, however, demands isolation, a willed disconnection from the purposive, instrumental, or communicative contexts into which we, as cultural beings, are almost always thrust. Derrida himself notes this aspect of the demonstration: in the darkened car, he observes that his hand wanders forth in a solitary manner *("s'aventure solitaire"),* accepting the "adventure" of kinesthesia but relinquishing the sight of the road. But if, for Sklar, "dropping awareness" into our bodies provides knowledge of sensations *apart* from their segmentation into linguistic categories, for Derrida, what is "felt" is instead the movement of segmentation or differentiation itself.[10] To inscribe—by means of writing, drawing, or graffiti (which binds writing and drawing together)—is to "to draw attention to *what one draws with the help of that with which one draws*, the body proper as an instrument . . . the play or work of the hand—drawing as *surgery*" [donner ainsi à remarquer *ce que l'on dessine à l'aide de ce avec quoi l'on dessine,* le corps propre comme instrument . . . le travail de la main, le dessin comme *chirurgie*]."[11] To access the writing body ("that with which one draws") is to access "the work of the hand" as it cuts open the flesh of a world. To inscribe, then, is to anatomize extension into discrete parts, and a kinesthetic awareness of gesturing gives us access to this process. At first glance, Derrida's hand does not appear to be sensing the *quality* of its own movements but only fingering the world as a "space of inscription,"[12] sketching out coordinates and differentiations produced by spac*ing,* the movement in space of a body seized as "instrument." Yet here, once again, we must pause. This cutting motion of the surgeon, in the context of the crepuscular drive, is experienced as a "caress." In other words, the exploratory movements ("feels its way," "gropes," "caresses," "inscribes") possess an "effort quality" (Laban); they are a particular type of kinesis *and not kinesis in general,* movement as embodied subjectivity and not simply "movement" as abstract, the movement of *différance,* or time in and as space.

Derrida's fascination at the end of his career with touching, groping, and gesturing is related to a kind of "return of the repressed," a growing concern with those aspects of phenomenology left behind in the deconstructionist dismantling of ontology. Clearly, for the later Derrida of *Memoirs of the Blind* (1990) and *Le Toucher: Jean-Luc Nancy* (2000) there remains a crucial element of phenomenological thinking—a reflection on the here and now of immediate sense experience—that remains to be explored. In *Le Toucher,* Derrida returns to the famous scene in Husserl's *Ideen, 2,* also treated by Merleau-Ponty in *Phenomenology of Perception,* in which the hand touching becomes the hand touched, in which the instrumental gesture yields a tactile sensation. The scene embraces many of the themes treated throughout this book. First, a body becomes a *"corps propre"* (a singular human body) through acts of gesturing, particularly through reaching out and touching with the hand. The "distinctive trait" of the body, Husserl claims, is that it becomes a "corps propre" by groping and palpating (Derrida's translation: *"tâtonner"* and *"palper"*).[13] Second, the gesture of touching is approached as instrumental; Husserl imagines the reaching hand as a type of technical prosthesis allowing us to become acquainted with the world. Third, the palpating, groping movements of the hand are also regarded as providing knowledge about the self: "It is upon this surface of the hand that I feel sensations of contact," Husserl writes.[14] Derrida asserts, though, that there is a "radical" break between the "phenomenological interiority" of the hand, that is, its sensation of being touched by the world, and the knowledge of the world that the touching hand receives.[15] In this passage, he does not evoke the quality of the movement itself as a part of the touching experience; he remains at the level of surface tactility, ignoring the kinetic quality of the *kind* of touch involved. This quality of movement is also felt by the touching hand, as Derrida recalls more vividly in *Memoirs of the Blind;* scribbling words on paper in the darkened space of the car, he engages more fully with the motions of scribbling, the "caress," than with the tactile apprehension of the fingers as they grip the pen or press the paper against the dashboard. His rich insight into the phenomenology of motility, into "phenomenological interiority," is thus glancing and indirect, but no less suggestive for that.

What graffiti reveal—illegible to the eye but tangible as "caress"— is that a gesture can be more than the instrumental probing of an object, the parsing of space, the production of a sign, or the apprehension of touch. As I hope this book has shown, a gesture can also be an experience of itself, that is, an experience of a particular way of *moving*—abruptly, in agitation, or, as in Derrida's darkened car, slowly, serenely, with care. Gestures—from physical movements of the body, limbs, or digits to phonic gesticulations—have a definite direction, a specific velocity, rhythm, scope, tonicity. When we perform physical gestures we can sense these qualities and we can also sense how comfortable or taxing it is to produce them. Paradoxically, however, in accessing these layers of sensation through movement, we also become peculiarly sensitive to the constructed nature of our acts; we become estranged momentarily from the practice in which we are engaged and recognize the presence of not only sensation but also cultural conditioning as it has been inscribed on our muscles and bones.

A point that never seems to arise in Derrida's scenes of touching, not even in his scenes of writing, is that we "caress" in culturally framed ways. Perhaps it requires movement practitioners to realize to what a great extent gestures *are not merely inscriptions in a metaphorical sense.* Gestures literally transform the bodies that perform them. "Phenomenological interiority" is thus also a profound experience of culture, of the *habitus* we share with others, of the exteriority we inevitably are. There is no need, then, to fear the "solipsism"[16] of interoceptive awareness (a fear Derrida evokes repeatedly in *Le Toucher* and *Memoirs of the Blind,* taking his cue from Freud's understanding of narcissism or his earlier critique of self-affection and Husserl's closed system of "interior monologue"). For the solitude in which we "adventure" during periods of somatic attention can lead to the discovery of what is not ours alone; it can even lead to the revision of congealed routines, if not to the toppling of gestural regimes. If performing gestures affords an opportunity to sense the discrepancy between what gestures *mean* (the meaning bestowed by cultural convention on them and therefore on the subjects performing them) and what gestures make us *feel* (the sensations we experience while performing them)—if, in other words, gesturing widens the gap between meaning and sensate being—*then gesturing can have the valence of critique.* This is the full meaning of the "gestural performative": on the one hand, gesturing can performatively bring a body into being; on the other, the performing body can critically bring a gesture into being, one that draws from the body's ability to differentiate, swerve, and remark.

The emergence of a robust new direction in performance studies, a form of dance and theater analysis abetted by cultural studies, represents the return of deconstruction's repressed. But it is important to stress that this is a return that could not have occurred without deconstruction in the first place.[17] As Mark Franko has astutely observed, the textual or discursive moment of poststructuralism has always been accompanied by a "gestural moment" (albeit one that does not last quite as long).[18] If post-structuralism "underplays the inscriptive *force* of gesture,"[19] Franko concedes, it nonetheless extends the phenomenological, Nietzschean, decidedly *non*structuralist interest in the moving body in a variety of ways. Among other examples, one can cite, of course, Derrida's meditations on *"tâtonnement"* and Foucault's interest in the body's pleasures; but riches are also to be found in Deleuze and Felix Guattari's fascination with virtual movement, Baudrillard's analysis of "gestural systems of control," and Agamben's approach to gesture as nonproductive "event."[20] Post-structuralist thinkers do not deny attention to the gestural; in fact, they often integrate gesture into a recursive loop, addressing it as part of a dialectical relationship with inscription, *technè*, or power. Unfortunately, this integration sometimes cancels out one of the major features of gesture, which is that it carries out a dialectic with the body *on its own terms*. Gestures, when repeated frequently and absorbed as habit, "pierce deeply enough into their host materials so as to create permanent marks," as Sally Ann Ness has written; but "they do not penetrate them so as to alter *the material's enduring character*."[21] And here is where the dialectic peculiar to gesture must be located: the gesture shapes a body that can perform—*re*form—the gesture in turn. That is, the "enduring character" of the body to which Ness alludes both invites and resists the inscriptions it receives. For Ness, moving bodies, from the moment they enter culture, are a "host material," a substance on which, and into which, the gestural routines of a specific group or gender are constantly being reinscribed. The urgent question, then, is to what extent the "enduring character" of the material (the body) remains available to the inward-turning awareness that kinesthesia demands. If the body is a text on which culture has inscribed its marks, then what, precisely, does a subject feel when she "drops down"? Where, in depth, is there to go?

For a theorist like Butler, and, at times, Bourdieu, we only ever experience and reexperience the habitual body, not the "host material," or natural body, before it has been subjected to cultural marking. In contrast, Ness's insistence on the "enduring character" of the body's "host material" preserves a possibility for *self-disclosing motility*, the subliminal agency of neuromuscular feedback, yes; but also, and equally important, the mindful agency of a body listening to itself. It is the latter possibility that I have repeatedly, and from several perspectives, attempted to elucidate here. If there is an enduring character to the material body, then it remains a source for new movements and experiences; it promises to disclose an aspect of human kinetic potential that has not previously been integrated into normative gestural routines. The motor body possesses a variety of agency that can help renovate the paradigms of construction and resistance, interpellation and identity, with which we normally conduct theoretical work.

As movement theorists from Mauss to Lowell Lewis have insisted, awareness of movement as self-disclosing (and thus potentially resistant to fixed representations) is particularly acute when the body is being subjected to new routines. In the future, it will be important for movement analysts to look more closely at these moments if we are to determine with any empirical purchase whether the body can remain aware of itself, whether the "host material" can talk back, despite the conditioning it receives. Stages of skill acquisition are often highly charged and ambiguous. They are moments when culture provides us with a Janus-faced gift: we submit to physical constraints but also discover a new "I can"; we receive the anonymous imprint of conditioning but are simultaneously enabled to feel ourselves moving in new ways. Like any element of a conventionalized language or procedure, gestures are iterable, but when performed *by me* they are not necessarily iterations. There is a first time for *my* body to perform what other bodies already have learned to do. And there is a first time for *my* body to perform the gesture in an idiosyncratic and potentially subversive way. Skilling and de-skilling can thus be singled out as those processes through which we confront movement not primarily as functional act in an operating chain, or segment of meaning in a gestural language, or even aesthetically compelling spatial shape in a choreography (although movement can still remain functional, significant, and aesthetic). Skilling and deskilling are processes through which we are given an opportunity to confront a gesture as contingent, part of a spectrum of possible movements, none of which exhausts the body's potential to move.

This is particularly important in the context of writing, or inscription in general, which remains in many societies a privilege of the elite. Although controlled and disseminated largely through institutions, inscriptive practices are often parodically altered by children and others whose access to these institutions—and their norms—is partial or nonexistent. Inscription is a power that goes far beyond that wielded by the copying scribe; because it can be learned and mobilized outside of pedagogical structures, it bears a relation to transgression, to magic, and to the conduct of trance.[22] To be sure, the gestural routines of inscription are violently disciplining; they can shape and suppress the individual body by submitting it to highly rigorous standards of execution. However, the process of making marks also offers opportunities for subversion: we can leave our marks in the wrong place, invent private or countercultural mark systems, or use mark making as an exploratory project, investigating how our bodies might move differently and thereby achieve materialization and cultural legibility in unexpected ways. Finally, we can choose to isolate ourselves from the demands of the *habitus* and write for, *and with,* that "host material" of the body, the articulation of which also makes demands. By "articulating the host material" I mean not simply inscribing in such a way as to index physical (or libidinal) impulses—as in abstract expressionism or childish *griffonnage.* I am suggesting instead that the gestural routines of inscription yield a kinesthetic experience that is a resource in its own right, a resource of sensation capable of subverting the institutions of inscription by promising new, unmarked material to record. In short, my wager is that the interoception provided by movement can be productive of new cultural meanings. Finding the means to express interoceptive awareness (in writing, but in images and choreographies as well) is intimately bound up with accessing the "host material" that is the corporeal substrate of writing. Testing our powers of articulation against the limits of articulation is the way we contribute to history, not just the history of our singular bodies as expressive and operational but also the history of what is given to humans to make into marks.

Notes

Introduction

1. Michel Foucault, *Discipline and Punish: The Birth of the Prison,* trans. Alan Sheridan (New York: Vintage, 1979), 132. In this regard, it is interesting to compare the famous scene of "the docile body" as it masters the "gymnastics" of handwriting in *Discipline and Punish* (152), or the passage in "Nietzsche, Genealogy, History" where he depicts the body as "totally imprinted by history" (*Language, Counter-Memory, Practice: Selected Essays and Interviews,* ed. and intro. Daniel F. Bouchard [Ithaca, N.Y.: Cornell University Press, 1977], 148), to his later musings on the "care," "cultivation" and "intensity of relations to self" in *History of Sexuality 3: The Care of the Self* (trans. Robert Hurley [New York: Vintage, 1988], 42). Foucault appears to evolve toward a position where his earlier model of the body as "totally" subjected (or resistant) to power is supplemented—and in some ways challenged—by an alternative model in which cultures offer multiple practices that actually encourage attention to bodily states (Roman practices of self-evaluation, for instance).

2. "Choreographing History," in *Choreographing History,* ed. Susan Leigh Foster (Bloomington: Indiana University Press, 1995), 15; added emphasis. Foster's claim finds confirmation in Marc Jeannerod's *Motor Cognition: What Actions Tell the Self* (Oxford: Oxford University Press, 2006). The neuroscientist provides evidence that somatosensory feedback "influences conscious experience" and decision making (56).

3. The degree to which we are conscious of somatosensory feedback is a matter of debate. See Jeannerod, *Motor Cognition,* and Antonio R. Damasio, *The Feeling of What Happens: Body and Emotion in the Making of Consciousness* (New York: Harcourt Brace, 1999), 23, 150, 153–154, 319. Damasio is unclear whether kinesthetic feedback is available to consciousness or not; part of the confusion may lie in the fact that he sometimes treats kinesthesia as a homeostatic function similar to temperature control. In contrast, many of the

philosophers and cognitive scientists I cite in this book (and on whom Damasio implicitly relies) approach kinesthesia as a rich background of impressions that we can access under appropriate conditions. In a provocative essay, "What Are We Naming," Maxine Sheets-Johnstone proposes that most of the terms we use to describe kinesthetic experience are misleading (*Body Image and Body Schema*, ed. Helena De Preester and Veroniek Knockaert [Amsterdam: John Benjamins, 2005], 211–231). She objects to the term "sensation" because it suggests that our experience of movement is punctual; movement "is quite unlike the proverbial touching hand and the proverbial touched hand, both of which may be spoken of as yielding sensations of touch. Everyday self-movement is in contrast a dynamically felt temporal phenomenon" (214). She prefers the word "perception," arguing that "if one did not *perceive* one's body, one would have no grounds for building or having such conceptual understandings or emotional attitudes" captured by the term "body image" (218; original emphasis). "Embodiment" is also a word Sheets-Johnstone would like to replace; she suggests "*bodily-kinetic* experience" (218; original emphasis). Although I sympathize with her point, I choose to preserve the traditional terms to highlight the continuity between my own work and that of earlier theorists. The reader should keep in mind, however, that when I say "sensation" I am thinking of something closer to what Sheets-Johnstone calls "the qualitative dynamics that any movement creates" (214). There is no reason why movement could not be said to produce both "sensations" (such as discomfort or pleasure) and proprioceptive and kinesthetic "perceptions." The way a hand experiences being touched is not static or punctual either; the hand also experiences an unfolding stream of perceptions of pressure, soothing caress, and so on.

4. The growing body of scholarship on affect and emotion includes Philip Fisher, *The Vehement Passions* (Princeton: Princeton University Press, 2002); Sianne Ngai, *Ugly Feelings* (Cambridge, Mass.: Harvard University Press, 2005); and Rei Terada, *Feeling in Theory: Emotion after the "Death of the Subject"* (Cambridge, Mass: Harvard University Press, 2001). I am particularly sympathetic to Terada's approach, which assumes that emotion, like kinesthetic sensation, destabilizes rather than defines the subject. For earlier accounts of the relation between emotion and motion, see Mabel Elsworth Todd, *The Thinking Body: A Study of the Balancing Forces of Dynamic Man*, with a foreword by E. G. Brackett (New York: Dance Horizons, 1937), and the summary of twentieth-century movement therapies contained in Richard Shusterman's "Somaesthetics," in *Pragmatist Aesthetics: Living Beauty, Rethinking Arts*, 2nd ed. (New York: Rowman and Littlefield, 2000). See also *The Affective Turn: Theorizing the Social*, ed. Patricia Ticineto Clough with Jean Halley, foreword by Michael Hardt (Durham, N.C.: Duke University Press, 2007), which contains essays clarifying the contributions of affect theorists Silvan Tomkins, Gilles Deleuze, and Eve Kosofsky Sedgwick. For a neuroscientist's approach, see Antonio R. Damasio, *Looking for Spinoza: Joy, Sorry, and the Feeling Brain* (Orlando, Fl.: Harcourt, 2003) and *The Feeling of What Happens*. A pertinent critique of the neuroscience approach can be found in Daniel M. Gross, *The Secret History of Emotion: From Aristotle's Rhetoric to Modern Brain Science* (Chicago: University of Chicago Press, 2006).

5. Francisco Varela, "The Reenchantment of the Concrete," in *Incorporations,* ed. Jonathan Crary and Sanford Kwinter (New York: Zone Books, 1992), 333.

6. Gilbert Simondon, for instance, calls kinesthetic sensations "unconscious stereotypes"; *L'Individuation psychique et collective* (Paris: Aubier, 1989), 99.

7. See, for starters, Susanne K. Langer, *Feeling and Form* (New York: Scribner's, 1953): "Gesture is vital movement; to the one who performs it, it is known very precisely as a kinetic experience" (174). See also Sally Ann Ness, *Body, Movement, and Culture: Kinesthetic and Visual Symbolism in a Philippine Community* (Philadelphia: University of Pennsylvania Press, 1992); Mark Franko, *Dancing Modernism/Performing Politics* (Bloomington: Indiana University Press, 1995), and *The Work of Dance: Labor, Movement, and Identity in the 1930s* (Middletown, Conn.: Wesleyan University Press, 2002); and Brenda Farnell, *Do You See What I Mean? Plains Indian Sign Talk and the Embodiment of Action* (Austin: University of Texas Press, 1995). Dee Reynolds makes a strong case in *Rhythmic Subjects: Uses of Energy in the Dances of Mary Wigman, Martha Graham and Merce Cunningham* (Hampshire, England: Dance Books, 2007): "Kinesthesia . . . is central to embodied experience. Movement events that disrupt normative, habitual ways of using energy in movement and produce innovations in production, distribution, expenditure and retention of energy in the body are acts of 'kinesthetic imagination.' These acts involve a delicate balance between determinism and agency" (4). Or, as Diana Taylor puts it, "Materials from the archive shape embodied practice in innumerable ways, yet never totally dictate embodiment" (*The Archive and the Repertoire: Performing Cultural Memory in the Americas* [Durham, N.C.: Duke University Press, 2003], 21).

8. Rudolf von Laban began publishing on "effort qualities" in his *Method of Kinetography* of 1928, extended his theory from dance to work-related movement in Laban and F. C. Lawrence, *Effort* (London: MacDonald and Evans, 1946), and systemized his notation method further in *Principles of Dance and Movement Notation* (London: MacDonald and Evans, 1956).

9. On the "frames" of experience, see Erving Goffman, *Frame Analysis: An Essay on the Organization of Experience* (New York: Harper and Row, 1974).

10. Thomas J. Csordas, "Somatic Modes of Attention," in *Body/Healing/Meaning* (New York: Palgrave MacMillan, 2002).

11. If in the past the study of technology has largely followed a materialist, even determinist bent (in the work of Friedrich Kittler, for instance), more recent investigations have introduced a phenomenological orientation. See José Gil, *Metamorphoses of the Body,* trans. Stephen Muecke (Minneapolis: University of Minnesota Press, 1998); Brian Massumi, *Parables for the Virtual: Movement, Affect, Sensation* (Durham, N.C.: Duke University Press, 2003); and Mark Hansen, *New Philosophy for New Media* (Cambridge, Mass.: MIT Press, 2004).

12. Tim Ingold, *The Perception of the Environment: Essays on Livelihood, Dwelling, and Skill* (New York: Routledge, 2000), 5.

13. Michel de Certeau, *L'Invention du quotidian 1: Arts de faire* (Paris: Union Générale d'Éditions, 1980), 21. See also de Certeau's critique of Foucault's binary model, which is similar to my own: pp. 13–14 and 101–108 .

14. The adjective "durable" as well as the terms "body *hexis*" are drawn from Pierre Bourdieu, *Outline of a Theory of Practice,* trans. Richard Nice (Cambridge: Cambridge University Press, 1977), 78 and 74: "Body *hexis* speaks directly to the motor function in the form of a pattern of postures that is both individual and systematic, being bound up with a whole system of objects, and charged with a host of special meanings and values" (74). Jean Baudrillard adopts Bourdieu's notion of the body as "bound up with a whole system of objects" but produces a more extreme determinist analysis; see *The System of Objects* (London: Verso, 1996). The Frankfurt School theorists locate gesture as one of the areas where a cultural transformation—here, capitalism and industrialization—has the power to deny the body access to its own sensations, its "lived experience" *(Erlebnis).* As a result, the hold of what Bertolt Brecht called the "social *gestus*" becomes permanent; see *Brecht on Theatre,* ed. and trans. John Willet (New York: Hill and Wang, 1996), 104. The same approach is taken by Giorgio Agamben in "Notes on Gesture," in *Means without End: Notes on Politics,* trans. Vincenzo Binetti and Cesare Casarino (Minneapolis: University of Minnesota Press, 2000).

15. See *Les origines du caractère chez l'enfant* (Paris: PUF, 1973; originally published 1934). For evidence against Wallon, see George Butterworth, "Origins of Self Perception in Infancy," *Psychological Inquiry* 3, no. 2 (1992): 103–111, and "An Ecological Perspective on the Origins of the Self," in Bermúdez et al., *The Body and the Self,* (ed. José Luis Bermudéz, Anthony Marcel, and Naomi Eilan [Cambridge, Mass.: MIT Press, 1995]), 101. I return to Wallon and his less known debate with Lacan in Chapter 5.

16. See Thomas J. Csordas, "Embodiment as a Paradigm for Anthropology," *Ethos* 18, no. 1 (March 1990) 5–47: and "Introduction: The Body as Representation and Being-in-the-World," in *Embodiment and Experience,* ed. Thomas J. Csordas (Cambridge: Cambridge University Press, 1994); and Andrew J. Strathern, "Embodiment," in *Body Thoughts* (Ann Arbor: University of Michigan Press, 1996).

17. See Edwin G. Boring, *Sensation and Perception in the History of Experimental Psychology* (New York: Irvington, 1942), especially 524–530 on the contributions of Charles Bell, François Magendie, Hermann von Helmholtz, and Sherrington. Boring does not discuss the experiments of Théodule Ribot in France, which confirmed the centrality of movement to cognition and were significant to Emile Durkheim and Mauss. On kinesthesia as the "first-person cue par excellence," see Jeannerod, 73.

18. Quoted in ibid., 535; added emphasis.

19. *The Brain's Sense of Movement,* trans. Giselle Weiss (Cambridge, Mass.: Harvard University Press, 2000); originally published as *Le Sens du movement* in 1997), 5. See also ed. Francisco J. Varela, Evan Thompson, and Eleanor Rosch, eds., *The Embodied Mind: Cognitive Science and Human Experience* (Cambridge, Mass: MIT Press, 1991); John Haugeland, *Having Thoughts: Essays in the Metaphysics of Mind (Cambridge, Mass.: Harvard University Press, 2000).*

20. Andrew Hewitt, *Social Choreography: Ideology as Performance in Dance and Everyday Movement* (Durham, N.C.: Duke University Press, 2005), 18. See also Amy Koritz, "Re/Moving Boundaries: From Dance History to Cultural

Studies," in *Moving Words: Rewriting Dance,* ed. Gay Morris (London: Routledge, 1996). Derrida's critique of "auto-affection" (a concept that emerges regularly in philosophy from Aristotle and Kant to Husserl and Bergson) follows a similar logic: something outside the self intervenes in its dialogue with itself. I return to these issues in Chapter 2 and the Conclusion.

21. According to Berthoz, recent experiments indicate that distortions of the body schema (based on kinesthetic and proprioceptive feedback) can be corrected through reeducation. "The possibility that the cortical structures involved in sensorimotor function are accessible to training was pretty much unthinkable. Recently, however, neuronal recording in the monkey and in humans using brain-imaging techniques have shown that neurons from the somatosensory areas of the cerebral cortex can reorganize the maps where these parts of the body are represented" (*The Brain's Sense of Movement,* 239). The tests Berthoz cites only confirm what movement therapists Moshe Feldenkrais and Frederick Mattias Alexander proved clinically in the 1920s; see *Bone, Breath, and Gesture: Practices of Embodiment,* ed. Don Hanlon Johnson (Berkeley: North Atlantic Books, 1995). See also Todd, *The Thinking Body,* 38–40.

22. Writing in 1937, Todd observed, as Mauss had two years earlier, that through conditioning "the sensory-motor chain of reactions in our nerves and muscles has been gradually modified through association of ideas derived, not from mechanical or physical considerations of what balance means or how a really straight back looks, but from moral, that is, social concepts" (*The Thinking Body,* 35). A readjustment to harmful but acquired and ideologically supported ways of moving might "produce at first the discomfort attending upon change" (40)—and thus, the body could, indeed, "lie." But this would not mean that there does not exist a right way to move for that body, if we take "right" to mean protective of the structure of muscles, tendons, ligaments, and bones.

23. Bloomington: Indiana University Press, 1994 (94).

24. In *The Nick of Time: Politics, Evolution, and the Untimely,* Grosz acknowledges the shortcomings of her earlier work, stating that she "failed there to adequately address [*sic*] how living matter, corporeality, allows itself cultural location, gives itself up to cultural inscription, provides a 'surface' for cultural writing—that is, how the biological induces the cultural rather than inhibits it" (New York: Routledge, 2000, 4). In a similar vein, Judith Butler sees the return of repressed sensation in symptoms of melancholy in *The Psychic Life of Power* (Stanford: Stanford University Press, 1997).

25. Ness, *Body, Movement, and Culture;* Paul Stoller, *Sensuous Scholarship* (Philadelphia: University of Pennsylvania Press, 1997); Deidre Sklar, *Dancing with the Virgin: Body and Faith in the Fiesta of Tortugas, New Mexico* (Berkeley: University of California Press, 2001). For a wide-ranging discussion of the senses, see Sally Banes and André Lepecki eds., *The Senses in Performance* (London: Routledge, 2007); Michael Jackson, *Paths toward a Clearing: Radical Empiricism and Ethnographic Inquiry* (Bloomington: Indiana University Press, 1989); David Howes, *Sensual Relations: Engaging the Senses in Culture and Social Theory* (Ann Arbor: University of Michigan Press, 2003); and David Howes, ed., *Empire of the Senses: The Sensual Culture Reader* (Oxford: Berg, 2005), which includes an essay by Constance Classen, a scholar of

the olfactory. In archeology, see Christopher Tilley and Wayne Bennett, *The Materiality of Stone: Explorations in Landscape Phenomenology* (Oxford: Berg, 2004) and Yannis Hamilakis, Mark Pluciennik, and Sarah Tarlow eds., *Thinking through the Body: Archeologies of Corporeality* (New York: Kluwer Academic, 2002).

26. Kathryn Linn Guerts, *Culture and the Senses: Bodily Ways of Knowing in an African Community* (Berkeley: University of California Press, 2002).

27. For a general account of the fate within the academy of "experience" as an epistemological category, see Martin Jay, *Songs of Experience: Modern American and European Variations on a Universal Theme* (Berkeley: University of California Press, 2005).

28. John A. Lucy, "Linguistic Relativity," *Annual Review of Anthropology* 26 (1997): 296.

29. *Culture and the Senses,* 231.

30. John Martin, *The Modern Dance* (New York: A. S. Barnes, 1933) and *Introduction to the Dance* (New York: Norton, 1939). Martin is the earliest dance theorist to make use of Bell's discovery of neuroreceptors in the muscles. He also anticipated the recent discovery of "mirror neurons" when he theorized the existence of "inner mimicry."

31. Ph.D. diss. (University of California, Santa Cruz, 1982), 13.

32. *Body Code: The Meaning in Movement* (London: Routledge and Kegan Paul, 1979).

33. Stern, *The Interpersonal World of the Infant* (New York: Basic Books, 2000), xvii-xviii; see also Berthoz on posture as anticipated action in *The Brain's Sense of Movement,* 137, and Damasio, *The Feeling of What Happens,* on permanent feedback, 150.

34. *Outline of a Theory of Practice,* 78. Bourdieu writes further that the principles of the *habitus,* embodied through motor action, "are placed beyond the grasp of consciousness, and hence cannot be touched by voluntary, deliberate transformation, cannot even be made explicit" (94).

35. See "Remembering Kinesthesia: An Inquiry into Embodied Cultural Knowledge," in *Migrations of Gesture,* ed. Carrie Noland and Sally Ann Ness (Minneapolis: University of Minnesota Press, 2008). See also Drew Leder, *The Absent Body* (Chicago: University of Chicago Press, 1990).

36. Adam Kendon, *Gesture: Visible Action as Utterance* (Cambridge: Cambridge University Press, 2004).

37. *The Perception of the Environment,* 292.

38. Ness, *Body, Movement, and Culture,* 4.

39. In *Consciousness Explained* (London: Little, Brown and Co., 1991), David Dennett argues that what we call "consciousness" is really the result of a probe into one of the many parallel streams of information running simultaneously in the brain. The probe focuses attention on some aspect of a perception, sensation, emotion, or thought. Dennett's approach allows us to rethink the blunt opposition between conscious and unconscious, intentional and unintentional.

40. See *Being and Time,* trans. Joan Stambaugh (Albany, N.Y.: State University of New York Press, 1996), 122. In "Engaged Agency and Background in Hei-

degger," Charles Taylor develops Heidegger's understanding of "being-in-the-world" into a theory of engaged (or what I am calling "distributed") agency (*The Cambridge Companion to Heidegger,* ed. Charles B. Guignon [Cambridge, Mass.: Cambridge University Press, 2006], 202–221): "To understand what it is to 'lie to hand' one has to understand what it is to be an agent with the particular bodily capacities that humans have. . . . The ways in which our world is so shaped define the contours of what I am calling engaged agency—what Heidegger sometimes referred to as the 'finitude' of the knowing agent" (204). Taylor acknowledges that it was Merleau-Ponty, with the help of Husserl, who transformed Heidegger's concepts into a fully elaborated theory of embodied perception.

41. *Gesture,* 109.
42. Peggy Phelan, *Unmarked: The Politics of Performance* (London: Routledge, 1993), 3. Yet another definition of performance is relevant here: Richard Schechner's understanding of performance as "restored behavior." "Restored behavior is symbolic and reflexive"; "Performance means: never for the first time"; "Performance is 'twice-behaved' behavior" (*Between Theater and Anthropology,* foreword by Victor Turner [Philadelphia: University of Pennsylvania Press, 1985], 36). Although "performance" as "restored behavior" suggests that the moving bodies of actors are doing something qualitatively different from the moving bodies of non-actors, Schechner would agree (37) that all cultural subjects (subjects of the *habitus*) are in some sense engaged in repeating behaviors already performed. André Leroi-Gourhan captures this sense of mindful repetition in everyday life when he refers to instrumental habitual movements (operating chains) as "performances." See *Le Geste et la parole,* 2 (Paris: Albin Michel, 1964), 75.
43. *Outline of a Theory of Practice,* 84.
44. Pierre Bourdieu, *The Logic of Practice,* trans. Richard Nice (Stanford: Stanford University Press, 1990), 55.

1. The "Structuring" Body

1. *Journal de psychologie* 32 (1935): reprinted in Mauss, *Sociologie et Anthropologie,* with an introduction by Claude Lévi-Strauss (Paris: PUF, 1973). (Page references will be to this volume [abbreviated as SA]; all translations are my own.)
2. For a summary of these contributions, see Adam Kendon, *Gesture: Visible Action as Utterance* (Cambridge: Cambridge University Press, 2004), chap. 1.
3. E. E. Evans-Pritchard published the earliest account of danced movement in Africa as serving "physiological and psychological" as well as collective needs; see "The Dance," *Africa* 1, no. 3 (1928): 446. Mauss's students and associates included Marcel Granet, Curt Sachs, Michel Leiris, and Alfred Métraux, all of whom produced pioneering studies of the role of dance movement in the transmission of belief systems. Mauss also taught André-Georges Haudricourt, whose works have inspired the next generation of technology scholars, such as Jean-Pierre Séris and Bernard Steigler.

4. André-Georges Haudricourt, "Relations entre gestes habituels, forme des vêtements et manière de porter les charges" (originally published in 1948), in Haudricourt, *La Technologie, science humaine: Recherche d'histoire et d'ethnologie des techniques* (Paris: Editions de la Maison des Sciences de l'Homme, 1987), 174.

5. Camille Tarot, *De Durkheim à Mauss: l'invention du symbolique: Sociologie et science des religions,* with a preface by Alain Caillé (Paris: La Découverte MAUSS, 1999), 647.

6. "Les Techniques du corps," in SA, 379.

7. André-Georges Haudricourt, "La technologie, science humaine" (1964), in Haudricourt, *La Technologie, science humaine,* 38.

8. SA, 366.

9. In *The Cambridge Companion to Merleau-Ponty,* ed. Taylor Carman and Mark B. N. Hansen (Cambridge: Cambridge University Press, 2005), 185 and 188.

10. The veracity of this story of the Maori girl is uncertain. Mauss borrowed it from the first volume of Elsdon Best's two-volume study of Maori customs, *The Maori* (Wellington, New Zealand: Harry H. Tombs, 1924). But Mauss gets the spelling of the name wrong, calling the gait *"l'onioi,"* whereas it appears in Best's text as *"onioni."* Furthermore, Best does not translate what the Maori mother says to her child, and I have not found anyone who can confirm that Mauss's translation is accurate. The passage in Best reads: "Native women adopted a peculiar gait that was acquired in youth, a loose-jointed swinging of the hips that looks ungainly to us, but was admired by the Maori. Mothers drilled their daughters in this accomplishment, termed *onioni,* and I have heard a mother says [*sic*] to her girl: *"ha! Kaore koe e onioni"* when the young one was neglecting to practise the gait" (408). Mauss bends the story to his own purposes, which include a desire to reveal the resistance of the girl to what appears *to an outsider* to be an "ungainly" walk. Mauss's spelling mistake in the French anthology, *Sociologie et anthropologie,* has been corrected in the new English anthology of his works on technology: *Marcel Mauss: Techniques, Technology and Civilization,* ed. and Introduction by Nathan Schlanger (New York and Oxford: Durkheim Press/Berghohn Books, 2006); see p. 81.

11. See, for instance, artist Simon Leung's *Squatting Project* (2003), based on Mauss in "Squatting through Violence," *Documents* 6 (Spring/ Summer, 1995): 92–101.

12. In *Human Evolution, Language and Mind: A Psychological and Archaeological Inquiry,* William Noble and Iain Davidson advance the hypothesis that the mastery of gestures such as aiming and throwing led to the development of the vocal apparatus: "Selection of the hand/arm which, through finer motor control, yields more effective results from throwing, may account for the close connection found between handedness and the brain hemisphere associated with both vocal utterance and control of facial and mouth muscles more generally" (Cambridge: Cambridge University Press, 1996), 219. For further background, see G. W. Hewes, "Gesture Language in Cultural Contact," *Sign Language Studies* 4 (1974): and David MacNeill, *Hand and Mind* (Chicago: Chicago University Press, 1992).

13. Mauss began lecturing on the subject of bodily techniques around 1920 at the Institut d'Ethnologie and then at the Collège de France. His writings on techniques and technology have been collected in *Sociology and Psychology,* trans. Ben Brewster (London: Routledge, 1979), *Marcel Mauss: Techniques, Technology and Civilization,* and *Oeuvres,* vols. 2 and 3, ed. Victor Karady (Paris: Minuit, 1968–1974).

14. Bruno Karsenti, *L'Homme total: Sociologie, anthropologie et philosophie chez Marcel Mauss* (Paris: PUF, 1997), 65. All translations are my own.

15. There are, however, hints in Durkheim's writings of an alternative approach. See Emile Durkheim, "Représentations individuelles et représentations collectives," in *Sociologie et philosophie* (Paris: PUF, 1996; originally published Alcan, 1924).

16. Paris: La Société Anonyme de la Grande Encyclopédie, 1901, 30:165–176, collected in Mauss, *Oeuvres,* 3.

17. Karsenti, *L'homme total,* 64. Durkheim, "Individual Representations and Collective Representations," 2; my translation.

18. Mauss indicates his distance from Bergson on this point in "Divisions et proportions des divisions de la socologie" (*Année sociologique* (1927), reprinted in *Oeuvres,* 3.

19. SA, 303; added emphasis.

20. The organism, observes Mauss, is profoundly "affected throughout its being by the smallest of perceptions or the least mental"; "Rapports réels et pratiques de la psychologie et de la sociologie," in SA, 306; reprinted from *Journal de Psychologie Normale et Pathologique* (1924). All translations are my own.

21. Mauss raises these questions directly in "Real and Practical Relations between Psychology and Sociology," but they had already been prefigured in articles he was writing earlier, most notably his *"comptes rendus"* on the works of Wilhelm Wundt, a German psychophysiologist and contemporary of William James who had proposed that every psychic phenomenon has its physiological double, especially in the case of expressive practices that, he argued, are based on the organic rhythms of the body. In a series of review articles Mauss published in 1905 and 1907, Mauss advances Wundt's proposition that rhythm, expressed through movement, is the physiological base, the corporeal substrate, from which all expressive culture issues. But although Mauss continues to praise Wundt for approaching rhythm as "à la fois physiologique, psychologique et sociologique," in later works Mauss seeks to revise Wundt, insisting, where Wundt does not, on the crucial role of socialization in the rhythmic patterning at the base of cultural production. For a contemporary application of Mauss's ideas on the relation between ritual gestures and spirituality lived on the order of the body, see Talal Asad, *Genealogies of Religion: Discipline and Reasons of Power in Christianity and Islam* (Baltimore: The Johns Hopkins University Press, 1993).

22. Karsenti does mention the importance of Ruth Benedict and Margaret Mead, who brought attention to the role of bodily acts in the making and transmission of culture; see the chapter "Mauss et la linguistique."

23. "The Study of Techniques as an Ideological Challenge: Technology, Nation, and Humanity in the Work of Marcel Mauss," in *Marcel Mauss: A Centenary*

Tribute, ed. W. James and N. Allen (Oxford: Berghahn Books, 1998), 194. Schlanger mentions one factor that might have played a role in Mauss's growing attention to bodily techniques: the interest in the body manifested by the Germans prior to and during World War II. It is probably no accident that "Techniques of the Body" was presented in 1934 and published in 1935 against the background of the Nazi fascination with the body as a racial, biological entity capable of perfection. "Techniques of the Body" can be read as Mauss's attempt to un-race the body, to reveal it as a creation of social conditioning.

24. "Sociologie," in collaboration with Paul Fauconnet, in *La Grande Encyclopédie* (Paris: Société anonyme de la grande encyclopédie, (1901), 30:165–176 (*Oeuvres*); "Yoga," in *La Grande Encyclopédie* (Paris: Société anonyme de la grande encyclopédie, 1901), 31:134–135 (not republished).

25. At the turn of the century, when Mauss was composing "Yoga," quite a bit more was known about the discipline/religion in nonacademic milieux. A lively interest in Indian culture was stimulated when Franz Bopp discovered in the early nineteenth century the relation between Indian and European languages. German Romanticism (through Friedrich Schlegel) piqued the interest of Victor Cousin, who lectured on Patanjali's *Yoga Sutras* and the Bhagavad-Gita in his Cours de Philosophie. In 1900, the Sorbonne held a Congrès International de l'Histoire des Religions, which Mauss might very well have attended. But these academic venues were separated by social barriers from the Theosophists, who were simultaneously inviting yogis from India, such as Vivekananda (in 1895), to visit France. For a fuller history of yoga in France, both as a philosophy studied at the Sorbonne and as a physical practice introduced and popularized by nonacademics over the course of the century, see Silvia Ceccomore, *Cent ans de Yoga en France* (Paris: Edidit, 2001).

26. Mauss followed Lévi's courses at the Ecole pratique des hautes études. Lévi was one of the three scholars (along with Emile Burnouf and Abel Bergaigne) who translated the Bhagavad Gita into French in 1901. On this period in Mauss's life, see Marcel Fournier, *Marcel Mauss* (Paris: Fayard, 1994). The study of Indian languages is, curiously, at the root of both an exclusively textual approach, that of Jean Starobinski and Saussure, and the Maussian approach I sketch out here.

27. "Introduction à l'oeuvre de Marcel Mauss," in SA, xiv.

28. *De Durkheim à Mauss,* 383.

29. Bergaigne quoted in *De Durkheim à Mauss,* 390. On the history of Indology as a discipline in France and its links to German Romanticism, see 375–391.

30. Mauss, *Oeuvres,* 1:214.

31. On the transmission of experience in Indian performance that confirms my reading, see Richard Schechner, "Rasaesthetics," in *Performance Theory* (New York: Routledge, 2003), 333–367.

32. *De Durkheim à Mauss,* 401. Reflecting on Sanskrit and Pâli texts, Mauss was led to develop, as Tarot has written, "hypotheses concerning the anteriority of rites with respect to myths, the genesis of forms from acts [*la genèse des formes à partir des actes*]" (392).

33. One could object that Durkheim had already pinpointed the significance of shared kinesthetic experience with his notion of "effervescence." However,

Durkheim was not concerned with the role of gestural routines in the effervescent experience of ritual, nor did he examine the relation between the gestures performed and the beliefs conveyed by verbal chants or formulas. It is specifically this relation between verbal and gestural orders that interests Mauss—and in more than ritual situations. See *Les formes élémentaires de la vie religieuse* (Paris: Alcan, 1912).

34. Marcel Granet, *Danses et légendes de la Chine ancienne* (Paris: PUF, 1959; originally published 1926).

35. Curt Sachs, *World History of Dance,* trans. Bessie Schonberg (New York: Norton, 1965; originally published 1937), 145. Sachs was not directly a student of Mauss; he was trained in Germany. However, when Sachs felt threatened in Germany, he moved to Paris and was welcomed by Mauss and the team at the Musée d'Ethnographie. He became a curator at the Musée and wrote an important essay to accompany his exhibition on ethnographic dance: "La danse sacrée: A propos de l'exposition au Musée d'Ethnographie au Troc," *Cahiers d'art* 5–8 (1934): 158–162.

36. Michel Leiris, *La Possession et ses aspects théâtraux chez les Ethiopiens de Gondar* (Paris: Plon, 1958); Alfred Métraux, *Le Vaudou haitien* (Paris: Gallimard, 1958).

37. *L'Homme total,* 66. It is on these grounds that Karsenti identifies Mauss's program with that of phenomenology: see 96–97. See also Merleau-Ponty, *Sens et non-sens* (Paris: Nagel, 1966), 155–158.

38. *L'Homme total,* 280; added emphasis.

39. Phenomenology has frequently been cast by poststructuralism as naively positing the authenticity of the subject's perspective and thus at odds with poststructuralism. In *Merleau-Ponty and Modern Politics after Anti-Humanism* (Lanham, Md.: Rowman and Littlefield, 2007) Diana Coole critiques Michel Foucault in particular for accusing Merleau-Ponty of a "phenomenological subjectivism" that, she claims, his work does not manifest (9). See also Karsenti, *L'Homme total,* 284; and Claude Lefort, *Les formes de l'histoire* (Paris: Gallimard, 1978). I am suggesting here that the opposition between phenomenology and poststructuralism is exaggerated and that phenomenology is sometimes caricatured in order to assert a clear distinction.

40. *L'Homme total,* 285.

41. Jean-François Lyotard, *La phénoménologie* (Paris: PUF, 1954).

42. New York: Routledge, 1993.

43. In a slightly different and less oppositional version, Adorno and Benjamin also carried on the debate concerning the authenticity of immediate experience, the explanatory potential, epistemological privilege, and ontological priority of the illuminating particular versus the abstracted structure of historical conditions that produces the particular. For Adorno, it is practically impossible to access any immediate, authentic experience of historical conditions—including the condition of the body—because of the deformation of consciousness that has resulted from ideology associated with those historical conditions.

44. SA, xi.

45. See SA, xxxix.

46. These questions are still raised by anthropologists: see Clifford Geertz, *Local Knowledge: Further Essays in Interpretive Anthropology* (New York: Basic Books, 1983) on the emic perspective (that of the subject) versus the etic perspective (that of the researcher) as well as Turner's meditations on what an anthropologist can know in *The Forest of Symbols: Aspects of Ndembu Ritual* (Ithaca, N.Y.: Cornell University Press, 1964) for influential post-Maussian accounts.

47. *Signes* (Paris: Gallimard, 1960), 126; added emphasis.

48. *Signes,* 125.

49. *Signes,* 126.

50. *Signes,* 126; added emphasis.

51. *Signes,* 126–127.

52. *Signes,* 127.

53. In *Phenomenology of Perception* Merleau-Ponty suggests that through practice, "the part of the body in question sheds its anonymity, is revealed by the presence of a particular tension, as a certain power of action within the framework of the anatomical apparatus"; trans. Colin Smith (London: Routledge, 2002; originally published as *Phénoménologie de la perception* in 1945), 125.

54. Charles Blondel, *Introduction à la psychologie collective* (Paris: Armand Colin, 1927), 64.

55. Ibid., 152.

56. Mabel Elsworth Todd, *The Thinking Body: A Study of the Balancing Forces of Dynamic Man,* with a foreword by E. G. Brackett, M.D. (New York: Dance Horizons, 1937), 31.

57. *The Thinking Body,* 30.

58. Thomas J. Csordas, *Body/Healing/Meaning* (New York: Palgrave Macmillan, 2002), 244: "The ways we attend to and with our bodies, and even the possibility of attending, are neither arbitrary nor biologically determined, but are culturally constituted" (246).

59. *The Thinking Body,* 31.

60. Gregory Bateson, *Steps to an Ecology of Mind,* with a foreword by Catherine Bateson (Chicago: University of Chicago Press, 2000), 141; 133–134.

61. J. Lowell Lewis, "Genre and Embodiment: From Brazilian Capoeira to the Ethnology of Human Movement," in *Cultural Anthropology* 10, no. 2 (May 1995): 229.

62. Jean Starobinski, "A Short History of Bodily Sensation," in *Fragments for a History of the Human Body,* vol. 2, ed. Michel Feher with Ramona Naddaff and Nadia Tazi, trans. Sarah Matthews (New York: Zone Books, 1989), 360. Starobinski is following Freud's essay "Narcissism" when he relates attention to the body to antisocial self-absorption.

63. "A Short History," 369. Starobinski also is interested in Blondel insofar as he marks a shift at the turn of the century "from [a consideration of] the body as a physiological object (primarily the producer of internal information destined to be filtered by language) to the body according to society (primarily carrying out messages bearing *meaning,* according to the collective codes and rules)" (361). A careful reading of Blondel, however, shows that he does not argue that a "normal mind" is "a mind in which the cenesthesic factor [is]

dominated and controlled by the impersonal system of socialized discourse" (360). On the contrary, for Blondel, kinesthesia remains a source of differentiated but not coded sensations. As we shall see in Chapter Five, Jean-Paul Sartre follows Blondel's lead when he speaks of cenesthesia as prediscursive in *L'Être et le néant*.

2. Gestural Meaning

1. *La Nature: Notes, cours du Collège de France,* ed. and annot. Dominique Séglard (Paris: Seuil, 1995); *Nature: Lectures and Course Notes* (Evanston, Ill.: Northwestern University Press, 2003). trans. Colin Smith (London: Routledge, 2002); *Phenomenology of Perception,* trans. Colin Smith (London: Routledge, 2002). (All further references to this edition will be indicated in the text as PP.)

2. Despite Michel Serres's claim in *Les Cinq sens* (Paris: Hachette, 1998) that Merleau-Ponty largely ignored sensation and thus the role of the sense organs in shaping understanding, most philosophers, dance theorists, and anthropologists would agree that Merleau-Ponty is occupied with the question of the subject's sensual engagement with the world and with kinesthesia in particular. Merleau-Ponty's approach is deeply indebted to Husserl's ideas concerning the primacy of movement and kinesthetic sensation. For a helpful rendering of these ideas in English, see Jean-Luc Petit, "Constitution by Movement: Husserl in Light of Recent Neurobiological Findings," in *Naturalizing Phenomenology: Issues in Contemporary Phenomenology and Cognitive Science,* ed. Jean Petitot, Francisco J. Varela, Bernard Pachoud, and Jean-Michel Roy (Stanford: Stanford University Press, 1999) and Soren Overgaard, "The Importance of Bodily Movement to Husserl's Theory of *Fremderfahrung*" in *Recherches Husserliennes* 19, (2003), 55–65.

3. For an analysis of the gestures of painting see, especially, "Indirect Language and the Voices of Silence," in *Signs* (Evanston, Ill.: Northwestern University Press, 1964).

4. *La Nature,* 374.

5. Ibid., 374.

6. Ibid., 375; original emphasis.

7. It would be difficult to overestimate Merleau-Ponty's debt to Gestalt psychologists Adhémar Gelb, Kurt Koffka, and Wolfgang Köhler, frequently cited in his early works. All three provided empirical evidence to support Husserl's understanding of the embodied mind as projecting *Gestalten,* or forms of behavior, that mediate sensory stimuli. It is no coincidence that Koffka and Köhler taught Bergson's ideas in Germany, therefore creating a lineage leading from Bergson to Merleau-Ponty. For a thorough account of this lineage, see Mitchell G. Ash, *Gestalt Psychology in German Culture, 1890–1967: Holism and the Quest for Objectivity* (Cambridge: Cambridge University Press, 1995.

8. Merleau-Ponty writes that the body seizes with its "motor knowledge" the meaning of the word "sleet" (PP, 468–469); he suggests that a "spoken word is a genuine gesture, and it contains its meaning in the same way as the gesture contains its" (PP, 213). The philosopher may be taking his notion of "phonic

gesticulation" from Marcel Jousse, whose theory of words as gestures *("gestes laryngo-buccaux")* influenced the entire interwar generation; see *L'Anthropologie du geste: Le parlant, la parole et le souffle"* (Paris: Gallimard, 1978).

9. Gabriel de Tarde's *Les lois de l'imitation: Étude sociologique* (1890) had a significant influence on Blondel and many others, including the theorists of mime who were important to Merleau-Ponty's generation: Marcel Jousse and Paul Guillaume. For an analysis of Tarde's contributions, see the introduction by Bruno Karsenti to *Les lois de l'imitation* (Paris: Editions Kimé, 1993).

10. Paris: Minuit, 1983, especially pt. 1, chaps. 6–7; see also *Le Bergsonisme* (Paris: PUF, 1966) and *Logique de la sensation* (Paris: Éditions de la Différence, 1981), vol. 1. Deleuze argues in the latter that intensities of sensation explain movement and not the other way around. My quarrel here is not with the significance of self-affection (or, in Michel Bernard's words, *"auto-affection"*—defined as *"la double face passive et active"* of a sensory impression) but rather with the failure of Deleuzian approaches (including Bernard's) to take into consideration the motor patterns the mind simulates *in anticipation of the impression;* see Bernard, *De la creation choréographique* (Paris: Centre National de la Dance, 2001), 97. The relation between movement and affect has been an area of inquiry since the origins of modern psychology. If Sigmund Freud focused our attention on the verbal expression of affective disturbances and Jean-Martin Charcot was fascinated by their visual performance, Pierre Janet and Théodule Ribot examined more closely their instantiation in movement (see especially Ribot's *La Vie inconsciente et le mouvement* [1914]). For important recent work concerning the relation between emotion and the mind, see Antonio R. Damasio, *Descartes' Error: Emotion, Reason, and the Human Brain* (New York: Putnam, 1994), and *Looking for Spinoza: Joy, Sorrow and the Feeling Brain* (New York: Harcourt, 2003).

11. Henri Bergson, *Matter and Memory,* 17, trans. N. M. Paul and W. S. Palmer (New York: Zone Books, 1988), (quoted by Hansen, *New Philosophy for New Media* [Cambridge, Mass.: MIT Press, 2004], 3), and 16, 45 (added emphasis), 64. (All further references to this edition will be indicated in the text as MM.) See Deleuze, *Image-Mouvement,* 92.

12. For "the normal person," "every movement is, indissolubly, movement and consciousness of movement . . . every movement has a *background [fond]* . . . the movement and its background are 'moments of a unique totality'" (PP, 127; 128; original emphasis). See also Antonio R. Damasio, *The Feeling of What Happens: Body and Emotion in the Making of Consciousness* (New York: Harcourt Brace, 1999), on kinesthetic "background," 7. For Damasio, this background is responsible for chiseling out the present from the past: "the same movement is rarely, if ever, replicated twice. Initial conditions of the limb change, the goals are different and the kinematics must be re-computed" (12).

13. Deleuze divides Bergson's "image" into three types: the "movement-image" (the first image of the stimulus filtered in such a way that the organism can react according to its own interest); the "perception-image" (the response based on memories of previous actions); and the "affection-image" (the attitude or emotional response). See *Image-Mouvement,* 91–96.

14. Ibid., 91.
15. For full list of titles, see the Getty exhibition catalogue *Bill Viola: The Passions,* ed. John Walsh (Los Angeles: J. Paul Getty Museum, 2003).
16. The actors, John Malpede, Weba Garretson, Tom Fitzpatrick, John Fleck, Dan Gerrity, sometimes grasp each other, but they remain wrapped up in their own emotional and physical space.
17. www.getty.edu/art/exhibitions/viola/index.html.
18. Bill Viola's notebook quoted in John Walsh, "Emotions in Extreme Time," in Walsh, *Bill Viola: The Passions,* 33.
19. Bill Viola in "A Conversation: Hans Belting and Bill Viola," in Walsh, *Bill Viola: The Passions,* 200.
20. Paul Ekman has found evidence that technically "putting-on" facial gestures is more effective in creating emotional states than searching the soul for emotional equivalents, as in the Method acting approach derived from Konstantin Stanislavsky's theory of "affective memory." See Ekman, R. W. Levenson, and W. V. Friesen, "Autonomic Nervous System Activity Distinguishes between Emotions," *Science* 221:4616 (1983): 1208–1210, and "Voluntary Facial Action Generates Emotion-specific Autonomic Nervous System Activity," *Psychophysiology* 27:4 (1990): 363–384. For an application of Ekman's ideas to acting, see Richard Schechner, "Magnitudes of Performance," in Richard Schechner and Willa Appel, eds., *By Means of Performance: Intercultural Studies of Theatre and Ritual* (Cambridge: Cambridge University Press, 1990), as well as Schechner's detailed discussion of the neuroscience of acting in *Performance Theory,* 2nd ed. (New York: Routledge, 1988), 301–306.
21. This is Weba Garretson describing Viola's process in an interview, quoted in Walsh, "Emotions in Extreme Time," 35.
22. Ibid., 36.
23. Hansen, *New Philosophy for New Media,* 6 and "The Time of Affect or Bearing Witness to Life," *Critical Inquiry* 30:3 (Spring 2004): 584–626.
24. See Hansen's discussion of the face and its privileged relation to the communication of affect in "Affect as Interface: Confronting the 'Digital Facial Image,'" in *New Philosophy for New Media,* 127–159.
25. See, for example, the blocking of the arms and torso in Bill Viola's *Silent Mountain* (2001), also included in *The Passions.* For an insightful meditation on Viola's actors and the paradox of representing that which overflows representation, see Richard Meyer, introduction to *Representing the Passions: Histories, Bodies, Visions* (Los Angeles: Getty Research Institute, 2003).
26. Hansen, "The Time of Affect," 611.
27. Ray L. Birdwhistell proved that involuntary movements can be learned when he videotaped facial gestures, played the videotape back in slow motion, analyzed the muscular motions, and then taught himself how to perform them; see *Kinesics and Context* (Philadelphia: University of Pennsylvania Press, 1970). Schechner observes astutely that what was demonstrated in Birdwhistell's experiments was not so much that communities share a limited variety of learned gestures ("kinemes," Birdwhistell calls them), but that it is only these gestures that are *recognized* as meaningful: "There is an American way of

flashing the eyebrows—or, perhaps it is more accurate to say, there is an American cultural context within which brow flashes communicate culture-specific meanings" (*Performance Theory*, 301).

28. See Merleau-Ponty, PP, 97.

29. "Organism: A Meshwork of Selfless Selves," in *Organism and the Origins of Self*, ed. Alfred I. Tauber (Dordrecht: Kluwer Academic, 1991), 89; original emphasis.

30. "The Reenchantment of the Concrete," in *Incorporations*, ed. Jonathan Crary and Sanford Kwinter (New York: Zone Books, 1992), 333. See also Francisco Varela, Evan Thompson, and Eleanor Rosch, eds., *The Embodied Mind: Cognitive Science and Human Experience* (Cambridge, Mass.: MIT Press, 1991).

31. Varela, "Reenchantment," 333; added emphasis.

32. Alain Berthoz, *The Brain's Sense of Movement*, trans. Giselle Weiss (Cambridge, Mass.: Harvard University Press, 2000; originally published as *Le Sens du mouvement* in 1997), 20.

33. Ibid., 163.

34. Ibid., 201; added emphasis.

35. Ibid., 187–188.

36. Ibid., 164. On the "plasticity" of the nervous system, see also Catherine Malabou, *What Should We Do with Out Brain?*, Foreword by Marc Jeannerod, trans. Sebastian Rand (New York: Fordham University Press, 2008).

37. Maxine Sheets-Johnstone, *The Primacy of Movement* (Amsterdam: Johns Benjamins, 1999). Compare to Merleau-Ponty: "Our bodily experience of movement is not a particular case of knowledge; it provides us with a way of access to the world and the object, with a '*praktognosia*,' which has to be recognized as original and primary" (PP, 162).

38. See Daniel Stern *The Interpersonal World of the Infant: A View from Psychoanalysis and Developmental Psychology* (New York: Basic Books, 1985).

39. Charles Darwin, *The Expression of the Emotions in Man and Animals*, originally published 1872. In chap. 3, Darwin explains the neurological and physiological bases of the expressive gestures linked to pain and suffering (extreme contraction of many muscles of the body); rage (impeded blood flow, labored respiration); joy or vivid pleasure (quickened circulation, excited sensorium); and terror (secretions of the alimentary canal and kidneys increased; releasing of the sphincter). However, in each case, Darwin insists that an element of habit—in the sense of *habitus*—determines how these corporeal intensities will be expressed on the level of the body and face.

40. The vitality affects that relay the body's sensations back to itself are the first matter on which cultural distinctions play. According to Stern (as well as Merleau-Ponty), the autonomous body is never available to us in its precultural purity, but we can, as I will soon indicate, catch glimpses of its resonance in the "embodied schemata" by which it is caught and brought into cultural (perceptual/cognitive) being. On "embodied schemata" (smooth versus rough, up versus down) as early cultural imprinting, see the groundbreaking work of Mark Johnson, *The Body in the Mind: The Bodily Basis of Meaning, Imagination, and Reason* (Chicago: University of Chicago Press, 1987).

41. Stern, *The Interpersonal World,* xvii (added emphasis); xvii-xviii.
42. Ibid., xviii.
43. Ibid., 54.
44. The actors in *Anima* are Page Leong, John Fleck, and Henriette Brouwers. *Anima* was completed in 2000; it measures 16½ by 75 by 2 inches and is mounted on three LCD flat panels, small computers with the maker's name, logo, etc., covered by a frame.
45. Hansen, "The Time of Affect," 594.
46. Sellers, "Bodies of Light," in Walsh, *Bill Viola: The Passions,* 161.
47. In his own comments on *Four Hands,* Viola recounts how he determined which gestures to include, explaining that he sought to display those that are found in many cultures or religious traditions, not just one. Viola's contention that some gestures are universal has provoked much controversy. For summaries of the relevant research in linguistics, see David McNeill, *Hand and Mind: What Gestures Reveal about Thought* (Chicago: Chicago University Press, 1992); and Adam Kendon, *Gesture: Visible Action as Utterance* (Cambridge: Cambridge University Press, 2004), 327–354. See also Maxine Sheets-Johnstone, "Corporeal Archetypes and Power: Preliminary Clarification and Considerations of Sex," in *Body and Flesh: A Philosophical Reader,* ed. Donn Welton (Oxford: Blackwell, 1988).
48. Explicitly correcting Bergson, Merleau-Ponty writes: "The part played by the body in memory is comprehensible only if memory is, not only the constituting consciousness of the past, but an effort to reopen time on the basis of the implications contained in the present" (PP, 210).
49. Berthoz, *The Brain's Sense of Movement:* "I have repeatedly emphasized that the multisensory character of perception includes signals that derive not from the senses but from the intention to move. The character of perception is evidenced by this profound influence of *the intentional character of gesture*" (86). One of Merleau-Ponty's longest allusions to Bergson actually contains a critique of Bergson's conviction that the gestural projections ("nascent movements") flowing from the past to address the present are somehow separate from consciousness, and thus denied the dignity of intelligence bestowed on the agentic mind. Merleau-Ponty objects that intelligence is in fact operating on the order of kinesthetic feedback, and that, as a corollary, becoming aware of the qualities of that feedback is merely reflecting on what the body already knows: "Attention to life is the awareness we experience of 'nascent movements' in our bodies" (PP, 90–91).
50. Andrew N. Meltzoff, "Imitation, Intermodel Co-ordination and Representation in Early Infancy" in *Infancy and Epistemology: An Evaluation of Piaget's Theory,* ed. George Butterworth (Brighton, England: Harvester Press, 1981), 96–103.
51. *Signs,* 40; original emphasis.
52. Julia Kristeva, *Polylogue* (Paris: Seuil, 1977).
53. For a reading of Merleau-Ponty (and phenomenology more generally) that supports my own, see Jan Patocka, *Le monde naturel et le mouvement de l'existence humaine* (Dordrecht: Kluwer Academic, 1998). I thank Mark Hansen for directing me to this work. See also Damasio, *The Feeling of What*

Happens, on "all the dispositions that were acquired through experience [but that] lie dormant" (228).

54. See Drew Leder, *The Absent Body* (Chicago: Chicago University Press, 1990).

55. Ibid., 21. See also Deidre Sklar, "Remembering Kinesthesia: An Inquiry into Embodied Cultural Knowledge," in *Migrations of Gesture,* ed. Carrie Noland and Sally Ann Ness (Minneapolis: University of Minnesota Press, 2008).

56. PP, 469: "One day I 'caught on' to the word 'sleet', much as one imitates a gesture, not, that is, by analyzing it and performing an articulatory or phonetic action corresponding to each part of the word as heard, but by hearing it as a single modulation of the world of sound, and because this acoustic entity presents itself as 'something to pronounce' in virtue of the all-embracing correspondence existing between my perceptual potentialities and my motor ones . . . This is why consciousness is never subordinated to empirical language, why languages can be translated and learned. . . . Behind the spoken *cogito,* the one which is converted into discourse and into essential truth, there lies a tacit *cogito,* myself experienced by myself."

57. Thomas J. Csordas, *Body/Healing/Meaning* (New York: Palgrave MacMillan, 2002), 244: "The ways we attend to and with our bodies, and even the possibility of attending, are neither arbitrary nor biologically determined, but are culturally constituted" (246).

3. Inscription and Embodiment

1. See Annette Michelson, "In Praise of Horizontality," *October,* 37 (Summer 1986), 3. The issue contains two essays by Leroi-Gourhan, "The Religion of the Caves: Magic or Metaphysics" and "The Hands of Gargas," both translated by Michelson (from *Le fil du temps* of 1973).

2. Margaret W. Conkey, "New Approaches in the Search for Meaning? A Review of Research in 'Paleolithic Art,'" *Journal of Field Archeology* 14 (1987): 414. For a survey that situates Leroi-Gourhan's findings with respect to contemporary scholarship, see Mary Copple, "Gesture and Speech: André Leroi-Gourhan's Theory of the Coevolution of Manual and Intellectual Activities," *Gesture,* 3, no. 1 (2003): 47–94 and Marc Groenen, *Leroi-Gourhan: Essence et contingence dans la destinée humaine* (Paris: De Boeck et Larcier, 1996). For a more critical view, see Donald Preziosi, *Rethinking Art History: Meditations on a Coy Science* (New Haven: Yale University Press, 1989). The problem with Preziosi's argument is that he looks only at the structuralist reading of cave art from the first edition of *Treasures of Prehistoric Art,* first published as *Préhistoire de l'art occidental* (Paris: Mazenod, 1965) but republished in 1971 with a new introduction by Leroi-Gourhan that places his own structuralist reading in question.

3. See Randall White, introduction to *Gesture and Speech,* trans. Anna Bostock Berger (Cambridge, Mass.: MIT Press, 1993), xviii. White claims that the number of propositions advanced in *Le Geste et la parole* that are "empirically outdated" are "remarkably few." He also suggests that closer study would reveal the influence of Leroi-Gourhan's ideas on Michel Foucault's *Archeology of Knowledge,* Pierre Bourdieu's *Outline of a Theory of Practice,* and Jacques

Derrida's *Of Grammatology* (xxi). (All further references to the English translation of *Gesture and Speech* will be abbreviated in the text as GS.)

4. *Technics and Time,* vol. 1, *The Fault of Epimetheus,* trans. Richard Beardsworth and George Collins (Stanford: Stanford University Press, 1998), 84.

5. *Technics and Time,* vol. 1, 137. (All quotations from volume 1 will be from the edition just cited; all quotations from volume 2 will be from *Technics and Time, 2: Disorientation,* trans. Stephen Barker (Stanford, Ca.: Stanford University Press, 2009).

6. *Technics and Time,* vol. 1, 141.

7. Leroi-Gourhan initially intended to write a thesis with Marcel Granet at the École des Hautes Études. Granet, a student of Mauss and the author of *Danse et légendes de la Chine ancienne,* died before Leroi-Gourhan finished his thesis. After Granet's death, Leroi-Gourhan opted to continue his work with Mauss, with whom he had already studied at the Institut d'Ethnologie de l'Université de Paris. It is significant that Claude Lévi-Strauss, as opposed to both Leroi-Gourhan and Merleau-Ponty, was not a student of Mauss. See Marcel Fournier, *Marcel Mauss* (Paris: Fayard, 1994), 694, 606; and Maurice Merleau-Ponty, "De Mauss à Claude Lévi-Strauss," in *Signes* (Paris: Gallimard, 1960), 143–157.

8. An important exception is Bruno Karsenti, who examines the influence of Mauss in Leroi-Gourhan's work in "Techniques du corps et normes sociales: De Mauss à Leroi-Gourhan," *Intellectica* nos. 1–2, (1998): 227–240.

9. "Les Techniques du corps," in *Sociologie et anthropologie,* with an introducation by Claude Lévi-Strauss (Paris: PUF, 1973), 384.

10. See Dominique Baffier, Francine David, Gilles Gaucher, and Michel Orliac, "André Leroi-Gourhan et l'ethnologie préhistorique," in *André Leroi-Gourhan ou Les Voies de l'homme: Actes du colloque du CNRS, Mars 1987* ed. Lucien Bernot (Paris: Albin Michel, 1988), 27–49.

11. "In Praise of Horizontality," 4.

12. True to the tendencies of his generation, Leroi-Gourhan was a historical materialist in the tradition of Marx, not a metaphysician like Reinach or Breuil. See Jacques Gutwirth, "André Leroi-Gourhan et l'ethnologie de la modernité," in *André Leroi-Gourhan ou Les Voies de l'homme,* 123–135.

13. *Le Geste et la parole,* vol. 1, *Technique et langage* (Paris: Albin Michel, 1964), 210. (Further references to this volume will appear in the text as GP I. References to volume 2 will appear as GP II. All English translations are my own, unless otherwise indicated. I have consulted the translations in *Gesture and Speech,* but sometimes find infelicities; for instance, lexical echos with *De la grammatologie* have been effaced.)

14. *Technics and Time,* vol. 1, 136.

15. See Edmund Husserl, *Méditations cartésiennes* (Paris: Colin, 1931), 81, and *The Idea of Phenomenology,* trans. Lee Hardy (Dordrecht: Kluwer Academic, 1999).

16. "We consider mobility to be the significant feature of evolution toward Man" (GP I, 41). It should be noted that Disability studies presents a challenge to Leroi-Gourhan's universalizing theory of human embodiment as linked to a particular mode of ambulation; see Susan S. Stocker, "Problems of Embodiment and Problematic Embodiment" in *Hypatia* 16:30 (Summer 2001): 30–55.

17. *The Primacy of Movement* (Amsterdam: John Benjamins, 1999). See also Mary

LeCron Foster and Lucy Jayne Botscharow, *The Life of Symbols* (Boulder, Colo.: Westview Press, 1990); Christopher Stringer and Clive Gamble, *In Search of the Neanderthals: Solving the Puzzle of Human Origins* (New York: Thames and Hudson, 1993); Randall White, Heidi Knecht, and Anne Pike-Tay, eds., *Before Lascaux: The Complex Record of the Upper Paleolithic* (Boca Raton, Fl.: CRC Press, 1993).

18. Maxine Sheets-Johnstone, *The Roots of Power: Animate Form and Gendered Bodies* (Chicago: Open Court, 1994), 205.

19. *The Primacy of Movement,* 21 and 23; original emphasis.

20. Tim Ingold, *The Perception of the Environment: Essays in Livelihood, Dwelling, and Skill* (New York: Routledge, 2000), 292. In a chapter entitled "'People Like Us': The Concept of the Anatomically Modern Human," Ingold presents his argument that modern geneticists have mistakenly resorted to "the language of information theory" (380). This distorts our understanding of the genome, he writes, because it suggests that a genetic endowment is a "code" that the body deciphers, whereas in fact DNA is not a coded "message" but a "developmental system": "just as a received message may be interpreted differently in different circumstances, so also the genotype will be 'realised' in different ways depending upon the environmental context, leading to observed variations in phenotypic form" (383); "Hence there is no 'decoding' of the genome that is not iself a process of development" (384).

21. *The Perception of the Environment,* 292.

22. Ibid.

23. See Alain Berthoz, *The Brain's Sense of Movement,* trans. Giselle Weiss (Cambridge, Mass.: Harvard University Press, 2000), 162–164.

24. To my knowledge, there is no English translation of *Évolution et techniques,* which is divided into two volumes: *L'Homme et la matière* (Paris: Albin Michel, 1943; rev. 1971) and *Milieu et techniques* (Paris: Albin Michel, 1945; rev. 1973). All translations are accordingly my own.

25. On "maximum grip" and the "intentional arc" of technically proficient activity, see Dreyfus, "The Current Relevance of Merleau-Ponty's Phenomenology of Embodiment," in *Perspectives on Embodiment,* ed. Honi Haber and Gail Weiss (New York: Routledge, 1996).

26. *L'Homme et la matière,* 385 and 384.

27. Ibid., 384.

28. Ibid., 385.

29. Ibid.

30. See Maxine Sheets-Johnstone, "What Are We Naming" in *Body Image and Body Schema: Interdisciplinary Perspectives on the Body,* ed. Helena De Preester and Veroniek Knockaert (Amsterdam: John Benjamins, 2005): "corporeal-kinetic intentionalities" is the name she gives to the agentic force determining the perpetual alterations of movement patterns, or gestures (221). See also Michel Bernard, *De la création chorégraphique* (Paris: Centre National de la Danse, 2001); José Gil, "The Dancer's Body" in *A Shock to Thought: Expression after Deleuze and Guattari,* ed. Brian Massumi (London: Routledge, 2002); and Sally Ann Ness, "Choreographies of Tourism in Yosemite Valley: Rethinking 'Place' in Terms of Motility" in *Performance Re-*

search 12:2 (2008): 79–84. Ness identifies the region of movement that pleasures or takes interest in itself as human "motility," as opposed to "mobility," which she understands to be "a capability for, or condition of movement, that is not necessarily experienced by the moving entity in any positive way." In contrast, "motility" is "a phenomenological and semiotic experience of movement as a life-sustaining condition of being" (79).

31. For summaries of recent research on the inter-implication of cognitive and motor development, or "the motor theory of perception," see Alain Berthoz *The Brain's Sense of Movement; The Body and the Self,* ed. José Luis Bermúdez, Anthony Marcel, and Naomi Eilan (Boston: MIT Press, 1995); and *The Cambridge Handbook of Situated Cognition,* ed. Philip Robbins and Murat Aydede (New York: Cambridge University Press, 2009).

32. *Technics and Time,* vol. 1, 139.

33. Ibid., 146.

34. *Phenomenology of Perception* (New York: Routledge, 2002), 106–107; added emphasis. All further references to this volume will be indicated as PP.

35. *Of Grammatology,* trans. Gayatri Chakravorty Spivak (Baltimore: Johns Hopkins University Press, 1976), 84. See also *De la grammatologie* (Paris, Minuit, 1967), 126. (All further references to the English translation will be abbreviated as OG. References to the French original will be abbreviated as DG).

36. Spivak's translation of *De la grammatologie* renders the French original, *"Délivrer l'unité du concept d'homme"* (DG, 124), as "To free unity from the concept of man" (OG, 83). To my mind, this makes no sense. In the relevant context, Derrida appears to be using *"délivrer"* in its second sense, not as "to free" but as "to provide" or "to return to." I have therefore inserted my own translation.

37. Writing—treated by Derrida as the "external" mode of programmation par excellence—enters the problematic of *Gesture and Speech* not as a prosthetic tool or mnemonic device but as an example of a *gestural activity.* Speaking of those "penumbral" gestures of which we can, at times, become aware, Leroi-Gourhan provides the examples of *"les gestes qu'on enchaîne au cours de la toilette, du repas, de l'écriture"* (GP II, 29). Echoing Leroi-Gourhan, the linguist Roy Harris has argued that writing may very well have originated independently of speech and that it bears a closer relation to other physical actions designed to alter the environment; see *Signs of Writing* (New York: Routledge, 1995). See also Vivian Sobchack, "'Susie Scribbles': On Technology, Technë, and Writing Incarnate," in *Carnal Thoughts: Embodiment and Moving Image Culture* (Berkeley: University of California Press, 2004).

38. See Melanie Klein, "The Role of the School in the Libidinal Development of the Child," in *Contributions to Psychoanalysis: 1921–1945* (London: Hogarth, 1948), 73–76, as well as Derrida's long note on Klein, OG, 333–334.

39. In order to bring home his point, Leroi-Gourhan cites a study conducted on adults afflicted with agraphia, the inability to write. He recalls that it occurs not when centers of high-order conceptualization are damaged but rather when lesions appear in the "motor zones of the hand" (GP I, 126). Symbolic activity, according to this reading, must be related to motor experience as well as conceptual skill. Leroi-Gourhan's thesis has recently been supported by the

work of Terence Deacon; see *The Symbolic Species: The Co-evolution of Language and the Human Brain* (New York: Penguin, 1997).

40. When Derrida states that the history of the *grammè* is the "history of life," he argues that all systems of differentiation are based on an on/off system, one composed of quantitative differences (force/no force, or charge/no charge). The analog is only an apparently qualitative system underwritten by a quantitative, or digital, system. The *grammè,* in this sense, opens the possibility of a *being there* through the constitution of the *being there/not being there* opposition. Hence he can say that that which constitutes life ("there," "on") constitutes it only in relation to its absence ("not there," "off," lack of charge, or death). Derrida presents the same structure as the death that underwrites life in "Freud and the Scene of Writing," in *Writing and Difference,* trans. Alan Bass (London: Routledge, 1978). On Derrida's neglect of a history of the qualitative actualization (as opposed to the structure itself), see Stiegler, *Technics and Time, 2, 30.*

41. For Leroi-Gourhan, writing is an animal affair. Humans are a part of the history of writing not because writing extends from genes to cybernetic programs (pace Derrida), but because writing arguably begins with bears. In *Préhistoire de l'art occidental,* Leroi-Gourhan studies, among other prehistoric sites, the cave of Rouffignac, where he speculates that the marks left by bear claws might have inspired humans to leave behind their prints as well. It is thus as gestural activity, not memory storage, that writing must be analyzed. Many of Leroi-Gourhan's paleoethnographic investigations are devoted to demonstrating the continuum between animal markings on cave walls and human-attributed forms of mark-making (see "The Hands of Gargas").

42. Leroi-Gourhan anticipates one of the founding principles of enactive cognition, or the "motor theory of perception," which teaches that solicitations to act and the protentive neuronal activity they trigger are essential to the development of the perceptual organs. The development of movement-dependent perceptual skills in turn makes it possible for the mind to function cognitively, symbolically, and hermeneutically. See P. Viviani, "Motor-perceptual Interactions: The Evolution of an Idea," in *Cognitive Science in Europe,* ed. Michel Imbert et. al. (New York: Springer-Verlag, 1987). J. J. Gibson is the originator of the ecological approach to perception on which later enactive approaches are based; see *The Ecological Approach to Visual Perception* (New York: Houghton-Mifflin, 1979). For a clear presentation of recent research confirming the seminal importance of movement experience for the development of animal and human neuromotor systems, see George Butterworth, "An Ecological Perspective on the Origins of Self," in *The Body and the Self,* ed. José Luis Bermúdez, Anthony Marcel, and Naomi Eilan (Cambridge, Mass.: MIT Press, 1995).

43. Derrida meditates on handwriting and its digitalization in *Paper Machine,* trans. Rachel Bowlby (Stanford: Stanford University Press, 2005).

44. Mark Poster and Mark Seltzer both contend that computer writing renders less immediate, more attenuated, the contact between the hand and its product, the inscription. See *The Mode of Information: Poststructuralism and Social*

Context (Chicago: Chicago University Press, 1990) and Mark Seltzer, *Bodies and Machines* (New York: Routledge, 1992).

45. http://studiocleo.com/cauldron/volume2/confluence/billmarsh/.
46. www.vispo.com/nio/index.html.
47. www.shadoof.net/in/riverisland.html.
48. www.vniverse.com/.
49. www.camilleutterback.com/textrain.html.
50. www.sitec.fr/users/akenatondocks/DOCKS-datas_f/collect_f/auteurs_f/C_f/ CASTELLIN_f/anim_f/lasomme_F/poeme.html. For a documentation of the installation as it was shown at Beaubourg, France, in 2002, see www.sitec .fr/users/akenatondocks/.
51. www.camilleutterback.com/.
52. Camille Utterback, personal communication, email, September 24, 2008.
53. For a supporting argument, see Mark Hansen, *Bodies in Code: Interfaces with Digital Media* (New York: Routledge, 2006) and *Embodying Technesis: Technology Beyond Writing,* foreword by N. Katherine Hayles (Ann Arbor: The University of Michigan Press, 2000).
54. Artist-engineer Simon Penny has cautioned that even aesthetic uses of digital platforms risk adopting some of the mechanical features (and associated ideologies) incorporated in their inception. He worries that the device may bring its industrial environment along with it, that it cannot be divorced from an ideology that unhinges action from perception: "There is thus, an underlying and seldom acknowledged conflict between the values reified in the hardware and software of computer technology, and the purposes to which these technologies are put"; "Experience and Abstraction: The Arts and the Logic of the Machine," *Fibreculture* 1 (2008): 8.

4. Inscription as Performance

1. Modernist primitivism might be considered an epiphenomenon of industrialization that emerged near the beginning of the twentieth century in Europe. It is characterized by a fascination with "tribal arts" (Picasso and the Surrealists); incantation (Dada); jazz *(tout Paris);* non-Western dance and ritual forms (Maya Deren, Curt Sachs); and "primitive" peoples (German and French ethnography). For persuasive accounts, see Tyler Stovall, *Paris Noir: African Americans in the City of Light* (New York: Houghton Mifflin, 1996); James Clifford, *The Predicament of Culture: Twentieth-century Ethnography, Literature, and Art* (Cambridge, Mass.: Harvard University Press, 1988); Petrine Archer-Straw, *Negrophilia: Avant-garde Paris and Black Culture in the 1920s* (London: Thames and Hudson, 2000); William Rubin, *Primitivism in Twentieth-Century Art: Affinity of the Tribal and the Modern* (New York: Museum of Modern Art, 1984); Carole Sweeney, *From Fetish to Subject: Race, Modernism, and Primitivism 1919–1935* (Westport, Conn.: Praeger, 2004).
2. From Jean-Dominique Rey, "L'Expérience des signes: Entretien avec Henri Michaux," in *Henri Michaux: Oeuvres choisies 1927-1984* (Marseille: Réunion des Musées Nationaux, 1993), 212.

3. The *"par"* of *"Par des traits"* is hard to translate: it can mean "with" or "by means of" or "through" or "taking the route of" lines.

4. Henri Michaux, *Oeuvres complètes,* vol. 3, ed. Raymond Bellour, Ysé Tran, and Mireille Cardot (Paris: Gallimard, 2004) abbreviated from here on as OC III), 1249–1250.

5. Michaux, in Rey, "L'Expérience des signes: Entretien avec Henri Michaux," 212.

6. Michaux's critics have been anxious to identify his turn toward the gestural with his desire for a liberation of the subject. See, in particular, Max Loreau; Henri Meschonnic, *La Rime et la vie* (Lagrasse: Verdier, 1989); and Gérard Dessons, "La Manière d'Henry: Prolégomènes à un traité du trait," in *Méthodes et saviors chez Henri Michaux,* ed. Gérard Dessons (Poitiers: La Licorne, 1993).

7. See Margit Rowell, *La Peinture, le geste, l'action: L'existentialisme en peinture* (Paris: Klincksieck, 1972); Michael Leja, *Reframing Abstract Expressionism: Subjectivity and Painting in the 1940s* (New Haven: Yale University Press, 1993); Richard Schiff, "Performing an Appearance," in *Abstract Expressionism: The Critical Developments,* ed. Michael Auping (New York: Abrams, 1987); Mary Kelly, "Reviewing Modernist Criticism," in *Art after Modern-ism: Rethinking Representation,* ed. Brian Wallis, with a foreword by Marcia Tucker (New York: New Museum of Contemporary Art, 1984); Amelia Jones, *Body Art: Performing the Subject* (Minneapolis: University of Minnesota Press, 1998).

8. Leslie Jones, "Prehistoric Re-Marks: Henri Michaux's Visual Exploration into the 'Origin of Painting'" (unpublished manuscript). Michaux's personal library contained accounts of prehistoric visual culture by Henri Breuil and Hugo Obermaier.

9. Abbé Henri Breuil and Dr. Hugo Obermaier, *The Cave of Altamira at Santillana del Mar, Spain,* trans. Mary E. Boyle (Madrid: Tipografia de Archivos, 1935).

10. See Jones, "Prehistoric Re-Marks," 3.

11. Georges Henri Luquet, *L'Art et la religion des hommes fossiles* (Paris: Masson, 1926).

12. Thus, Michaux evokes "prehistory"—as a discourse and as a mode of representation—by doing precisely what the prehistorians do: he groups together sequences of seemingly related (visually similar) motifs without taking into account their semantic or syntaxic relations, that is, without attending to the meaning or order they might have had within their indigenous cultural environments or sites. As Georges Braatschi has remarked, Michaux's ink drawings possess "the character of collector's cabinets"; see "Michaux, calife de l'intérieur," *Tribune de Genève,* October 26, 1984.

13. Michel Cournot's description of Michaux's work space testifies to this variety of sources: "Une table de bois, près de la fenêtre, n'est qu'une confusion de pinceaux chinois, de grattoirs, de revues étrangères de chimie, de géographie, de papier déchirés couverts, de guingois, d'une minuscule écriture illisible"; "Michaux sur le bout des doigts," *Le Nouvel observateur,* January 11, 1985, 63.

14. Interview by the author with Micheline Phamkin, December 2004. The cheap paper was bought at an art supply store, and thus was intended as a support not for writing but for drawing studies and exercises.

15. Henri Michaux, *Oeuvres Complètes,* vol. 2, ed. Raymond Bellour and Ysé Tran (Paris: Gallimard, 2001) abbreviated from here on as OCII, 598.

16. A similar sequence is repeated in each section, reinforcing the impression that Michaux himself actually drafted the ink drawings in that particular order, that he himself progressed from making small, tightly knit, constrained figures to thrusting greater amounts of ink with greater force onto the page. Michaux obviously approved of the order in which Bertelé arranged the pages, so to some extent he is responsible for it. And yet again he refused to take responsibility for Bertelé's choices.

17. René Bertelé, "Préface à Parcours," OC III, 432.

18. "Mouvements," in *Mouvements* (OC II, 440); added emphasis.

19. "Le signe peut exprimer mieux que n'importe quoi, le "MOI-JE" ("Signes," in OC II, 431).

20. Michaux first visited China—which is his principal reference for calligraphy—in 1930. He was also influenced by Paul Klee's line drawings: see "Aventure des lignes," in OC II, 360–363.

21. Frances Morris, Introduction to *Paris Post War: Art and Existentialism 1945–55,* ed. Frances Morris (London: Tate Gallery, 1993), 144.

22. Leslie Jones, "'A Barbarian in Asia': Henri Michaux's Works in Ink, 1927–55" (diss., Institute of Fine Arts, New York University, 2003), 155–156. I am not convinced this last point is true; it seems to me that Michaux often does follow a stroke order. I return to this question in my reading below.

23. "A Barbarian in Asia," 156. See also ed. Anne-Élisabeth Halpern and Véra Mihailovich-Dickman, eds., *Quelques orients d'Henri Michaux,* (Éditions Findlay, 1996), and Richard Sieburth, "Signs in Action: The Ideograms of Ezra Pound and Henri Michaux," in *Untitled Passages by Henri Michaux,* ed. Catherine de Zegher (New York: Drawing Center, 2000).

24. For a review of calligraphic script styles and their history, as well as a revealing comparison between calligraphy and the practices of Jackson Pollock and Willem de Kooning, see Robert E. Harrist, Jr., "Reading Chinese Calligraphy" in *The Embodied Image: Chinese Calligraphy from the John B. Elliott Collection,* ed. Harrist and Wen C. Fong, (New York: Abrams, 1999), 3–27.

25. Max Loreau, "La poésie, la peinture et le fondement du langage," in *La Peinture à l'oeuvre et l'énigme du corps* (Paris: Gallimard, 1980), 46.

26. At times, Michaux restrained himself further, using only the center of the paper and leaving large margins on all sides blank. In some of his later unpublished ink drawings, Michaux even pencils in this square. I thank Micheline Phamkin for showing me a series of ink drawings in the style of *Mouvements* that contain penciled squares inside of which the mark clusters appear.

27. OC II, 430–431.

28. For an overview of gestural painting during Michaux's period, see Rowell and Geneviève Bonnefoi, *Les Années fertiles: 1940–1960* (Villefranche-de-Rouergue: Mouvements Éditions, 1988).

29. See Henri Michaux, *Oeuvres completes,* vol. 1, ed. Raymond Bellour and Ysé Tran (Paris: Gallimard, 1998) (abbreviated from here on as OC I). The editors list Michaux's first exhibition as occurring June 3–23, 1937 (224).

30. "Chronologie," cxxiv. In Michaux's own words: "Vu l'expo Dubuffet. Plein de qualities de peintre ce Dubuffet. J'ai été conquis. Depuis, je me reprends . . . un peu" (quoted cxxiv). During 1946–47, Dubuffet made at least seven portraits of Michaux in either India ink, pencil, or oil on canvas. See *Catalogue de travaux de Jean Dubuffet plus beaux qu'ils croient: Portraits* (Paris: J. J. Pauvert, 1964–1991).

31. Sarah Wilson, "Paris Post War: In Search of the Absolute," in Morris, *Paris Post War,* 34.

32. "Préambule," in *L'Afrique fantôme* (Paris: Gallimard, 1981; originally published 1934, without the "Préambule"), 7.

33. This is Micheline Phamkin's rendering of a sentence Michaux pronounced to her in reference to Dubuffet's works. Interview by the author, December 2004.

34. Bonnefoi, *Les Années fertiles,* 22.

35. Claude Gregory quoted by Alfred Pacquement in Hélène Seikel, Daniel Abadie, and Alfred Pacquement, *Paris–New York* (Paris: Centre Pompidou, 1977), 540.

36. The chronology supplied in OC II lists three major exhibits in which Pollock was displayed with Michaux: "Un art autre" (Paris, December 1952); "Vitalita nell'arte" (Venice, summer 1959); and an exhibition in Turin in 1963 that reunited Dubuffet, Fautrier, Mathieu, Wols, Tobey, Pollock, and Michaux (OCII, xxx).

37. Geneviéve Bonnefoi, "Entretiens et témoignages sur l'oeuvre peint [*sic*] d'Henri Michaux," in *Cahiers de l'Herne: Henri Michaux,* ed. Raymond Bellour (Paris: Minard, 1966), 377; my translation.

38. Apparently, in contrast, Mathieu and Degottex both gave themselves an intense training in calligraphy and practiced for hours before they placed the definitive paraphe on the canvas.

39. Bonnefoi in Bellour, *Cahiers de l'Herne,* 375.

40. Rowell, *La Peinture, le geste,* 49; all translations are my own.

41. Ibid., 112.

42. Ibid., 42.

43. Ibid., 42 and 47.

44. Ibid., 47.

45. The discovery of a set of small canvases that may have been painted by Pollock during 1944–45 while working with the photographer Herbert Matter complicates the distinction I am trying to support. It may be that Pollock, inspired by Matter's abstract light experiments, tried out his drip techniques on smaller canvases before moving to the larger scale. See Ellen G. Landau's essay "Pollock Matters," www.pollockexhibit.com.

46. See Jones, *Body Art,* especially the chapter entitled "The Pollockian Performative."

47. See Schiff, "Performing an Appearance." As Jones and Richard Schiff have both suggested, the "Pollockian performative" is a painterly utterance in which the artist (here Michaux), rather than leaving traces of his deepest psychological impulses, produces these impulses in the act of inscription itself.

48. See also Michael Newman, "The Marks, Traces, and Gestures of Drawing," in *The Stage of Drawing: Gesture and Act: Selections from the Tate Gallery,* selected by Avis Newman, curated by Catherine de Zegher (New York: The Tate and the Drawing Center, 2003).

49. T. J. Clark, *Farewell to an Idea: Episodes from a History of Modernism* (London: Yale University Press, 1999), 323.

50. To be fair, deskilling techniques were prefigured by Breton's technique of changing the speed, or *"vitesse,"* at which he allowed his hand to scribble down thoughts. Breton even differentiated between five different speeds of writing, each of which was identified with another layer of deconditioning.

51. *The Open Work,* trans. Anna Cancogni, with an introduction by David Robey (Cambridge, Mass.: Harvard University Press, 1989), 103; added emphasis.

52. Ibid., 103; original emphasis.

53. *Émergences, resurgences* (Geneva: Albert Skira, 1972), 9; original emphasis.

54. "Préface à Parcours," 432.

55. The grid structure has many implications, only some of which I can evoke here. For a brief but suggestive summary, see Rosalind E. Krauss, "Grids," in *The Originality of the Avant-garde and Other Modernist Myths* (Cambridge, Mass.: MIT Press, 1987): "grids are not only spatial to start with, they are visual structures that explicitly reject a narrative or sequential reading of any kind" (13); "the grid is a way of abrogating the claims of natural objects to have an order particular to themselves" (9).

56. Several critics allude to Michaux's kinesthetic experience, mostly with respect to the mescaline drawings, but without applying or generating a theory of kinesthetic experience as central to the act of inscription itself. See Dessons, Loreau, Meschonnic, and the psychoanalytic reading of Michaux's *grapho-manie* in Anne Brun, *Henri Michaux ou le corps halluciné* (Paris: Institut d'édition Sanofi-Synthélabo, 1999).

57. OC II, 429.

58. OC II, 344. Introduced into France and Belgium at the end of the nineteenth century, Swedish gymnastics was based on medical rather than military principles. See Gilbert Andrieu, *L'Éducation physique au XXe siècle: Une histoire des pratiques* (Paris: Actio, 1993). Ironically, Andrieu compares Swedish gymnastics to hatha yoga, the very form Michaux idealizes as superior to the training he received.

59. Precisely which form of Hindu dance Michaux is referencing in his note to "Observations" is impossible to determine. Similar in this regard to Artaud, Michaux makes the mistake of assuming that Eastern movement traditions remain faithful to the natural body ; see OC II, 344.

60. OC II, 313–314.

61. OC II, 372.

5. The Gestural Performative

1. First published as "Performative Acts and Gender Constitution: An Essay in Phenomenology and Feminist Theory," in *Performing Feminisms: Feminist Critical Theory and Theatre,* ed. Sue-Ellen Case (Baltimore: Johns Hopkins University Press, 1990).

2. Introduction to *Gender Trouble: Feminism and the Subversion of Identity* (New York: Routledge, 2006; originally published 1990), 8. (All further references to this edition will be abbreviated in the text as GT.)

3. There is nothing original in asserting that Butler does not attend sufficiently to somatic experience. A growing body of feminist scholarship takes Butler to task for neglecting it; see in particular Maxine Sheets-Johnstone, *The Roots of Power: Animate Form and Gendered Bodies* (Chicago: Open Court, 1994); Susan Bordo, *Unbearable Weight* (Berkeley: University of California Press, 1993); and Vicki Kirby, "Corporeal Habits: Addressing Essentialism Differently," in "Feminism and the Body," special issue, *Hypatia*, 6, no. 3 (1991): 4–24. For more recent scholarship, see Diana Taylor, *The Archive and the Repertoire: Performing Cultural Memory in the Americas* (Durham, N.C.: Duke University Press, 2003).

4. Butler in fact uses the example of a girl baby being "interpellated" in *Bodies That Matter: On the Discursive Limits of "Sex"* (London: Routledge, 1993): "Consider the medical interpellation which (the recent emergence of the sonogram notwithstanding) shifts an infant from an "it" to a "she" or a "he," and in that naming, the girl is "girled," brought into the domain of language and kinship through the interpellation of gender. But that "girling" of the girl does not end there; on the contrary, that founding interpellation is reiterated by various authorities and throughout various intervals of time to reenforce or contest this naturalized effect" (7–8). (Further references to this volume will be abbreviated as BTM.)

5. *Throwing Like a Girl and Other Essays in Feminist Philosophy and Social Theory* (Bloomington: Indiana University Press, 1990), 141–159. Young has published a reflection on this essay, "'Throwing Like a Girl': Twenty Years Later," in *Body and Flesh: A Philosophical Reader,* ed. Donn Welton (Oxford: Blackwell, 1998). She worries that her model of motility—derived from Heidegger's *Being and Time* and Merleau-Ponty's *Phenomenology of Perception*—might be incomplete, but otherwise does not revise her former position.

6. *Throwing Like a Girl,* 146.

7. Ibid., 151.

8. Ibid., 148 and 151; original emphasis.

9. Ibid., 151.

10. André Leroi-Gourhan, *Le Geste et la parole II: La mémoire et les rythmes* (Paris: Albin Michel, 1964), 29.

11. BTM, 10.

12. *Excitable Speech: A Politics of the Performative* (London: Routledge, 1997), 5.

13. See, in particular, Butler's critique of Lacan in "The Lesbian Phallus and the Morphological Imaginary," BTM, 57–91. Butler embraces the Lacanian axiom that *percipi* are only sustained "through nomination" (80); however, she pushes Lacan to say that such nomination must, by the very nature of the distortion, be repeated in order to sustain its effects: "the ego established through this identificatory relation is itself a relation, indeed, the cumulative history of such relations. As a result, the ego is not a self-identical substance, but a sedimented history of imaginary relations . . ." (74).

14. Michel Foucault, *The Archeology of Knowledge and the Discourse on Language,* trans. A. M. Sheridan Smith (New York: Routledge, 2002), 26. (All further references to this edition will be abbreviated in the text as AK.)

15. See *The History of Sexuality: An Introduction* (New York: Vintage Books, 1990), 102. In *Bodies That Matter,* Butler writes: "The paradox of subjectivation *(assujetissement)* is precisely that the subject who would resist such norms is itself enabled, if not produced, by such norms. Although this constitutive constraint does not foreclose the possibility of agency, it does locate agency as a reiterative or rearticulatory practice, immanent to power, and not a relation of external opposition to power" (BTM, 15).

16. See Gilles Deleuze's description of the *"énoncé"* in *Foucault* (Paris: Minuit, 1986); 16–17 and 23.

17. "Thus conceived," Foucault concludes, "discourse is not the majestically unfolding manifestation of a thinking, knowing, speaking subject, but, on the contrary, a totality, in which the dispersion of the subject and his discontinuity with himself may be determined" (AK, 55).

18. Jacques Derrida, "Signature, Event, Context," in *Limited, Inc.* (Baltimore: Johns Hopkins University Press, 1977), 57.

19. "Signature, Event, Context," 67.

20. The page from *Of Grammatology* cited by Butler indicates Derrida's debt to Jean Starobinski's *Les mots sous les mots: Les Anagrammes de Ferdinand de Saussure,* trans. Gayatri Chakravorty Spivak (Baltimore: Johns Hopkins University Press, 1997), 379, which provides deconstruction's founding textual model of authorial agency as an aleatory epiphenomenon of writing.

21. Butler's move to deny the "fiction of the ego as master of circumstance" and to redefine agency is motivated by a need to correct what she considers to be an infelicitous interpretation of her conclusion to *Gender Trouble,* "From Parody to Politics," in which she appears to identify the practices of drag with intentional denaturalization, the instrumental parodic citation of a norm by an "ego" who masters the circumstances of articulation. "Although many readers understood *Gender Trouble* to be arguing for the proliferation of drag performances as a way of subverting dominant gender norms, I want to underscore that there is no necessary relation between drag and subversion" (BTM, 125). Butler must argue this point—that there is "no necessary relation" between a speech act and its effects—if she is to remain consistent with Derrida's critique of Austinian speech act theory. To wit, no act can be governed entirely by the intention, serious or parodic, in which it was initiated. As works on drag such as Esther Newton's *Mother Camp* clearly show, the conventions ensuring the reception of a discursive act as parodic and subversive are as rigid and as vulnerable to failure as those ensuring any other scene of interpretation. See *Mother Camp: Female Impersonators in America* (Englewood Cliffs, N.J.: Prentice-Hall, 1972). For a salient critique of Butler's position on drag, see Sue-Ellen Case, who distinguishes "feminine masquerade" from "feminist masquerade" in "Toward a Butch-Femme Aesthetic," in *Making a Spectacle,* ed. Lynda Hart (Ann Arbor: University of Michigan Press, 1989). Much of the work of Case, Peggy Phelan, Elin Diamond, and, more recently, Diana Taylor has been devoted to nuancing Butler's stern linguistic orientation.

22. "Signature, Event, Context," 60.

23. Some sensitive work has been done on Butler's melding of "performance" and "the performative"; see *Performance and Performativity,* ed. Andrew Parker and Eve Kosofsky Sedgwick and with an introduction by Andrew Parker (New York: Routledge, 1995); and Shannon Jackson, "Theatricality's Proper Objects: Genealogies of Performance and Gender Theory," in *Theatricality,* ed. Tracy C. Davis and Thomas Postlewait (Cambridge: Cambridge University Press, 2003), 186–213.

24. BTM, 10. Note that for Butler, the somatic is always reduced to the morphological, that is, it becomes a matter of bodily contour, rather than a sensing of bodily processes, such as movement.

25. For Butler's further thoughts on this issue, see *The Psychic Life of Power: Theories in Subjection* (Stanford: Stanford University Press, 1997.

26. In a limited manner, Shoshana Felman does the reverse, treating speech as an act engaging the body; see *The Scandal of the Speaking Body,* trans. Catherine Porter, with an afterword by Judith Butler (Stanford: Stanford University Press, 2003).

27. Adam Kendon, *Gesture: Visible Action as Utterance* (Cambridge: Cambridge University Press, 2004), 108.

28. Sha Xin Wei, "Resistance Is Fertile: Gesture and Agency in the Field of Responsive Media," *Configurations: A Journal of Literature, Science, and Technology* 10, no. 3 (Fall 2002): 444–445. On the difference between gestures and words, see also Brian Rotman, "Corporeal or Gesturo-haptic Writing," 423–438 in the same issue.

29. Gestures (including the gestures of speech and writing) can indeed be parsed into units, broken up into what Kendon calls "excursion" gestures (the gestures leading toward the "stroke"), "stroke" gestures (gestures executing the identifiable, freeze-frame gesture-sign), and "noise gestures" (the in-between gesticulations which, taken on their own, bear no cultural meaning). See also Wei, "Resistance Is Fertile," 445; and Vilém Flusser, *Les gestes* (Paris: D'ARTS Ecole Nationale Supérieure d'Arts Cergy et Art 95, 1999).

30. *Being and Nothingness,* trans. with an introduction by Hazel E. Barnes (New York: Washington Square Press, 1984), 432.

31. *Being and Nothingness,* 432.

32. "The Lived Experience of the Black Man," in *Black Skin, White Masks,* trans. Richard Philcox, with a foreword by Kwame Anthony Appiah (New York: Grove Press, 2008), 89; translation modified. (All further references to this volume will be abbreviated in the text as F. For modifications of the English translation, I have consulted the French edition: *Peau noire, masques blancs* [Paris: Seuil, 1952].)

33. In *The Threshold of the Visible World* (New York: Routledge, 1996), Kaja Silverman also reads *Black Skin, White Masks* as a struggle to overcome the hegemony of a body image—here negative and unassimilable—that is "immanent within the collective white look" (28): "*Black Skin, White Masks* helps us to understand, first of all, that our identifications [Sartre's *"relation à l'autrui"*] must always be socially ratified. It also teaches us that only certain subjects have access to a flattering image of the self, and that others have imposed upon them an image so deidealizing that no one would willingly

identify with it" (29). See also Kelly Oliver, *The Colonization of Psychic Space: A Psychoanalytic Social Theory of Oppression* (Minneapolis: University of Minnesota Press, 2004).

34. I have modified the English translation, which renders the French word for knowledge, "*connaissance,*" as the English word "image." This confuses the issue. Fanon never speaks of a body "image." See *Peau noire, masques blancs* (Paris: Seuil, 1952), 89. For a sensitive treatment of this passage, see Ronald A. T. Judy, "Fanon's Body of Black Experience," in *Fanon: A Critical Reader,* ed. with an introduction and translations by Lewis R. Gordon, T. Denean Sharpley-Whiting, and Renée T. White (Oxford: Blackwell, 1996). See also Robert Bernasconi, "The European Knows and Does Not Know: Fanon's Response to Sartre," in *Frantz Fanon's Black Skin, White Masks: New Interdisciplinary Essays,* ed. Max Silverman (Manchester: Manchester University Press, 2005).

35. *Being and Nothingness,* 464.

36. Fanon's describes the construction of his body schema before it is eclipsed by an image projected on him by the white world; his description follows the classic understanding introduced by Head and adopted by Lhermitte: "I know that if I want to smoke, I shall have to stretch out my right arm and grab the pack of cigarettes lying at the other end of the table. As for the matches, they are in the left drawer, and I shall have to move back a little. And I make all these moves not out of habit, but by implicit knowledge. A slow construction of myself as a body in a spatial and temporal world—such seems to be the schema. It is not imposed on me; it is rather a definitive structuring of my self and the world—definitive because it creates a genuine dialectic between my body and the world" (F, 90–91).

37. According to David Macey, until 1947, Fanon did not declare his intention to study psychiatry and would not have been intimate with the major thinkers in that discipline. However, there is clear evidence that he read phenomenology and existentialism during the period he was writing *Peau noire, masques blancs* (roughly 1947–51). As Macey notes: "The central term in Fanon's analysis is 'lived experience.' The French *expérience vécue* is the normal translation of *Erlebnis,* the technical term used by Husserl and Heidegger and then popularized by Merleau-Ponty in particular. While Fanon had not read Husserl and Heidegger, he does cite Merleau-Ponty, and the notion of *Erlebnis* was current in the psychiatric circles in which he moved in Lyon" (164). Jean Lhermitte is also the "primary source for Merleau-Ponty's account of the 'synthesis' of the body in *Phenomenology of Perception*"; *Frantz Fanon: a Life* (London: Granta Books, 2000), 165; see also 128–29 and 163–65.

38. On melodrama in Lacan, see Wallon: "to speak as the psychoanalysts do of a return to the 'abysses' of childhood, to look upon the child as a tortured soul in search of body wholeness, or like Lacan to evoke 'dislocation, dismemberment, emasculation, cannibalism, entombment,' is to invent a tragic reality to which nothing in the child's behavior actually attests. The child's researches concerning himself and the objects about him are informed by the same lively and often joyful curiosity that he brings to his perceptual and motor learning. To feel dislocated, he would have to be endowed with some kind of fore-knowledge of his future bodily unity, and there is no evidence to support this

idea"; "Kinesthesia and the Visual Body Image in the Child," in *The World of Henri Wallon,* ed. Gilbert Voyat (New York: Jason Aronson, 1984), 123.

39. Paul Schilder, *The Image and Appearance of the Human Body* (New York: International Universities Press, 1950): "The optic and the tactile material are used in the body-image according to the situation. But sometimes the optic material may determine our tactile impression and, with that, the model of the body" (107). Schilder generalizes this observation, arguing that while different sensations—optic, tactile, proprioceptive, and kinesthetic—often reinforce one another, one can take precedence over another in both normal and abnormal cases. It bears repeating that for Schilder, no sensation—optic or otherwise—can function in isolation to create a coherent body image; exteroceptive and interoceptive sensations combine to build an evolving image, one that ultimately depends upon the performance of movement, through which correction and correlation are effected (see 112–113). For a contemporary account of the interaction between kinesthetic sensation and visual information, see Antonio R. Damasio, *The Feeling of What Happens: Body and Emotion in the Making of Consciousness* (New York: Harcourt Brace, 1999), 76–77.

40. Recent clinical support for Fanon's position can be found in *Body Image and Body Schema,* ed. Helena De Preester and Veroniek Knockaert (Amsterdam: John Benjamin, 2005); and Jose Luis Bermudéz, Anthony Marcel, and Naomi Eilan, eds., *The Body and the Self* (Cambridge, Mass.: MIT Press, 1995). In the latter, see especially Shaun Gallagher, "Body Schema and Intentionality." Gallagher points out that a major misunderstanding was created by Merleau-Ponty's English translator, Colin Smith, when he translated the author's reference to the *"schéma corporel"* as "body image." This confusion is not corrected by Elizabeth Grosz when she discusses the role of the body "image" in *Phenomenology of Perception* (see *Volatile Bodies: Toward a Corporeal Feminism* [Bloomington: Indiana University Press, 1994]).

41. Jean-Paul Sartre, *Black Orpheus,* trans. S. W. Allen (Paris: Présence Africaine, 1963).

42. *Being and Nothingness,* 433.

43. See ibid., 444; original emphasis.

44. Ibid., 403; *L'Être et le Néant,* (Paris: Gallinard, 1976) 344; original emphasis.

45. Fanon is explicit alluding to Langston Hughes' "The Negro Speaks of Rivers," but for the moment he rejects the vision of ancestral solidarity the poem evokes.

Conclusion

1. Walter Ong, *Orality and Literacy: The Technologizing of the Word* (New York: Methuen, 1982), 7.

2. Following the example of Hegel and Husserl, Sartre also illustrates the tug of the unreflected on reflection with an anecdote concerning writing. In *Esquisse d'une théorie de l'émotion* he notes: "at this moment, I write but I have no consciousness of writing. Will it be said that habit has made me unconscious of the movements my hand makes while tracing letters? That would be absurd.

Perhaps I'm habituated to writing, but by no means habituated to writing *these* words in *this* order" (Paris: Hermann, 1975; originally published 1938), 40; my translation. Yet Sartre also emphasizes that during the act of writing our concentration is so fixed on the meaning—rather than the shaping—of the words that we can easily lose awareness of the gestures of the hand that we have acquired: "In the instant I trace a word, I pay no notice to each of the gestures [*jambages*] that my hand makes" (40). Sartre proposes that our absorption in the act of finding the right words for the new situation (we have never written *these* words in *this* order before) both obscures and highlights what our hand is doing.

3. See G. W. F. Hegel, *The Phenomenology of Spirit,* trans. A. V. Miller, with an analysis and foreword by J. N. Findlay (Oxford: Oxford University Press, 1977): "'What is Now?', let us answer, e.g. 'Now is Night.' In order to test the truth of this sense-certainty a simple experiment will suffice. We write down this truth; a truth cannot lose anything by being written down. . . . If *now, this noon,* we look again at the written truth we shall have to say that it has become stale" (60); "The Now is pointed to, *this* Now. 'Now'; it has already ceased to be in the act of pointing to it" (63).

4. See Edmund Husserl, *Idées directrices pour une phénoménologie,* trans. Paul Ricoeur, 8th ed. (Paris: Gallimard, 1950), 112: "Let's start with a few examples. Here, before me, in the half-light, this white paper. I see it, touch it. This visual and tactile perception of the paper, which constitutes my fully concrete lived experience *of the paper-that's-here* [*le vécu pleinement concret du papier-que-voici*], the paper given exactly with these qualities, appearing exactly in this relative obscurity, in this imperfect discrimination, according to this orientation—is a *cogitatio,* a lived experience of consciousness [*un vécu de conscience*]" (original emphasis ; my translation). In *La Voix et le phénomène* (Paris: PUF, 1967) Derrida analyzes Husserl's understanding of symbolic gestures (communicative gestures accompanying speech), identifying them as the idea's "empirical body" analogous to vocalized words and thus the falling away of thought from its ideal, nonindexical expression. But there is another order of the gestural in Husserl pertaining to the inextricability of movement and perception; Merleau-Ponty derives his emphases from this less often treated aspect of Husserl's phenomenology of the moving body.

5. Maurice Merleau-Ponty, *The Phenomenology of Perception* (London: Routledge, 1962), 429; added emphasis. (All references to this edition will be abbreviated in the text as PP.)

6. Jacques Derrida, *Memoirs of the Blind: The Self-portrait and Other Ruins,* trans. Pascale-Anne Brault and Michael Naas (Chicago: University of Chicago Press, 1993), 3; *Mémoires d'aveugle: L'Autoportrait et d'autres ruines* (Paris: Editions de la Réunion des musées nationaux, 1990), 11.

7. See Jacques Derrida and Paule Thévenin, *Antonin Artaud: Dessins et portraits* (Paris: Gallimard, 1986, 63). Here, gesture is reconceived as a support for nothing other than itself, profoundly antirepresentational yet requiring, in order to mark its passage, the vehicle of "letters" (77).

8. Deidre Sklar, "Remembering Kinesthesia: An Inquiry into Embodied Cultural Knowledge," in *Migrations of Gesture,* ed. Carrie Noland and Sally Ann

Ness (Minneapolis: University of Minnesota Press, 2008), 86, 91. Sklar is careful to avoid positing an acultural "universal bodily experience"; "In different sociocultural and historical circumstances, people learn to emphasize and value different sensory details of form and quality, different perceptual and expressive media, and different ways of processing somatosensory information" (95). See also Deidre Sklar, *Dancing with the Virgin: The Enactment and Embodiment of Religious Belief* (Berkeley: University of California Press, 2001).

9. "Remembering Kinesthesia," 91.

10. By employing the word *"solitaire,"* Derrida appears to be troping on Husserl's scene of autoaffection in which internal monologue, the *"discours solitaire,"* is privileged as undivided consciousness (*La Voix,* 106).

11. *Memoirs of the Blind,* 4-5; *Mémoires d'aveugle,* 12; original emphasis.

12. Jacques Derrida, *Of Grammatology,* trans. Gayatri Chakravorty Spivak (Baltimore: Johns Hopkins University Press, 2003), 44.

13. Jacques Derrida, *Le Toucher: Jean-Luc Nancy* (Paris: Galilée, 2000), 184; Derrida is quoting from Edmund Husserl, *Ideen,* 2:210–211.

14. *Ideen,* 2:213; *Le Toucher,* 199.

15. *Le Toucher,* 198.

16. Ibid.

17. For an attempt to theorize dance through cultural studies, see Jane C. Desmond, ed., *Meaning in Motion: New Cultural Studies of Dance* (Durham, N.C.: Duke University Press, 2003). In her introduction, Desmond asks the vital questions "What is kinesthetic subjectivity? How does it shape and get shaped by other social formations of the self, and of communities? How and what do we come to know through kinesthesia as a historically particular register of meaning? How do we theorize it?" (2).

18. See Mark Franko, "Mimique": "French poststructuralist thought of the 1960s employed the terms 'stage' *(scène)* and 'gesturality' as models of deconstructed philosophy, as if performance were that 'outside' always denied an ontological dimension in thought. Poststructuralist critical theory self-consciously constituted itself as a performative enterprise, indeed as the project of a theater through its emphasis on the gestural"; in *Bodies of the Text: Dance as Theory, Literature as Dance,* ed. Ellen Goellner and Jacqueline Shea Murphy (New Brunswick, N.J.: Rutgers University Press, 1995), 208. However, as André Lepecki observes in "Inscribing Dance," movement only returns in Derrida as "deferment," or deferral: "the conditions of possibility for Derrida's project on writing as différance and for his critique of presence are grounded on the imperative insertion of movement in grammatology. For Derrida this movement is called deferment"; in *Of the Presence of the Body: Essays on Dance and Performance Theory,* ed. André Lepecki (Middletown, Conn.: Wesleyan University Press, 2004), 137.

19. Franko, "Mimique," 211; original emphasis.

20. See Jean Baudrillard, *The System of Objects,* trans. James Benedict (London: Verso, 2005); and Giorgio Agamben, "Notes on Gesture," in *Means without End: Notes on Politics,* trans. Vincenzo Binetti and Cesare Casarino (Minneapolis: University of Minnesota Press, 2000).

21. Sally Ness, "The Inscription of Gesture: 'In'-ward Migrations in Dance," in Noland and Ness, *Migrations of Gesture,* 4–5.

22. See Georges-Henri Luquet, *L'Art primitif* (Paris: Doin, 1930), and Anne-Marie Christin, *L'Image écrite, ou la déraison graphique* (Paris: Flammarion, 1995). Extending Luquet's observations, Christin claims that writing, far more than reading, offers a mode of subversion within culture. On the potential duplicity of writing and its relation to hermetic practices, see Marcel Griaule, *Silhouettes et graffiti abyssins* (Paris: Larose, 1933). Finally, a number of archeologists and anthropologists are now interpreting the earliest forms of mark making as implicated in rituals involving trance and collective hallucination. See Jean Clottes, *The Shamans of Prehistory: Trance and Magic in the Painted Caves,* trans. Sophie Hawkes (New York: Abrams, 1998).

Acknowledgments

While writing this book, I was generously supported by three institutions: the Camargo Foundation in Cassis, France, the American Philosophical Society, and the University of California Humanities Research Institute. I thank the directors and boards of all three for taking such good care of me.

Parts of this book were previously published elsewhere. An earlier version of Chapter 3 appeared as "Motor Intentionality: Gestural Meaning in Bill Viola and Merleau-Ponty," *Postmodern Culture,* 17, no. 3 (Fall 2007); an earlier version of Chapter 4 was published as "Miming Signing," in *Migrations of Gesture,* ed. Carrie Noland and Sally Ann Ness (Minneapolis: University of Minnesota Press, 2008); and extracts of Chapter 3 appeared as "Digital Gestures," in *New Media Poetics,* ed. Adalaide Morris and Thom Swiss (Cambridge, Mass.: MIT Press, 2005). Thanks are due to the editors and publishers for allowing me to publish revised versions here.

On a more personal note, I would like to thank my dear friends and most perspicacious critics, Sally Ann Ness and Deidre Sklar. Meeting them quite simply changed the way I think. Their work has been for me exemplary in its originality and rigor; their conversation and comradery have been a source of joy and comfort. Sally and Deidre relieved the loneliness I have often felt in academia and gave me the courage to move into entirely new realms in my writing. If I have not managed to move as far as they might wish, it is because I lag behind, entangled in texts.

Other friends in academia have reached out to me and have supported my work at crucial moments in my career and personal development. Longtime supporters and interlocutors include Richard Terdiman, Barrett Watten, Michael Davidson, and Amelia Jones. John Mowitt at the University of Minnesota and Catherine Soussloff at the University of California, Santa Cruz, furnished occasions to rehearse the arguments of this book and offered invaluable criticism and support. I also extend my warm thanks to colleagues at the University of California, Irvine, who suggested readings, invited me to speak, or took the time to critique my work: Simon Penny, Bill Maurer, Yvonne Rainer, Bryan Reynolds, and—with special gratitude—Étienne Balibar for turning me on to Bruno Karsenti. Many cherished friends have lifted my spirits through the long years of writing and rewriting: Marjorie Beale and Bill Myerhoff, Kathy Ragsdale and Michael Fuller, Susan Klein and Joe McKenna, Victoria Bernal, Ketu Katrak, David Meyer, Kay and Doug Ryals, Stephanie Wales, and Charlie Chubb. In France, Cecile Gry, Christiane Girelli, Vincent Poujardieu and Esther Peyroles got me through the long dark months of a year on my own.

Generous colleagues at other institutions shared their work with me and went way beyond the disciplinary call of duty to find me sources, establish contacts, and just generally cheer me up: for this, I thank Leslie Jones, Blake Stimson, Lesley Stern, Jonathan Flatley, Joyce and Max Kozloff, and Jayne Fargnoli. Excellent suggestions for revision were forthcoming from Mark Franko, Amelia Jones, Felicia McCarren, and anonymous readers for journals and presses. The book I have written is in many ways a response to the inspiration they provided. The team at Harvard University Press, Humanities Editor Lindsay Waters and Phoebe Kosman, and Tonnya Norwood have been encouraging and patient throughout the entire process.

Finally, I thank my rambunctious family, my greatest source of pride, Julian and Francesca, and my beloved husband, Christopher Beach: *Namaskar.*

Index